DEVELOPING VOCABULARY AND ORAL LANGUAGE IN YOUNG CHILDREN

The Essential Library of PreK–2 Literacy

Sharon Walpole and Michael C. McKenna, *Series Editors*
www.guilford.com/PK2

Supporting the literacy development of our youngest students plays a crucial role in predicting later academic achievement. Grounded in research and theory, this series provides a core collection of practical, accessible resources for every teacher, administrator, and staff developer in the early grades. Books in the series contain a wealth of lesson plans, case examples, assessment guidelines, and links to the Common Core State Standards. Issues specific to each grade—and the essential teaching and learning connections between grades—are discussed. Reproducible materials in each volume are available online for purchasers to download and print in a convenient 8½″ × 11″ size.

**Reading Intervention in the Primary Grades:
A Common-Sense Guide to RTI**
Heidi Anne E. Mesmer, Eric Mesmer, and Jennifer Jones

Developing Word Recognition
Latisha Hayes and Kevin Flanigan

Developing Vocabulary and Oral Language in Young Children
Rebecca D. Silverman and Anna M. Hartranft

**Developing Fluent Readers:
Teaching Fluency as a Foundational Skill**
Melanie R. Kuhn and Lorell Levy

**Developing Reading Comprehension:
Effective Instruction for All Students in PreK–2**
Katherine A. Dougherty Stahl and Georgia Earnest García

Developing Vocabulary and Oral Language in Young Children

Rebecca D. Silverman
Anna M. Hartranft

Series Editors' Note by
Sharon Walpole and Michael C. McKenna

THE GUILFORD PRESS
New York   London

KH

© 2015 The Guilford Press
A Division of Guilford Publications, Inc.
72 Spring Street, New York, NY 10012
www.guilford.com

Printed in the United States of America

This book is printed on acid-free paper.

Last digit is print number: 9   8   7   6   5   4   3   2   1

Library of Congress Cataloging-in-Publication Data

Silverman, Rebecca D.
  Developing vocabulary and oral language in young children / Rebecca D. Silverman,
Anna M. Hartranft.
    pages cm — (The essential library of prek-2 literacy)
  Includes bibliographical references and index.
  ISBN 978-1-4625-1788-6 (paperback)—ISBN 978-1-4625-1825-8 (cloth)
  1. Language arts (Early childhood) 2. Vocabulary—Study and teaching (Early
childhood) I. Hartranft, Anna M. II. Title.
  LB1139.5.L35S545 2015
  372.6'044—dc23
                                                            2014023303

8/12/15

Every one has experienced how learning an appropriate name for what
was dim and vague cleared up and crystallized
the whole matter. Some meaning seems almost within reach,
but is elusive; it refuses to condense into definite form;
the attaching of a word somehow (just how, it is almost
impossible to say) puts limits around the meaning, draws it
out from the void, makes it stand out as an entity
on its own account.

—JOHN DEWEY (1910, p. 173)

To A and Z, whose words inspire me every day

—R. D. S.

For my mother, who first taught me how to apply for a library card, and
who subsequently funded that as-yet-unnamed east wing
of the library from all my late fees—does this cover it?

—A. M. H.

About the Authors

Rebecca D. Silverman, EdD, is Associate Professor in the College of Education at the University of Maryland, where she teaches classes and conducts research on reading and writing in early childhood and elementary school classrooms and serves as Director of the Maryland Language and Literacy Research Center. A former elementary school teacher, Dr. Silverman's research focuses on the vocabulary and comprehension of children from diverse backgrounds, particularly English language learners and children from low socioeconomic backgrounds. She has conducted numerous studies on vocabulary and comprehension development and instruction in prekindergarten through fifth grade; has led two federally funded grants focused on vocabulary and comprehension; and has authored several studies in journals including the *Journal of Educational Psychology, Contemporary Educational Psychology, Reading Research Quarterly, Scientific Studies of Reading*, and the *Elementary School Journal*.

Anna M. Hartranft, MEd, is Faculty Research Associate in the Department of Counseling, Higher Education, and Special Education at the University of Maryland. Ms. Hartranft has managed several locally and federally funded projects that have investigated the development and response to intervention of students from diverse backgrounds. Her research focuses on the instruction and inclusion of students with disabilities and their peers in the areas of reading and writing. She has contributed to presentations at conferences of the American Educational Research Association, the Council for Exceptional Children, and the Society for the Scientific Study of Reading and coauthored publications in journals such as *Reading Research Quarterly* and the *Elementary School Journal*.

Series Editors' Note

It takes a special author team to bridge the worlds of language and literacy, early childhood and reading education, and research and practice. Rebecca D. Silverman and Anna M. Hartranft are just such a team. In this wonderful book, they bring together knowledge from several fields to craft a message of immediate value for any early primary teacher. They successfully merge the lessons of experience with the newest research, and they write in a voice that is at once accessible and authoritative. Their message is simple, coherent, and urgent: Building vocabulary breadth and depth is essential for children's success. In every chapter, they articulate this message with care, showing how this goal can be reached through rich language exchanges that enhance, rather than supplant, other important early primary goals.

Many school leaders know that they must make vocabulary development a schoolwide goal, but they lack the guidance to move forward. Improvement efforts are often superficial and disjointed. One reason, we suspect, is that there are few comprehensive models for enriching children's vocabulary during the time that they are also building their beginning reading skills. Vocabulary instruction, too frequently, is an add-on, with language development taking a backseat to foundational skills instruction. This need not be the case. And it must not be if children are to face challenging texts with well-developed background knowledge. These authors point the way to a schoolwide program that equips them with that knowledge.

One of the most difficult aspects of continuous improvement, however, is acknowledging that teachers already have busy days and full agendas. They cannot simply do more, despite knowing full well that children at risk need more. This book provides reasonable but nuanced possibilities for building vocabulary breadth and depth in ways that restructure the time that teachers have available.

The authors acknowledge the complex character of the diverse classroom as they advocate realistic improvements that can have large payoffs in language development. They attend to the necessity of differentiating for children at risk, but they acknowledge the need for a balanced approach to teaching and learning.

You will also find a fresh and evidence-based perspective on technology in this book. That is not surprising, for these authors are active researchers into practical uses of multimedia in early primary classrooms. Our own experience tells us that teachers need to know exactly how and why technology can help them serve children, and they will not be disappointed here.

In short, this book is in every way an "essential" for the early primary classroom. We have not read one that rivals it, and we look forward to using it ourselves as we work with teachers who are committed to building children's vocabulary knowledge every day they are in school and to extending invitations to parents and caregivers to partner in this important effort.

SHARON WALPOLE, PhD
MICHAEL C. McKENNA, PhD

Preface

Over the past several years, we have worked with a number of early childhood and elementary school teachers to develop, implement, and evaluate vocabulary programs. Nothing could be more rewarding than hearing children confidently using words that they learned from our instruction. Maya beams as she says, "Look at my *structure*. Isn't it *intricate*?" Lucas glows as he says, "I can *identify* how they are *similar*!" And Devon's pride is palpable when he exclaims, "I have a *strategy* to solve this *problem*!" Helping children discover words is the most magical part of what we do. But this task is not without its challenges. With our teacher collaborators, we have struggled with choosing which words to teach, determining how best to teach them, and trying to differentiate instruction to meet the needs of children with vastly different levels of vocabulary knowledge. We imagine you have struggled with these issues too.

There has been a proliferation of books on vocabulary in recent years (e.g., Beck, McKeown, & Kucan, 2002, 2013; Biemiller, 2010; Blachowicz, Fisher, Ogle, & Watts Taffe, 2013; Graves, 2006; Kame'enui & Baumann, 2012; Marzano & Simms, 2013), and these books provide a wealth of guidance on how to teach vocabulary. However, none of these books focuses solely on teaching vocabulary in prekindergarten through second-grade classrooms. Given that most children in this grade range are not yet reading fluently and independently, vocabulary instruction for students in these early grades is qualitatively different from vocabulary instruction for students in the later grades. And, considering the importance of early vocabulary for later academic success, we believe an entire book should be dedicated to helping prekindergarten through second-grade teachers determine how to develop and implement effective vocabulary instruction for young children.

Therefore, for you and teachers like you, we document in this book what we have learned from our own research and the research of others about how to best teach vocabulary to young children. We have been strongly influenced by the work of Isabel Beck, Margaret McKeown, and Linda Kucan (2002, 2013), Andrew Biemiller (2010), and Michael Graves (2006), in particular, but we also bring to this book our own experience working with teachers and children in prekindergarten through second-grade classrooms in making recommendations for vocabulary instruction. Expanding on the work of Beck et al. (2002, 2013) and Biemiller (2010), we discuss the need for instruction in the early years that supports vocabulary *breadth* and *depth*. In other words, we emphasize the need for children to learn a vast number of words (i.e., vocabulary breadth) and to learn many different facets of words (i.e., vocabulary depth) in order to succeed in school and beyond. And, extending the work of Graves (2006), we suggest principles for instruction geared toward promoting vocabulary learning and describe how these principles play out in prekindergarten through second-grade classrooms. Based on our own work and recent research in the field (e.g., Christ & Wang, 2011; Collins, 2010; Coyne, McCoach, Loftus, Zipoli, & Kapp, 2009; Hindman & Morrison, 2011), we discuss the importance of differentiating instruction, using multimedia to support word learning, and developing home–school connections to foster vocabulary development in and out of school.

Given the strong focus on vocabulary in the Common Core State Standards, many teachers around the country will be taking a close look at their curriculum to see whether vocabulary instruction is optimally addressed. Many will find they need to supplement their curriculum or revise their current practices to help children meet the high expectations set forth in the Standards. If you are one of these teachers, we envision this book as a resource you can use to identify effective, research-based practices with which to optimize your vocabulary instruction. In Chapter 1, we discuss the importance of vocabulary, provide some background on how vocabulary develops, and introduce the role of instruction in supporting vocabulary development. In Chapter 2, we suggest three principles for choosing words, texts, and materials for instruction, and we propose six principles of effective vocabulary instruction that can be used to guide curriculum planning and revisioning. In Chapters 3 through 9, we delve into these principles in depth, and we provide many examples from teachers with whom we have worked to demonstrate the principles in action. And, in Chapter 10, we discuss how to put all components of instruction together and share some vignettes of classroom instruction that show multiple principles at work at the same time. Finally, in the Appendix, we list additional resources that we invite you to use to find appropriate words, books, and multimedia tools to implement effective vocabulary instruction in your classroom.

We recognize that the pressure on early childhood and early elementary grade teachers is mounting. It seems that children are expected to know more and do more and, therefore, teachers are expected to teach more and more every day. But given the importance of vocabulary for children's learning in school, focusing on vocabulary in the curriculum is essential. The good news is that since word learning is fun and can fit into almost any activity in the school day, prioritizing vocabulary is actually not that hard to do. We hope that in this book we have given you an array of suggestions and recommendations that will make building vocabulary your number-one instructional priority moving forward.

Contents

Purchasers can download and print select materials from
www.guilford.com/silverman-forms.

CHAPTER 1
· · · · · · · · · · ·
The Importance of
Vocabulary Breadth and Depth

GUIDING QUESTIONS
· ·

- What are vocabulary breadth and depth, and why are they important?
- How do children develop vocabulary, and what affects its development?
- What is the role of instruction in supporting vocabulary breadth and depth?

Ms. Davis has been meeting one on one with Marcus, a struggling second grader, every day since the beginning of the school year to help him learn to read. She has systematically taught the sight words and phonics skills he needs to read second-grade text, and he has been improving every day. Ms. Davis decides Marcus is finally ready to read *Frog and Toad Together* (Lobel, 1979), and he is very excited. He begins to read a story from the book called "The Garden." About six pages into the story he reads, " 'You are shouting too much,' said Frog. 'These poor seeds are afraid to grow.' " Ms. Davis asks Marcus, "So why does Frog think the seeds aren't growing?" Marcus says, "They're mad at the shouting." Ms. Davis says, "Well, it says the seeds were *afraid*. What does that mean?" Marcus looks quizzically at Ms. Davis and says, "They're mad?" In that moment, Ms. Davis realizes she has been focusing so much on helping Marcus read the words that she has forgotten to focus on teaching him about what they mean.

As the currency of communication, vocabulary is critical to comprehension and expression of thoughts and ideas. From understanding simple directions and conveying basic needs to understanding complex text and conveying intricate information, vocabulary is central across the range of social and academic domains. In fact, research on the role of vocabulary shows that children with greater word knowledge tend to have better social skills (Cohen & Mendez, 2009; Monopoli & Kingston, 2012), fewer behavior problems (Hooper, Roberts, Zeisel, & Poe, 2003), and better academic outcomes (Duncan, et al., 2007; Johnson, Beitchman, & Brownlie, 2010).

The importance of vocabulary is especially pronounced in school because of the strong connection between vocabulary and reading and writing (e.g., Coker, 2006; Cunningham & Stanovich, 1997; Duin & Graves, 1986; Perfetti, 2010; Snow, 1991). Children who have substantial word knowledge may find it easier to comprehend text and communicate through writing on a variety of topics in school. And children who have an easier time with reading and writing will likely have more exposure to words and more practice using words on their own. In fact, early vocabulary knowledge serves as a catalyst for a lifelong process of learning words and using words in reading and writing across subjects in school and beyond.

In this introductory chapter, we delve into the connection between vocabulary and reading and writing and the distinction between and the importance of vocabulary breadth and depth. We also review how vocabulary breadth and depth typically develop and discuss why some children show a different developmental trajectory. Next, we discuss research on the role of instruction in supporting vocabulary breadth and depth in prekindergarten through second-grade classrooms. Finally, we consider the prominence of vocabulary in the Common Core State Standards (CCSS), which are poised to transform the educational landscape. At the close of this chapter, we will provide an overview of the book, which we envision as a guide you can use to plan instruction that effectively supports the vocabulary breadth and depth of children in early childhood and elementary school classrooms.

The Importance of Vocabulary

A useful framework for thinking about how vocabulary contributes to reading and writing is the simple view. In the simple view of reading, reading comprehension, the ultimate goal of reading, is a product of decoding and linguistic comprehension (Gough & Tunmer, 1986; Hoover & Gough, 1990). Figure 1.1 represents this relationship. Decoding is the ability to translate letters and letter patterns into words. Linguistic comprehension refers to the ability to understand words, phrases, sentences, paragraphs, and texts. According to the simple view, decoding and linguistic comprehension are each necessary but insufficient components of reading comprehension. Importantly, as will be explained below, vocabulary is implicated in both of these main components of reading comprehension.

The relationship between vocabulary and linguistic comprehension is clear. Children need to be able to understand the words they are reading in order to

FIGURE 1.1. The simple view of reading. Based on Gough and Tunmer (1986).

understand what they read (Perfetti, 1985). In fact, readers need to know the meaning of 98% of the words in text to gain adequate comprehension (Carver, 1994; Hu & Nation, 2000). Consider the four passages in Figure 1.2, which contain four distinct ratios of known to unknown words. For the purposes of this exercise, the unknown words have been replaced with nonsense words to mimic the experience of a novice reader who is simultaneously decoding and making meaning of individual words while trying to understand the text as a whole. Although the original passage, the common English nursery rhyme "Row, Row, Row Your Boat," contains simple language, as more and more of the words are unknown, the meaning of the larger rhyme is quickly lost. Similarly, young readers must understand the vast majority of words in a passage in order to form a coherent understanding of the text.

While the relationship between vocabulary and linguistic comprehension is fairly straightforward, the relationship between vocabulary and decoding is perhaps less obvious. As children learn words as infants, toddlers, and young children, they use information about words, such as what they mean and how they sound, to store and retrieve words in memory. As children's vocabularies expand, they have to be strategic. They begin to compare and contrast sounds phonemically. For example, they learn that *high, pie, eye,* and *sky,* though they sound similar, refer to very different things. A 3-year-old would be unlikely to be overheard telling his mom, "Look Mommy! Airplane in the *eye!*" By comparing and contrasting how words sound, children develop phonemic awareness, which is essential for later decoding (Metsala & Walley, 1998; Nagy, 2005). Additionally, knowing the

Try This: How many words must be known in order to understand the passage?	
Passage 1 with 78% unknown words: *Chawv, Chawv, Chawv urp daop, Conplantly talp* the *shreab. Slriply, Slriply, Slriply, Slriply, Phand* is but a *broud.*	**Passage 1 with 50% unknown words:** *Chawv, Chawv, Chawv urp daop, Conplantly* down the *shreab* Merrily, merrily, merrily, merrily, *Phand* is but a *broud.*
Passage 1 with 22% unknown words: Row, Row, Row *urp daop,* Gently down the *shreab.* Merrily, merrily, merrily, merrily, *Phand* is but a dream	**Passage 1 with 6% unknown words:** Row, Row, Row your *daop,* Gently down the stream. Merrily, merrily, merrily, merrily, Life is but a dream.

FIGURE 1.2. An example of the effect of unknown vocabulary on comprehension.

meanings of words helps children as they begin to decode because as they sound out words they connect the sound and meaning of the words in memory.

In the simple view of reading, decoding skills and linguistic comprehension are simultaneously exercised in order for the reader to understand a word or text. Similarly, the simple view of writing (see Figure 1.3) suggests that writing proficiency is the product of encoding and ideation (Juel, 1988; Juel, Griffith, & Gough, 1986). In this model, being able to spell words (encoding) and use words effectively to communicate ideas (ideation) are necessary for proficiency in writing.

Encoding involves matching sounds to letters, which, like decoding, requires phonemic awareness and alphabet knowledge. Having a large vocabulary at an early age serves as a catalyst for these key skills that are important for reading *and* writing. Also, knowing the meaning of a word can help anchor the representation of how that word is spelled in memory. Ideation involves the translation of ideas from language into text. Communicating ideas, obviously, requires vocabulary, and having rich vocabulary knowledge enables more efficient and effective communication of precise and complex ideas in writing. Research by Kim and colleagues (2011) with kindergarteners and Coker (2006) with first graders suggests that vocabulary is an important predictor of writing proficiency.

Vocabulary is central to both reading and writing development, but it serves other academic purposes as well. In order to understand a lecture, make a presentation, or draft a report, being able to understand and use advanced vocabulary is necessary. In fact, formal education is dependent on language, and vocabulary is necessary for learning in school. To gain knowledge and interact with information about the wide range of content area topics introduced in school, vocabulary knowledge is critical. Of particular importance in the context of school is academic vocabulary, which refers to a specific class of words used in reading and writing and academic language that may not necessarily appear in everyday conversational speech. Academic vocabulary includes general academic words such as *analyze, identify, issue, method,* and *source,* which cut across curriculum areas and appear to a greater extent in academic talk rather than nonacademic or conversational talk. Academic vocabulary also includes specific academic words such as *isotope* in science, *polynomial* in mathematics, *citizenship* in social studies, and *stanza* in language arts, that are important to understanding content in specific academic domains. Nagy and Townsend (2012) argue that academic vocabulary words are tools children need to access content within and across subjects in school. Without academic vocabulary knowledge, children may struggle in math, science,

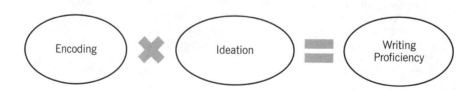

FIGURE 1.3. The simple view of writing. Based on Juel, Griffith, and Gough (1986).

Academic language refers to the kind of formal and syntactically complex language used in school and professional settings to discuss abstract concepts and complex content. Academic language is the language of written texts, and, as such, is necessary for reading comprehension and writing proficiency in the classroom context. Academic language is often contrasted with social language, which is language used in everyday conversations outside of the classroom environment. For example, when a child is asked by a friend on the playground, "What are you doing?" a child might respond, "Makin' a mud pit." But when asked this same question by a teacher during centers time, a child might respond, "I am constructing a building with the blocks."

Academic vocabulary consists of general academic words that are often abstract and more frequent in academic rather than social settings and domain-specific words that refer to specific subject matter (e.g., math, science, social studies) in school and professional settings. Academic vocabulary is often contrasted with basic vocabulary, which includes high-frequency words used in everyday conversations outside of the classroom environment. For example, *see, look,* and *find* are more basic words, whereas *notice, identify,* and *observe* are more academic words.

social studies, and language arts throughout their school careers (Townsend, Filippini, Collins, & Biancarosa, 2012). Given the importance of vocabulary across domains, teachers must devote time and energy here. It is particularly important that teachers focus on early vocabulary since it serves as a foundation for later language, literacy, and more.

Dimensions of Vocabulary

There are many ways to conceptualize word knowledge, but in this book we will focus on breadth and depth of vocabulary as two dimensions of vocabulary knowledge that are important for academic success. They are represented in Figure 1.4.

Vocabulary breadth refers to having at least surface-level knowledge of a wide range of words. For example, you might have heard the word *picayune* and know that it means something about being small, but you might not feel comfortable using it in your speech or writing. In order to understand content and concepts across a variety of academic subjects, children need to comprehend enough about a vast number of words to make sense of what they hear and read in school. For example, even though children may not be able to give a sophisticated, dictionary-like definition of the following words, knowing that *counting* refers to "how much," *habitat* refers to "where animals live," and *voting* refers to "making a choice about something" will allow children to understand content across subjects in school.

Vocabulary breadth refers to having at least surface-level knowledge of a wide range of words.

Vocabulary depth refers to having robust knowledge of many different facets of words.

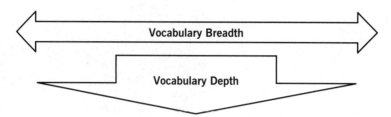

FIGURE 1.4. The relationship between vocabulary breadth and vocabulary depth.

Vocabulary depth refers to having robust knowledge of individual words and words in general. As shown in Figure 1.5, vocabulary depth includes knowledge of many different facets of words, including the phonology, orthography, and morphology of words as well as the syntactic, semantic, and pragmatic properties of words. The phonology of a word is how it sounds and the orthography of a word is how it is spelled. The morphology of a word is the different forms of words that can be used across different syntactic (i.e., grammatical) constructions. The semantics of a word is what a word means and how it is related to other words. And the pragmatics of a word is how it can be used in context to convey an intended meaning. To illustrate these facets of word knowledge, let's take the example of the words *right* and *write*. To fully know these words, children must be able to do the following:

- When they hear the words *right* and *write*, children must be able to distinguish them from other words that sound similar, like *light* and *ride* (phonology).
- When they encounter the words *right* and *write* in their reading, children must know or figure out that the *gh* in *right* and the *w* in *write* are silent (orthography).

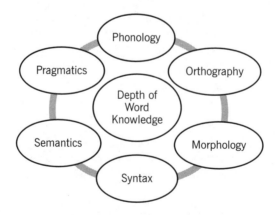

FIGURE 1.5. Depth of word knowledge.

- When children hear the words *wrote, written,* and *rewrite,* they must realize that these are other forms of the word *write* (morphology), and they must recognize that *wrote* should be used in sentences with past-tense constructions such as "Jamey wrote in her journal" (syntax).
- When children hear the word *write* as in to make marks on paper, they must be able to distinguish it from *right* as in the direction, *right* as in being correct, and a *right* as in something that you are allowed to do (semantics).
- Finally, when children hear their teachers say, "Is that right?" they must understand that the teachers likely want them to check their answer and, perhaps, try again (pragmatics).

Knowing about the many different facets of words allows children to more fully comprehend what they hear or read. In fact, the National Early Literacy Panel (2008), in a synthesis of research on early literacy, found that depth of vocabulary was much more predictive of later decoding and reading comprehension than breadth of vocabulary. And research shows that breadth and depth of academic vocabulary, in particular, are important for reading comprehension and academic success (e.g., Carlo et al., 2004; Townsend et al., 2012).

Vocabulary Development

Knowing that vocabulary breadth and depth are important is not the same as knowing how they develop. Children initially acquire words in their home environment from conversations with and among adults during everyday routines, pretend play, and book reading (Snow, Barnes, Chandler, Goodman, & Hemphill, 1991). During these activities, parents and caregivers use words to label and describe what children see and do, and children have the opportunity to practice using new words in appropriate contexts. The greater the number and sophistication of the words parents and caregivers use, the more breadth and depth of word knowledge children are likely to develop. For example, consider the difference between a caregiver saying, "Drink your milk" versus "Drink your milk so you can grow up big and strong." Parents and caregivers who use more language expose their children to a greater diversity of words and a greater complexity of word use. Children learn these words and, eventually, begin to use them on their own.

The number of words children have in their expressive vocabulary is estimated to be 4–6 words at 15 months, 20–50 words at 18 months, 200–300 words at 24 months, 900–1,000 words at age 3, 1,500–1,600 words at age 4, and 2,100–2,200 words at age 5 (Bates et al., 1994). Beyond age 5, children's vocabularies continue to grow at impressive rates. Biemiller (2005) estimates that, on average, children know 6,000 words by the end of second grade and 10,000 by the end of sixth grade.

The first words children learn are often related to people and objects in their immediate environment (e.g., *mommy*, *cup*, and *ball*) and to actions and adjectives that are related to these people and objects (e.g., *eat* and *more*). Later, children learn more abstract words (e.g., *find* and *later*). (See Figure 1.6 for a sampling of language milestones at various ages.)

Learning decontextualized language (language that is not tied to the here and now) is critical to literacy development and academic success. (Figure 1.7 shows how contextualized and decontextualized languages differ.) It serves as the foundation for children's ability to comprehend and produce descriptions and explanations of concepts and content beyond their immediate experience. For example, when observing a child using building blocks, a parent could use contextualized language and say, "It looks like you are making a tall building." Then, a parent could use decontextualized language and say, "Your building reminds me of the giant skyscraper we read about in your book about different kinds of buildings." The first statement describes something in the immediate environment, which helps children learn words in context. The second statement connects something in the immediate environment with something outside of the here and now, specifically a book the parent and child read together on another occasion. In using language to describe things outside of the here and now, parents help children learn how to use words to understand and convey meaning across space and time, which is exactly what children need to be able to do to be proficient in academic reading and writing in school.

How does this really impressive vocabulary growth occur? Even from the first encounter with a word, children begin to learn about its meaning. The initial connection between a word and its referent is called *fast mapping* (Carey & Bartlett, 1978). From the context in which the word appeared, children develop a general sense of the word and how it is used in that context. The more words children have fast-mapped to meanings, the greater their breadth of vocabulary knowledge. Thus, sheer exposure to words can serve to enhance vocabulary breadth. In fact, research shows that the more words children hear, the more likely they are to have larger vocabularies (e.g., Huttenlocher, Waterfall, Vasilyeva, Vevea, & Hedges, 2010).

Contextualized language is language that refers to people, objects, and actions that are present in the immediate context.

Decontextualized language is language that is beyond the here and now. For example, talk about abstract ideas, past and future time, and objects and events that are not physically present all involve decontextualized language.

While children may have unique pockets of word knowledge depending on their interests and experiences, they generally learn words with at least a surface level of understanding in a somewhat predictable order (Biemiller & Slonim, 2001; Leung, Silverman, Nandakumar, Qian, & Hines, 2010). This likely occurs for a number of reasons. First, adults use some words more frequently than others in their everyday speech, and children learn the words they hear most frequently first.

	Receptive Word Awareness	Expressive Word Awareness
By the end of Year 1	• Follows simple commands and understands simple questions ("Roll the ball," "Kiss the baby," "Where's your shoe?"). • Points to pictures in a book when named.	• Uses some one- or two-word questions ("Where kitty?" "Go bye-bye?" "What's that?"). • Puts two words together ("more cookie," "no juice," "Mommy book").
By the end of Year 2	• Understands differences in meaning ("go–stop," "in–on," "big–little," "up–down"). • Listens to and enjoys hearing stories for longer periods of time.	• Uses two or three words to talk about and ask for things. • Often asks for or directs attention to objects by naming them.
By the end of Year 3	• Hears you when you call from another room. • Answers simple "Who?," "What?," "Where?," and "Why?" questions.	• Talks about activities at school or at friends' homes. • Uses a lot of sentences that have four or more words.
By the end of prekindergarten	• Pays attention to a short story and answers simple questions about it. • Hears and understands most of what is said at home and in school.	• Uses sentences with details ("The biggest peach is mine") and tells stories that stick to topic. • Uses the same grammar as the rest of the family.
By the end of kindergarten	• Follows one to two simple directions in a sequence. • Listens to and understands age-appropriate stories read aloud.	• Answers "yes/no" questions and open-ended questions (e.g., "What did you have for lunch today?") • Retells stories or talks about prior events.
By the end of first grade	• Remembers information from stories and experiences. • Follows two- to three-step directions in a sequence.	• Tells and retells stories and events in a logical order. • Asks and responds to "wh" questions (who, what, where, when, why). • Stays on topic and takes turns in conversation.
By the end of second grade	• Follows three to four oral directions in a sequence. • Understands direction words (e.g., location, space, and time words). • Correctly answers questions about grade-level stories.	• Clarifies and explains words and ideas. • Uses oral language to inform, to persuade, and to entertain. • Stays on topic, takes turns, and uses appropriate eye contact during conversation.

FIGURE 1.6. The developmental progression of word learning. Adapted from American Speech–Language–Hearing Association (ASHA, n.d.). Copyright 2013 by ASHA. Used with permission.

Contextualized Language	Decontextualized Language
Contextualized language is used to negotiate interpersonal relationships.	Decontextualized language is used to "convey novel information to audiences who are at a distance from the speaker and who may share only limited amounts of background information with the speaker" (Snow, 1991, p. 7).
Contextualized language capitalizes on interpersonal cues, such as intonation, gestures, and facial expressions, to support communication.	Decontextualized language relies on purely linguistic information, often including low frequency vocabulary and complex syntactic constructions, to convey meaning.
Contextualized language utilizes shared background knowledge, listener feedback, and situational cues to facilitate meaning-making.	Decontextualized language does not depend on shared background knowledge or the communicative context.
Contextualized language is typical of everyday conversation in and out of school contexts.	Decontextualized language is typical of academic conversation in school contexts.

FIGURE 1.7. Contextualized versus decontextualized language.

> **Fast mapping** is the act of learning at least minimal information about a word from initial and brief exposure.

Second, children have many similar experiences (e.g., eating meals with family, playing on the playground, going to school), and they learn words they hear used in those contexts. Third, some words are more concrete and less difficult than others, and children are cognitively able to learn these words more quickly than more abstract or difficult words. Thus, children firt acquire knowledge of more frequent and concrete words they experience regularly and then build their knowledge of less frequent and more abstract words they encounter less regularly in their everyday lives over time and, thereby, develop breadth of vocabulary knowledge over their lifespan. Teachers can evaluate how children are progressing in developing vocabulary breadth compared to their peers using assessments based on this general progression of word learning.

Just as breadth of word knowledge grows gradually over time, so too does depth of word knowledge (Stanovich & Cunningham, 1993). Research suggests that *repeated exposure* to words over time and across contexts is needed for *extended mapping* of words, which leads to deeper word knowledge, and this word knowledge progresses from partial to complete knowledge (e.g., phonological and orthographic representations, morphological and syntactic properties, and semantic and pragmatic relations). As children learn words, they are typically first able to understand them receptively and then, over time, use them expressively. Researchers have outlined how increasing depth of word knowledge for specific words may develop.

> **Extended mapping** is the act of acquiring depth of word knowledge through repeated and rich exposure to a word over time.

For example, Dale (1965) suggested that word knowledge develops in four stages:

- Stage 1: Never saw it before.
- Stage 2: Heard it, but don't know what it means.
- Stage 3: Recognizes it in context as having something to do with _____.
- Stage 4: Knows it well.

And Beck, McKeown, and Omanson (1987) suggested a continuum of five stages:

1. Null (i.e., having no knowledge of a word) to
2. Connotative (i.e., having a general sense of the word) to
3. Contextual (i.e., having narrow context-bound knowledge of a word) to
4. Circumscribed (i.e., having knowledge of a word but not being able to recall it readily enough to use in appropriate situations) to
5. Decontextualized (i.e., having rich knowledge of a word's meaning, its relationship to other words, and its extension to morphological uses).

These stage models can be operationalized to estimate children's depth of knowledge of any given word. For example, we adapted the stages of word knowledge described above to rate kindergarten children's knowledge of words we taught during an intervention. We asked children, "What does the word _____ mean?" for a set of words that we had targeted. We rated children's explanations using the following rubric: 0 = no knowledge, 1 = connotative knowledge, 2 = contextual knowledge, and 3 = decontextual knowledge. This rubric helped us get a sense of the level of knowledge the children had about the words. For example, when we asked, "What does the word *climate* mean?" we heard the full range of explanations from no knowledge to contextual knowledge, as demonstrated by the examples below:

- A child who said, "It means like *climbing* a ladder" showed **no knowledge** of the target word, though he was trying to draw on knowledge of a word that sounded similar, *climb.*
- A child who said, "I think you need to wear warmer clothing, kind of" showed that she had **connotative knowledge** of the word because she knew that the word means something about temperature and how people dress appropriately for that temperature.
- A child who said, "The *climate* was warm today" showed that she had **contextual knowledge** of the word by using the word in a particular situation (i.e., the weather in her immediate context).
- And, a child who said, "The climate is the weather in a place. Like, the climate in Florida is hot in the summer" showed that he had **decontextual knowledge** of the word in that he knew how to objectively describe the word and use it flexibly across contexts.

While it is helpful to consider growth in word knowledge as moving from less to more over time, it is important to note that children may learn about different facets of words somewhat independently (Nagy & Scott, 2000). For example, a child may know one meaning of a word but not others, a child may know what a word means in one context but not another, and a child may know a definition or example of a word but not how it is related to other words with which it typically appears. Thus, growth in word knowledge may not necessarily be as neat as the scale we used above might suggest. Additionally, it is important to recognize that children may be at different stages of word knowledge for different words. At any given time, there are words children know with great depth and words that children know at only a surface level. In Figure 1.8, we provide an example of the word knowledge shown by one kindergarten student when asked about a series of words during a single assessment session. The child showed decontextual knowledge of *environment*, contextual knowledge of *responsibility*, connotative knowledge of *atmosphere*, and no knowledge of *contribute* on the same assessment.

Carey (1978) hypothesized that children may be working on up to 1,600 word mappings at once, suggesting that they are at various stages of knowledge or know different kinds of information about a vast number of words at any given time. Beck et al. (1987) suggest that to learn a word well enough to use it to aid comprehension, children may need upwards of 10–15 encounters with a word.

In addition to developing depth of knowledge of particular words, children must develop depth of knowledge of words in general. In other words, they must learn about different facets of words that are important for language and literacy development. Just as knowledge of what words mean (i.e., semantics) evolves over time as described above, other aspects of language including phonology, morphology, syntax, and pragmatics develop over time as well. For example, *phonological awareness* develops from being able to distinguish larger units of sound (e.g., rhyme) from smaller units of sound (e.g., phonemes). In the area of *morphological awareness*, inflectional morphology (e.g., *dog + s = dogs*) develops earlier than awareness of compound (e.g., *tooth + brush = toothbrush*) and derivational (e.g., *electric + ity = electricity*) morphology. With *syntactical awareness*, children progress from

Level of Word Knowledge	Student's Definition of the Word
No knowledge of *contribute*	"I don't even know that word!"
Connotative knowledge of *atmosphere*	"It means up in the air."
Contextual knowledge of *responsibility*	"Like I am responsible for my sister because she is younger than me."
Decontextual knowledge of *environment*	"The environment is the air and water and everything around where we live."

FIGURE 1.8. Examples of one student's varying levels of knowledge across words.

shorter and simpler words and phrases (e.g., *ball, throw ball, daddy throw ball*) to longer and more complex words, phrases, and sentences (e.g., *Daddy, throw the ball to me so I can make a basket*). Finally, in the area of *pragmatic development*, children develop from simply using language to call attention and make requests in their immediate environment to asking and answering why and how questions about abstract ideas and using different registers (i.e., styles of language used in particular settings) in social and academic contexts. As children develop in each of these linguistic areas, they are better able to distinguish between words that sound similar, use the appropriate morphological form of words across different syntactic constructions, and employ the correct word or word form depending on the situation. Understanding vocabulary depth and broader language abilities can serve to indicate the extent to which children know particular words and the extent to which they have general depth of vocabulary (i.e., general knowledge of the form and function of words).

Eventually, children begin to see words in print. Ideally, children will understand most of the words in the texts they first attempt to read so that they can focus on quickly developing decoding skills. They can continue to develop their vocabulary skills as they learn to decode through conversations and read-alouds with their caregivers and teachers. At this stage, children will know the meanings of many more words than they can actually read. In time, as they become more fluent decoders, they can begin to focus on learning new vocabulary from reading (Blachowicz & Fisher, 2000; Nagy, Herman, & Anderson, 1985). If children read texts at the right level, if they know most but not all of the words in text, and if they know how to figure out the meaning of words from word parts, context clues, and other resources, an upper-elementary-grade student could learn as many as 2,000 new words a year through wide reading alone. Thus, the focus of vocabulary instruction in prekindergarten through second grade, when children are not yet fully fluent readers, should be on building children's oral vocabulary and word learning skills so that they are ready to understand and learn from what they read once they become independent readers.

Individual Differences

Children arrive in school with vastly different levels of vocabulary breadth and depth. In terms of vocabulary breadth, Biemiller (2005) suggested that though the average number of root words known by children at the end of second grade is 6,000, children in the highest quartile know as many as 8,000 root words, and children in the lower quartile know only 4,000 root words. Biemiller goes on to say that second-grade children in the lower quartile know

> **Root words** are words without any affixes. **Affixes** are word parts added to root words that modify meaning (e.g., plural *s*, past tense *-ed*, prefixes, and suffixes).

only as many words as children at the average in kindergarten. Finally, Biemiller states that this gap in word knowledge remains steady over time as typical instruction does not seem to close the gap between children at different levels of word knowledge.

Besides having limited vocabulary breadth, many children have much less depth of vocabulary knowledge than their peers. Moats (2001) argues that many children have "partial knowledge of word meanings, confusion of words that sound similar but that contrast in one or two phonemes, limited knowledge of how and when words are typically used, and knowledge of only one meaning or function when there are several" (p. 8). There are a variety of reasons why some children arrive at school with advanced levels of word knowledge and others arrive at school with rudimentary word knowledge. Factors related to individual differences can be external and/or internal.

Externally, children learn words from the environment around them. Thus, differences in the language environment result in differences in children's vocabulary. Some differences in language environment are related to socioeconomic and racial, ethnic, and linguistic background (Snow, Burns, & Griffin, 1998). Socioeconomically, parents who are highly educated and earn higher incomes may be more likely to use academic language at home and to provide more books, materials, and experiences (e.g., trips to museums, theaters, zoos, and farms) that foster early vocabulary development than parents who are not highly educated and earn lower incomes. Racially, ethnically, and linguistically, children from African American and Hispanic homes and English language learners (ELLs)[1] may be more likely to experience a mismatch between the dialect or language and cultural experiences valued at home and school (Heath, 1983; Moll, Amanti, Nell, & Gonzáles, 1992). While knowing how to "code-switch" between two or more dialects or languages and cultures is ultimately productive for academic and professional success, children from African American and Hispanic homes and ELLs may struggle in school as they learn to navigate home and school languages and cultures that differ. In fact, according to the 2011 NAEP Vocabulary Report Card (National Center for Education Statistics, 2012), of the fourth graders who scored at or below the 25th percentile on the vocabulary scale, 73% were eligible for free or reduced-cost school meals, which indicates low socioeconomic status, 25% were African American, 35% were Hispanic, and 24% were ELLs. In contrast, of the students who scored at or above the 75th percentile, only 24% were eligible for free or reduced-cost school meals, 7% were African American, 10% were Hispanic, and 2% were ELLs. These statistics highlight the need for increased attention on vocabulary instruction to better prepare students from diverse socioeconomic, cultural, and linguistic backgrounds to master the academic vocabulary required in school and beyond.

---

[1]Many other terms have been used to refer to students who speak a language other than English at home and are learning English in school. Some of these terms are "English learners," "dual-language learners," and "language-minority learners." For consistency, we refer to these students as English language learners throughout this book.

"**Socioeconomic status** is commonly conceptualized as the social standing or class of an individual or group. It is often measured as a combination of education, income and occupation" (*www.apa.org/topics/socioeconomic-status/index.aspx*).

English language learners (ELLs) are students who are non-native speakers of English and who have difficulty listening, speaking, reading, and/or writing in English. ELLs may have difficulty learning English vocabulary, particularly academic English vocabulary.

Children's vocabulary development may be related to other factors in the home beyond socioeconomic, linguistic, and cultural background. For example, parent anxiety, stress, and depression have all been associated with limited vocabulary in children, likely because these factors affect how parents talk with their children (e.g., Chapin & Altenhofen, 2010; Sylvestre, et al., 2012). In addition, some studies suggest that birth order is related to vocabulary growth in that children who are first- and second-born children tend to have larger vocabularies than children who are born later in their families (e.g., Berglund, Eriksson, & Westerlund, 2005; Thal, Bates, Goodman, & Jahn-Samilo, 1997). Since parents may have more limited time to talk with later-born children while they are managing the needs of multiple children at once, this effect is likely also due to how parents talk with their children at home. The bottom line is that parental language is associated with major differences in how much vocabulary children have when they enter formal schooling.

Another external source of difference across children stems from the quality of child care for children who are in day care settings. Research here is sobering. Many children are enrolled in day care settings for large portions of the day, and the language input they receive in these settings can serve as an important influence on their language development. For example, Belsky et al. (2007) found that children in higher-quality child care settings were more likely to have higher vocabulary scores on a norm-referenced measure of receptive vocabulary than children in lower-quality child care settings. Quality child care can be defined as child care with a high degree of positive interaction between caregivers and children. Specifically, the more language that is directed at children in the child care setting, the more likely children are to have higher vocabulary upon school entry. So, the more caregivers talk to children about their lives and activities in and out of school and the more caregivers read books to children and talk about books with children, the more children will develop their early language skills. For instance, Wasik and Hindman (2011) showed that preschool children in classrooms where teachers provided more high-quality language input and feedback showed greater gains in vocabulary than their peers in classrooms where teachers provided less of this kind of input and feedback. The flip side of the coin is that children in low-quality child care settings that are not optimally supportive of language learning may have limited vocabulary compared to their peers in high-quality child care.

Specific language impairment (SLI) is a communication disorder that affects receptive and expressive language skills. Children with SLI have difficulty understanding directions and engaging in conversation with others. **Specific learning disability (SLD)** is a language-based disorder that affects spoken and written language ability. Children with SLD have difficulty with comprehension and expression, and, in particular, reading and writing. Neither of these disabilities is associated with physical disabilities (e.g., vision or hearing loss), developmental disabilities, emotional or behavioral disorders, cultural or linguistic differences, or socioeconomic disadvantage.

Internally, vocabulary acquisition depends on a number of important skills including, among others, hearing, vision, attention, working memory skills, processing ability, linguistic awareness, and social skills. Children need to be able to hear, see, and attend to caregivers to adequately perceive the input they need to learn new words. They need working memory skills and processing ability to be able to connect words and their referents when they hear them. They need linguistic awareness skills to be able to distinguish words that are similar (i.e., phonological awareness), appreciate how words and word forms are related (i.e., semantic and morphological awareness), and understand word use across contexts (i.e., syntactic and pragmatic awareness). And they need social skills to be able to interact with others as they acquire and practice using new words. All of these skills are likely reciprocal with vocabulary in that these skills support vocabulary development and vice versa. For children who struggle with attention, memory or processing, or linguistic awareness for any reason (e.g., attention deficit disorders, autism spectrum disorders, developmental disabilities, visual or hearing difficulties) vocabulary may be an area of difficulty. Children with a range of internal differences may experience difficulty in the area of vocabulary, which can impact reading and writing ability. Of particular concern are children with or at risk for language-related disabilities (e.g., specific language impairment or specific learning disability), which directly affect how they perceive and produce spoken or written language. However, supporting the vocabulary development of these children can provide them with important keys to unlocking their full potential in school and beyond. Therefore, we turn next to the role of instruction in supporting vocabulary development.

Vocabulary Instruction

Since young children learn much of their vocabulary through natural interactions with parents, caregivers, and others (e.g., siblings, peers, neighbors) and through exposure in their environment (e.g., books, television, and the Internet), why even teach vocabulary? Children learn through incidental exposure incrementally over time, gaining a small amount of knowledge about particular words and the linguistic characteristics of those words with each new encounter. Some words, particularly sophisticated words, may appear in the speech or text in children's environment fairly infrequently. For example, words like *seed, harvest,* and *autumn* appear in speech only 10 times in a million words. However, these words may be important to understanding literary texts set in the fall, social studies texts about agriculture, and science texts about the life cycle of plants. These words could be taught early so that children are ready to comprehend text across content areas that contain these words when they encounter them in school. Leaving word learning until children encounter words in text on their own is ineffective for many children for two main reasons. First, the context in which the words are encountered may not be ripe with clues with which children can figure out word meaning. For example, Beck et al. (2002, 2013) suggest that many contexts are misdirective, nondirective, or general rather than directive and therefore may lead children to incorrect or overly vague understandings of words to which they are exposed without instruction. Second, being able to use context to figure out words requires knowledge of the content surrounding the unknown word and skill in being able to identify and then put together the clues embedded in the text to get at the meaning of the word. This is not an easy task! In fact, the probability of learning a word from context upon first encountering it is only .15 (Nagy et al., 1985). After encountering a word enough times across contexts, children may eventually figure it out, but learning words this way is certainly not efficient for words that are needed for comprehension in school.

Without systematic and explicit instruction, leaving word learning up to incidental exposure would be haphazard and slow. Systematic and explicit instruction serves as a more efficient way of supporting vocabulary. Teachers can call children's attention to words that are likely to be unknown, which can support breadth of vocabulary knowledge, and they can plan for repeated exposure of particular words multiple times over the short and long term and offer definitional and contextual information that will support children's depth of word knowledge across those exposures. Systematic and explicit vocabulary instruction can enhance the reading, writing, and speaking and listening ability of all children, but it is particularly important for children who have limited vocabulary due to individual differences noted above. Children who experience external or internal factors that constrain their vocabulary learning need more than increased incidental exposure to words, though that, of course, is important too. They also need explicit instruction to help them learn individual words and strategies for word learning.

Unfortunately, observational studies suggest that there is relatively little explicit instruction of vocabulary in many classrooms (Al Otaiba et al., 2008; Biemiller & Boote, 2006; Ness, 2011; Wright, 2012). For example, in a study of kindergarten classrooms, Al Otaiba et al. (2008) found that instruction on vocabulary occurred much less frequently than instruction on phonological awareness and phonics even though vocabulary is, arguably, just as important. Additionally, in a study of prekindergarten and kindergarten classrooms, Silverman and Crandell (2010) found that even in schools where teachers had received professional development on the importance of vocabulary and effective approaches of vocabulary instruction, teachers varied widely in their use of these practices. Some teachers used them quite often, but other teachers used them hardly at all. Furthermore, in general, teachers attended more to vocabulary breadth (e.g., defining words and using them in the given context) than vocabulary depth (e.g., analyzing words).

A recent study by Wright (2012) echoed these findings. Wright noted that kindergarten teachers in her study most often provided brief definitions of words and rarely provided deep discussion or repeated exposure to words that they had introduced. Perhaps most disturbing is Wright's observation that "Teachers serving in economically advantaged schools provided more of these teachable moments and addressed more challenging words than teachers serving in predominantly low-income schools. Therefore, rather than ameliorating or potentially closing the vocabulary gap, the current state of vocabulary instruction could potentially exacerbate this gap" (p. 355). This trend appears similar in grades beyond prekindergarten and kindergarten. For example, Ness (2011) found that less than 3% of instruction attended to vocabulary in grades 1–5. Biemiller (2001) made the point over a decade ago that "schools now do little to promote vocabulary development, particularly in the critical years before grade 3" (p. 29).

One possible reason for the absence of high-quality explicit vocabulary instruction in schools is that curricula have not been structured to support teachers in teaching vocabulary. Neuman and Dwyer (2009), analyzing prekindergarten curricula for approaches to vocabulary instruction, found that "curriculum programs lacked focus, measurable objectives, instructional flow, and sequence of skills for teaching vocabulary instruction in pre-K" (p. 398). Disconcertingly, beyond the deficient vocabulary content of the programs under review, Neuman and Dwyer discovered that the early literacy programs offered scant advice for how exactly to teach new vocabulary explicitly. Wright and Neuman (2013) conducted a similar analysis of vocabulary instruction in kindergarten reading curricula and found similar results. These authors note that instruction in these curricula "does not reflect the current research base for vocabulary development and may not be systematic enough to influence children's vocabulary learning trajectories" (p. 386).

The good news is that intervention studies show that explicit instruction can be effective at supporting children's vocabulary. Intervention studies evaluate the effect of instruction under controlled conditions. In these studies, researchers design the instruction, teach teachers how to implement the instruction, monitor instruction throughout the intervention, and provide support for intervention implementation, if needed. In one study, Silverman, Crandell, and Carlis (2013) found that prekindergarten children who received explicit and extended vocabulary instruction learned more words than children who did not. In another study, Biemiller and Boote (2006) found that kindergarten, first-grade, and second-grade children learned more words that were explicitly taught than words that were not instructed. Finally, Beck and McKeown (2007) showed that kindergarten and first-grade students' learning was greater when words were taught more rather than less. Meta-analyses look at the effects of interventions across available studies, and, recently, Marulis and Neuman (2010) demonstrated an overall positive effect of intervention on children's vocabulary learning. Another meta-analysis of vocabulary interventions with children in prekindergarten through 12th grade by Elleman, Lindo, Morphy, and Compton (2009) revealed positive effects of vocabulary instruction on comprehension as well, particularly for students with reading difficulties.

In fact, instruction may enable children with limited vocabularies to catch up to their peers with more advanced vocabularies. For example, Wasik, Bond, and Hindman (2006) found that prekindergarten children from low-income backgrounds in classrooms where teachers provided research-based vocabulary instruction made gains in receptive and expressive vocabulary that suggest they were beginning to close the gap between themselves and their more advantaged peers. Similarly, when provided with rich instruction on breadth and depth of vocabulary, Silverman (2007a) found that kindergarten ELLs began to catch up with their non-ELL peers in vocabulary. And Loftus, Coyne, McCoach, Zipoli, and Pullen (2010) showed that children with lower levels of vocabulary who received supplemental instruction gained in word knowledge such that they seemed to be catching up to their peers with greater levels of vocabulary knowledge. While these results from individual studies are encouraging, Marulis and Neuman (2010), in the meta-analysis mentioned above, noted that when they disaggregated the results of the interventions they reviewed by students' background, vocabulary gains for children from low-income backgrounds were not substantial enough to "close the gap" between them and their peers from middle- to upper-income backgrounds. These authors suggest much more attention is needed to developing and implementing vocabulary instruction that meets the needs of all learners. Rather than "one-size-fits-all" instruction, vocabulary instruction may need to be more differentiated and individualized for children most in need of support than is typical in everyday early childhood and elementary school classrooms.

Vocabulary in the Common Core State Standards

The Common Core State Standards (CCSS) (National Governors Association Center for Best Practices & Council of Chief State School Officers [NGA & CCSSO], 2010), adopted by most states in the United States, have the potential to transform education in schools as teachers strive to support all children in meeting the rigorous standards established to prepare children for academic and professional success. We are glad to see that vocabulary knowledge and skills are featured prominently in the CCSS. Considering that word knowledge is essential for the advanced reading and writing skills required in college and beyond, it is no surprise that vocabulary is highlighted conspicuously in the CCSS English language arts strands for reading, writing, speaking, and listening, which focus on expressive and receptive oral and written language proficiency.

While the vocabulary skills pervade the CCSS English language arts standards for each of these English language arts strands, specific standards for vocabulary knowledge can be found in the language strand. According to these standards, children should be able to:

- Determine or clarify the meaning of unknown and multiple-meaning words and phrases based on grade-level reading and content.
  o Use context clues, affixes (i.e., word parts), and resources like dictionaries and glossaries to figure out word meanings.
- Demonstrate understanding of word relationships and nuances in word meanings.
  o Identify connections between words and their uses and distinguish shades of meaning.
- Use words and phrases acquired through conversations, reading and being read to, and responding to texts.

These standards encourage teachers at all grade levels to emphasize (1) independent word learning, (2) connections between and among words, and (3) use of words across contexts. Our take on the way vocabulary is described in these standards is that we must emphasize *both* breadth of vocabulary and depth of vocabulary as defined in this chapter. The CCSS suggest that "students will grow their vocabularies through a mix of conversations, direct instruction, and reading" (NGA & CCSSO, 2010). The challenge then, for all of us, is to create an environment that is ripe for vocabulary learning.[2]

Summary

In this chapter, we have discussed the importance of vocabulary and provided an overview of research on vocabulary development and instruction, which will serve as a foundation for the recommendations we make in the rest of this book.

---

[2]The CCSS are intended to set high standards for all learners, including ELLs. However, considering that ELLs are faced with the task of acquiring English-language proficiency *and* meeting the same CCSS standards as other children, teachers may need to provide additional support for them in language development and vocabulary learning. The WIDA English Language Development Standards (World-Class Instructional Design and Assessment, 2012), developed by the Wisconsin Center for Education Research and aligned with the CCSS, provide a road map for supporting the English language development of ELLs.

We have defined key terms such as vocabulary *breadth* and *depth* that we will use throughout the book. And we have described the role of vocabulary in the CCSS that promise to transform education in the years to come. We hope that this introduction has awakened or reawakened your appreciation of the importance of vocabulary and inspired you to read on to explore the multitude of ways you can promote vocabulary breadth and depth in the young children in your class. In the next chapter, we present principles to guide vocabulary instruction in prekindergarten through second-grade classrooms that will support students in meeting the expectations for vocabulary in the CCSS.

CHAPTER 2
. . . .

Principles of Effective Vocabulary Instruction

GUIDING QUESTIONS
....

- How should teachers choose words and texts for vocabulary instruction?
- What principles should guide vocabulary instruction?

At the end of one of our professional development sessions on effective vocabulary instruction, we noticed Mrs. Calhoun staring wearily at her handouts. We asked if everything was OK. She just sighed and said, "What I really need is a road map." We had presented Mrs. Calhoun with a lot of theory and research, but we didn't provide a comprehensive overview of how it all fit together. Other books on vocabulary have provided such an overview of vocabulary instruction across the grade spans, and we base our own work on much of what has come before us. But here, for Mrs. Calhoun and for you, we provide a road map with specific principles for effective vocabulary instruction for prekindergarten through second grade.

In Chapter 1, we argued that vocabulary breadth and depth are important and that instruction can play an important role in promoting vocabulary development in young children. However, we also noted that vocabulary instruction is not always optimal. That need not be the case. Over the past couple of decades, researchers have amassed enough knowledge about characteristics of effective vocabulary instruction that we can make well-founded recommendations about what to teach and how to teach it. In this chapter, we summarize what we know from the research about which words and skills to teach, how to address vocabulary breadth and depth, and what kinds of texts and materials to use to teach them. We propose six principles of effective vocabulary instruction in prekindergarten through second-grade classrooms that you can use when planning how to best support vocabulary development in young children. We also provide an overview of each principle and review the research base supporting it. In subsequent chapters, we delve into each principle in much more detail and provide recommendations on how to implement it in early childhood and elementary classrooms.

What Should Be Taught to Promote Vocabulary Breadth and Depth?

Nagy and Anderson (1984) estimate that there are roughly 88,000 different words in the books children will encounter from grade 1 through grade 12. If teachers tried to teach all of these words, they would need to teach over 7,000 words per year. Teaching thousands of words per year is neither practical nor necessary! If teachers ensure that all children have a solid foundation of word knowledge and word learning skills, children will acquire many words on their own. Thus, teachers in kindergarten through second-grade classrooms should teach the words and skills children need to become lifelong and independent word learners. Since children can learn and retain at least 2 new words per day, Biemiller (2005) suggests that teachers focus on at least 10 new words per week in kindergarten through second-grade classrooms. He estimates that teachers typically teach only 100 to 200 new words per school year, but he suggests that, for optimal support of children's vocabulary, they should teach 300 to 500 new words across the school year. Teaching an ample number of words is especially important for children with limited vocabulary knowledge compared with their peers. Though a lot more reasonable than teaching 7,000 words, teaching 300 to 500 words is still an overwhelming task. In working with teachers on vocabulary projects over the years, we have found that teachers often have the same fundamental questions: First, with so many words to choose from, which words should we teach? Second, with so many words to teach, in how much depth should we teach each word? Third, since children ultimately need to learn many more words on their own, what else do we need to teach to support children's word learning? Finally, which texts and materials provide the best context for teaching words and word learning skills to children in prekindergarten through second grade? In this section, we tackle these questions that we feel are central to effective vocabulary instruction.

Choosing Words to Teach

The task of choosing words to teach can be daunting. Unlike with phonemic awareness or phonics, in which there is a somewhat circumscribed number of sounds and letters and skills to teach, with vocabulary instruction the possibilities are seemingly endless.[1] Over the past few decades, researchers have proposed different approaches to choosing words to teach. In the following section, we will review these approaches and extract some overarching principles from across these approaches that teachers can use to determine which words to target through instruction.

Previous Approaches to Choosing Words to Teach

Perhaps the most widely adopted view of choosing words to teach has been proposed by Beck et al. in *Bringing Words to Life* (2002, 2013) and *Creating Robust Vocabulary* (2008). These authors suggest categorizing words into three tiers according to their utility or role in language (see Figure 2.1). Specifically, these authors define Tier One words as basic words that commonly appear in everyday conversation such as *happy, little,* and *people.* Tier Three words are low frequency words such as *bureaucracy, electron,* and *sediment* that are used primarily in specific domains of content such as science or social studies. Finally, these authors define Tier Two words as "words that are high utility for mature language users and are found across a variety of domains. Examples include *contradict, circumstances, precede, auspicious, fervent,* and *retrospect*" (p. 9). Beck et al. argue that Tier One words do not need to be taught, except perhaps briefly for students with limited vocabulary, because children will experience and acquire these words through everyday experiences. They suggest that Tier Three words only need to be taught within the context of specific domains to understand the content in those domains. They propose that Tier Two words, which appear across domains but are not readily encountered in everyday situations, should be the focus of instruction.

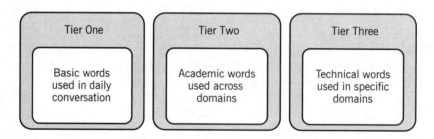

FIGURE 2.1. Word tiers. Adapted from Beck, McKeown, and Kucan (2002, 2013). Copyright 2013 by The Guilford Press. Adapted by permission.

---

[1]Note that when we refer to teaching *vocabulary* in this book, we are talking about teaching word meanings. Sometimes, teaching *vocabulary* is also used to refer to teaching sight words (e.g., "We need to build our first graders' sight word vocabulary."). Sight words are words that children need to learn to read by sight because they are phonetically irregular or highly frequent. And the sight words children need to know to read text at different grade levels are fairly well delineated. We are not focused on teaching sight words in this book; and, to avoid confusion, we generally refrain from using the word *vocabulary* to talk about sight words.

The three-tiered approach to classifying and choosing words provides a useful heuristic for teachers to use in thinking about the utility of words across academic language and content areas. However, other perspectives on choosing words warrant consideration as well. Biemiller and Slonim (2001) present an alternative perspective based on their study of word acquisition in prekindergarten through sixth-grade classrooms. These authors suggest that word acquisition occurs in a fairly predictable fashion, and, therefore, to accelerate word learning, teachers should assess which words children know and then, especially for children with limited vocabulary, teach the words that would typically be acquired next in development. To facilitate this approach, Biemiller (2010) published a list of words that, based on previous research (Biemiller & Slonim, 2001; Dale & O'Rourke, 1979), he rated according to six categories shown in Figure 2.2. Low-priority words (i.e., rated "L" for *low priority*) are concrete words that would be clear in context (e.g., *jaguar, lightening, slip*), whereas high-priority words (i.e., rated "T" for *teach*) require definition and explanation. To close the gap between children with high- and low-vocabulary knowledge early, Biemiller (2010) recommends teaching high-priority words known by 40% to 80% of children by the end of grade 2 as early as kindergarten. The other two categories ("E" for *easy* and "D" for *difficult*) are not recommended for instruction unless either: (1) they have not been previously acquired or (2) they are needed to understand a specific text.

In an alternative perspective, Hiebert (2005) proposes thinking of words according to word zones, which correspond to the frequency of words in written text. Using the corpus of words found in *The Educator's Word Frequency Guide* (Zeno, Ivens, Millard, & Duvvuri, 1995), which is derived from texts used in schools and colleges in the United States, Hiebert (2005) identified zones of words with ten or more occurrences in one million words of written text and suggested that teaching these words by the end of fourth grade would enable children to access most text they would encounter in school. The word zones Hiebert identified are outlined in the Figure 2.3.

Word Rating	Description
Easy	Words known by most children by the end of grade 2. (Not recommended for K–6 instruction.)
Teach in grades K to 2	Words known by 40–80% of children by the end of grade 2.
Low-priority in grades K to 2	Words known by 40–80% of children by the end of grade 2.
Teach in grades 3 to 6	Words known by 40–80% of children by the end of grade 6.
Low-priority in grades 3 to 6	Words known by 40–80% of children by the end of grade 6.
Difficult	Words known by fewer than 40% of children by the end of grade 6. (Not recommended for K–6 instruction.)

FIGURE 2.2. *Words Worth Teaching* word ratings. Adapted from Biemiller (2010). Copyright 2010 by The McGraw-Hill Companies. Adapted by permission.

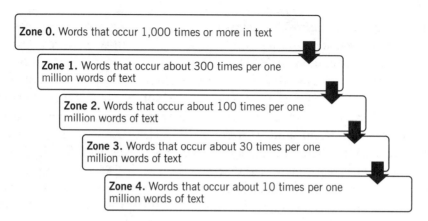

FIGURE 2.3. Word zones. Adapted from Hiebert (2005). Copyright 2005 by L. Erlbaum Associates. Used with permission.

Hiebert hypothesizes that children learn progressively less frequent words over time. Thus, as with Biemiller's approach, Hiebert suggests that teachers identify which zone(s) children already know and teach the next zone of words to accelerate children's word learning. Hiebert also suggests that, in general, first-grade teachers should teach Zone 1 words, second-grade teachers should teach Zone 2 words, and so on in order to ensure that children know all words in the four word zones by the end of fourth grade. In addition to Hiebert's word zones from *The Educator's Word Frequency Guide* (Zeno et al., 1995), there are other sources that consider the frequency of words in academic texts, such as the Academic Word List (AWL; Coxhead, 2000, 2011) and the Corpus of Contemporary American English (COCA) Academic Vocabulary List (AVL; Gardner & Davies, 2013). These resources omit the most frequent words in text and focus primarily on words that are prevalent in academic texts but uncommon in general conversation or everyday texts (i.e., newspapers and magazines). Using these resources can help teachers identify words children need for college and career readiness.

Another way to think about choosing words to teach is by how they are related to a theme or topic and how they are related to each other. For example, Marzano and Marzano (1988) organized 7,230 words found in common texts for elementary school students into 61 meaning clusters. Meaning clusters were focused on common themes such as *transportation, communication,* and *occupations.* Marzano and Marzano (1988) suggest that teaching words in these clusters can help children learn words relevant to the school context. The thematic approach to choosing words was used in a study focused on *habitats* set in prekindergarten through second-grade classrooms (Silverman & Hines, 2009). Across four habitats (i.e., the rainforest, the savannah, the desert, and the coral reef), teachers taught words such as *adapt, camouflage, creature, depend, shelter, surroundings, survive,* and *territory.* Teachers also highlighted words specific to the habitats such as *humid, tropical, arid,* and *stony.* Over the course of the intervention, children learned these words and showed increased knowledge of the science content of habitats.

Neuman and Dwyer (2011) argue that teaching words taxonomically (i.e., according to groups of like things) could be even more supportive of children's word learning than teaching children words thematically (i.e., according to groups of things that interact). They suggest that teaching words taxonomically can be helpful because it supports children's learning of key features of words that determine group membership and generalize those features to other words in the group. Thus, in the *wild animals, animals in the water,* and *insects* units included in their World of Words (WOW) preschool curriculum, teachers taught words such as *giraffe, tiger, zebra, crab, shark, whale, lizard, moth,* and *spider.* They also included words needed to discuss the categories, such as *habitat, camouflage, gills, antennae,* and *pond.* Results from research on the WOW program showed that children learned properties of categories such as *wild animals* and were able to determine, for example, whether animals that were not taught were *wild* or not.

More research comparing thematic and taxonomic approaches to teaching vocabulary is needed, but it is likely that both approaches are useful in supporting children's concept development. Additionally, choosing words to teach based on whether they are related semantically (e.g., synonyms or antonyms) or morphologically (e.g., prefixes and suffixes) is likely helpful for supporting children's vocabulary depth as they learn about different facets of words and how to use word knowledge to comprehend text (Baumann, Edwards, Boland, & Olejnik, 2003).

Our Approach to Choosing Words to Teach

Using the approaches described above, teachers might focus on whether a word is (1) useful, (2) known, (3) frequent in academic texts, or (4) related to the theme, content, or other words when considering words to teach. To most effectively choose words to teach, we believe that drawing on each of these different ways of choosing words is optimal. Thus, we propose three principles for choosing words to teach that are derived from the approaches described in the previous section. These principles appear in Figure 2.4 and are described in more detail below.

Our first principle focuses on choosing words to teach that are useful for comprehending academic texts across the content areas. These words can be considered high-leverage words because understanding them will help children learn in a variety of subjects in school. For this principle, we draw from Beck et al. (2002, 2013), who suggest that instruction should focus on Tier Two words, which they define as useful across domains. We also draw from Hiebert's work on the frequency of words in school texts, and Coxhead (2000, 2011) and Gardner and Davies (2013) on academic vocabulary. For example, Beck et al. (2013) highlight *insist* and *drowsy* as Tier Two words that could be taught in the context of *A Pocket for Corduroy* (Freeman, 1978). The word *insist* could be considered a high-leverage word in that

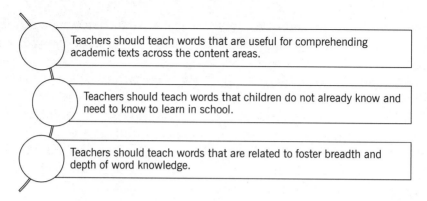

FIGURE 2.4. Principles for vocabulary selection.

it may be useful for understanding not only literary texts but also social studies and science texts (e.g., members of Congress *insist* their bill should be passed, and scientists *insist* that following the scientific method is crucial for obtaining valid results during experimentation). It is unlikely that *drowsy* would be similarly useful across content areas. In fact, while *drowsy* does not appear on any of lists noted above that suggest words to teach, *insist* appears in Zone 4 on Hiebert's Word Zones list and on the AVL (Gardner & Davies, 2013), although it is not on Biemiller's Words Worth Teaching list or the AWL (Coxhead, 2000, 2011). Thus, teachers may need to draw on multiple sources of information as well as common sense to decide which words are high-leverage words. (We provide a list of the resources for choosing words that we have discussed thus far in the Appendix.)

Our second principle focuses on teaching words that children do not yet know but need to know to understand text and content in school. It would be ridiculous to spend precious school time teaching words children have already learned. Similarly, it would be a waste of time to teach words children will rarely ever encounter. Therefore, in alignment with Hiebert's (2005) focus on frequency, we believe teachers should teach unknown words that are frequent in school texts for children with average and advanced vocabulary. For children with below-average vocabulary, we believe teachers should teach the same words as they do to the children with average and advanced vocabulary, but they should also teach words these children do not know that are known by their peers with greater word knowledge. This approach is aligned with Biemiller's (2005) focus on helping children with below-average vocabulary catch up to their peers. While Biemiller (2005) and Beck et al. (2002, 2013) suggest that, for most children, teachers can ignore very frequent or basic words because children will likely learn them naturally themselves, these words warrant instruction for children with limited vocabulary knowledge, including ELLs (August, Carlo, Dressler, & Snow, 2005). For example, while teachers of children in second grade may focus on *ahead* and *behind*—both found in Word Zone 2 (Hiebert, 2005)—with all children, they may also need to focus on *before* and *after*, both in Word Zone 1 (Hiebert, 2005), for children with more limited word knowledge. By focusing on words children need in order to comprehend grade-level text and, for children with limited vocabulary, words they need to catch up to their peers, teachers can ensure that all children are getting optimal support for vocabulary learning.

Our third principle focuses on teaching words that are related because we believe learning how words are related can be an important way to build children's concept knowledge and to foster their linguistic awareness and word learning skills. Thematically, children learn which words often appear together in context and how to use this knowledge to understand what they are learning in school. Taxonomically, children build conceptual knowledge, which is intricately related to vocabulary knowledge, and they learn how to use words to classify and categorize in general. And, linguistically, children learn how words are semantically and morphologically related, which helps them develop skills needed for later independent word learning when they use available information to figure out what words mean in context. Teaching words based on how they are related can be an invaluable way of supporting children's depth of vocabulary knowledge as children learn a great deal about important aspects of words and concepts they are learning. So, when teachers are considering which words to teach, they should privilege words that are somehow related to foster vocabulary depth. For example, in *It's Mine* by Leo Lionni (1985), teachers might choose to teach *quarrel, quibble,* and *bicker* instead of *appear, endless,* and *subsided* because teaching the former three would help children build a semantic network around the concept of arguing (which could also be taught even though it isn't in the book)[2], whereas teaching the latter three would not help children make connections between and across words.

We believe teachers should use these three principles in tandem when choosing words to teach, which means that teachers may have to weigh principles against each other as they consider which words deserve the most attention. Words that satisfy all three of the principles above are the best candidates for instruction and deserve the most attention in school. To illustrate how these three principles work together, let's consider some words from a book we have read aloud to kindergarteners called *Chicken Big* (Graves, 2010). This book is about a little bitty hen that lays a *big, giant* egg, out of which comes a chick, who is *gigantic, humongous,* and *enormous.* In addition to the words italicized in the previous sentence, some of the words to consider in the text are *brave, panic, missing, protect, thrilled,* and *coop.* All of these words are important to the text. (We didn't discuss importance to the text as a guiding principle, but when teaching words through read-alouds it is important to teach words that are important to foster comprehension. Additionally, children will have an easier time learning words that are central rather than peripheral to the text.) See Figure 2.5 to get a sense of how these words would be rated using the various approaches to choosing words we reviewed earlier in this chapter.

---

[2]Teachers can teach words that are not in a given text if the words are related to the concept and content of instruction and if they can be used to discuss the text at hand.

Target Word	Tier[1]	WTW[2]	Word Zone[3]	AWL[4]	AVL[5]
big	1	Easy	1	NA	NA
large	1	Easy	1	NA	NA
huge	2	Easy	2	NA	NA
giant	2	Easy	3	NA	NA
gigantic	2	Easy	3	NA	NA
humongous	2	NA	NA	NA	NA
enormous	2	NA	3	YES	NA
brave	2	Easy	4	NA	NA
panic	2	NA	4	NA	NA
missing	2	NA	3	NA	NA
protect	2	Easy	3	NA	YES
thrilled	2	T2	NA	NA	NA
coop	3	NA	NA	NA	NA

FIGURE 2.5. Word ratings by system. Sources: [1]Tier (Beck et al., 2002, 2013); [2]WTW = Words Worth Teaching Level (Biemiller, 2010); [3]Word Zone (Hiebert, 2005), [4]AWL = Academic Word List (Coxhead, 2000, 2011), [5]AVL = Academic Vocabulary List (Gardner & Davies, 2013). NA = "Not Applicable," which means the word does not appear on the list.

All of these words except *coop* are useful for children to know across contexts. Most of the children in our audience would have known word *big*, but the children with limited vocabulary would not have known *large*, and most of the children in the class would not have known the rest of the words. Finally, some words were semantically related to the concept of *size*, which could foster children's depth of word knowledge. Thus, the final list of words we chose included *large, huge, giant, humongous,* and *enormous.* The semantic gradient (i.e., continuum of words in order of degree) in Figure 2.6 shows how these words are conceptually related. Graphic organizers such as this one can help children understand how words are related.

By using these guiding principles for choosing words and simultaneously supporting children's foundational and advanced word knowledge, teachers can scaffold and accelerate children's word learning and prepare them for success in reading and writing in school. Much more research is needed on word choice, which ideally will provide teachers with more specific and tailored resources for choosing words to teach in the early childhood and elementary school years. In the meantime, teachers should think carefully about the words they choose to teach and use their best judgment to identify words that will provide the most bang for the buck for children's vocabulary learning.

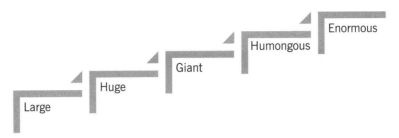

FIGURE 2.6. Semantic gradient of words relating to size.

Balancing Breadth versus Depth

When it comes to vocabulary instruction, all words do not need equal treatment. Teachers can teach some words at a surface level to build vocabulary breadth and others at a deeper level to build vocabulary depth. The depth of instruction for vocabulary words is intimately related to how words are selected—words that meet all of the principles outlined above are likely those that deserve the most depth of instruction. If words satisfy one or two but not all of the principles listed above, they may be appropriate for brief attention. For example, even though *appear* is not related thematically to words about *arguing* in *It's Mine*, discussed above, it is a useful word that may not be known by many prekindergarten through second-grade children. Thus, it should be taught at least briefly so children understand the story and gain initial knowledge of the word on which they can build in future encounters with it.

In addition to using the principles we have defined to guide the depth of focus for various words, teachers may also want to consider word difficulty. Notice that none of the approaches we discussed above mentions word difficulty. However, we think it is an important aspect of words to take into account. Children may learn frequent words easily because they experience these words repeatedly in familiar contexts. For example, children may learn the word *food* because parents and teachers use it a lot when they point to the child's food and say, "Eat all of your *food*, please." However, there are other aspects of words that make them easy or difficult. Words that are more abstract may be more difficult than words that are less abstract. For example, words like *dream, truth, courage, patience, danger, safety,* and *freedom* can be challenging for children because they cannot be easily perceived by the senses and cannot be easily explained without lots of examples. Additionally, positional words like *in front of, in back of, above, below, over, under, through,* and *around* are highly frequent but somewhat difficult because of their relativity. Max can be simultaneously *in front of* Sam and *in back of* Leo. (*We're Going on a Bear Hunt*, by Michael Rosen, 1997, is a great book for teaching positional words.) Thus, children have difficulty inferring the meaning of these words from context. Another set of words that can be difficult to learn is multiple meaning words. Words like *base, change, plane, ring,* and *turn* can be hard for children to learn because they change meaning depending on the context. We believe words that are more abstract and complex require more instructional attention than words that are less abstract and complex.

In addition to attending to word difficulty, teachers may offer different levels of instruction on words depending on whether children know the concept underlying the target word and whether they know the words that are related to the target word. For example, if children understand the concept of *quickly*, teaching the word *swiftly* will require less instruction. But if children do not understand the concept of *counting*, teaching the word *calculating* will require more time and effort. For most children, whether or not they know the underlying concept and related words will be tied to the difficulty level of a word, but many children with limited vocabulary knowledge may not understand basic concepts needed for understanding certain words. Thus, teachers may need to spend more time supporting the conceptual knowledge of some children so they can grasp the vocabulary they are learning in school.

Teachers may also adjust their focus on words depending on their goal. Sometimes, teachers may want to provide a brief, initial exposure to a word in context so children know what it means for immediate comprehension and so children can build on this surface-level word knowledge upon future encounters with the word. For example, while teachers may not focus in depth on *brave, panic, missing, protect*, and *thrilled* when reading *Chicken Big* aloud, they may briefly define these words in context. Other times, teachers may want to spend an entire lesson or multiple lessons on words, particularly words that are related to a thematic unit or major content area covered in class, so that children can learn about words in more depth and apply these words in a variety of activities. When reading *Chicken Big* in the context of a unit on shape and size, for example, teachers may spend a great deal of time having students compare and contrast the words *large, huge, giant, humongous*, and *enormous* and use these words across content areas (e.g., math and science). Thus, considering the goal of instruction can be useful for determining in how much depth to teach given words.

When teachers focus on breadth of word knowledge and immediate comprehension, they can just define words and refer to the immediate context. For depth of word knowledge, however, teachers need to focus on many more aspects of words. As discussed in Chapter 1, knowing a word in depth involves knowing its phonology, morphology, and semantics and understanding how to use it across syntactical and pragmatic contexts. Teachers, obviously, can't teach about all of these aspects of words for every word they teach, so they must balance when to teach for breadth and depth depending on how well the word aligns with our three principles of choosing words , how difficult a word is to learn, and what the goal of instruction may be. In addition to teaching specific words for breadth or depth, teachers must attend to supporting children's word awareness and teaching children word learning strategies so that once they become readers, they can use word knowledge and the skills they have acquired to become independent word learners throughout their lives. Finally, teachers must extend vocabulary instruction beyond the focus on individual words to instruction about language, comprehension, and writing in general so children learn to use vocabulary knowledge effectively in school and beyond.

Texts and Materials for Vocabulary Instruction

Now that we have established some principles for choosing words and discussed balancing breadth and depth of instruction, we briefly turn to determining which texts and materials to use for vocabulary instruction. We believe that engaging children's books should be at the center of any vocabulary program. Children's books, particularly those that are meant to be read aloud to children, are ideal sources for choosing words for vocabulary instruction. These books introduce children to a wide variety of contexts and include a vast supply of words that are not typically part of children's everyday conversations. Thus, teachers can use children's books to set the scene for word learning and introduce new words through the context of the books they are reading. In selecting books that provide fertile ground for vocabulary instruction, teachers should keep a number of principles in mind. Next we review a few principles, shown in Figure 2.7, that we adapted from an article by Shedd and Duke (2008) on planning for read-alouds.

First, teachers should choose books with rich language and vocabulary. Teachers can use children's book awards as a starting point for finding books with rich language on a wide variety of subjects. We provide information about book awards and book lists in the Appendix. Teachers can evaluate the words in books using the principles we defined earlier in this chapter.

Second, teachers should use different genres for introducing words. Fictional storybooks have been the mainstay of vocabulary interventions for quite some time, which is warranted, given the rich text and detailed pictures that are typically included in such books. However, recent research suggests that informational books provide another important context for teaching vocabulary. Combining fictional and informational texts in the same thematic units, as done in research by Silverman et al. (2013) in preschool and Silverman and Hines (2009) in prekindergarten through second grades, is a way to capitalize on both text types.

Language	Genre	Support	Complexity	Diversity
Teachers should choose texts with rich language and vocabulary.	Teachers should choose texts across genres.	Teachers should choose texts with ample pictorial support.	Teachers should choose texts that are optimally challenging.	Teachers should choose texts that reflect diverse cultures and experiences.

FIGURE 2.7. Principles for selecting texts for vocabulary instruction. Based on Shedd and Duke (2008).

Third, teachers should use texts with lots of picture support. For example, books with photographs or drawings provide visual representations of words, which help children learn them more readily. Looking up winners of the American Library Association's Caldecott Medal, awarded to illustrators of children's books, is a great place to start identifying books with remarkable pictures.

Fourth, teachers should choose texts at the right level of complexity. Since children can understand text at much higher levels than they can read at this age, teachers can introduce complex content that children cannot access through texts on their own. These texts should be challenging enough to be interesting, but not so advanced that children become disengaged. Considering children's background knowledge will be key to determining whether texts are at the right level of complexity for children in a given class.

Finally, teachers should choose texts that represent children's home culture and expose them to diverse cultures and experiences besides their own through words and pictures. Children develop a sense of security when they see their home culture valued in the texts they hear and read and school. Children also develop curiosity and interest about the world around them when they learn about new cultures and experiences. Thus, teachers should use texts that resonate with children's lived experiences as well as texts that expand children's knowledge base.

To supplement traditional texts, teachers can also choose to use digital texts for vocabulary instruction. These texts often offer the same content as traditional texts, but instead of just pictorial support, they also include multimedia features such as animations and pop-up definitions. In addition to the range of texts teachers should consider for vocabulary instruction, there are many different materials they can use to support word learning. For example, using pictures, props, and videos to show words in different ways can support word learning (e.g., Apthorp et al., 2012; Silverman & Hines, 2009; Wasik et al., 2006). Also, using picture sorts (i.e., sorting pictures into categories), word games (e.g., the Vocabulary Building Games Library for Grades 1–3 by Lakeshore), and computer games (e.g., vocabulary building games at *http://pbskids.org/games/vocabulary*) could be useful for reinforcing vocabulary knowledge through children's active engagement with words. For all these different types of materials, teachers should consider

The principles of text selection we discuss here are relevant to text selection as indicated in the CCSS. For example, in the CCSS, children are expected to ask and answer questions about unknown words in *literature* and *informational* text (e.g., CCSS.ELA–Literacy.RL.K.4 and CCSS.ELA–Literacy.RI.K.4). And the CCSS note that children should be able to use information from *pictures* to demonstrate understanding of text and explain how pictures contribute to and clarify text (e.g., CCSS.ELS–Literacy.RL.2.7 and CCSS.ELA–Literacy.RI.2.7). Finally, the CCSS call for students to engage with texts selected from a wide range of cultures and periods. (See Standard 10 on Range, Quality, and Complexity.)

(1) whether materials convey the meanings they are teaching, (2) whether materials are supportive of word learning, and (3) whether materials promote active participation in word learning.

Summary

In this section of the chapter, we reviewed previous approaches to word selection and explained our own approach to choosing words to teach. We also discussed balancing breadth and depth of instruction and described how to identify texts and materials for teaching children about words. With all of these nuts and bolts in place, we now consider how teachers should teach vocabulary to foster vocabulary breadth and depth.

What Principles Should Guide Vocabulary Instruction?

Over the past few decades, researchers have learned a great deal about vocabulary learning and instruction, and the principles of instruction we propose are built on this foundation. In particular, we draw on the work of Michael Graves, whose book *The Vocabulary Book* (2006) has greatly influenced our thinking about how to teach words. However, *The Vocabulary Book* focuses mostly on upper-elementary-grade students and above. Thus, we also draw on our own work in prekindergarten through second-grade classrooms (e.g., Silverman, 2007a, 2007b, 2013; Silverman & Crandell, 2010; Silverman et al., 2013; Silverman & Hines, 2009) and the work of others (e.g., Beck et al., 2002, 2013; Biemiller & Boote, 2006; Coyne et al., 2009) in adapting the principles Graves (2006) proposed for teaching vocabulary to young children. We list the principles of instruction that we have identified in Figure 2.8. In the remainder of this chapter, we provide an overview of the principles and a summary of the research supporting the principles. In subsequent chapters, we discuss the principles in depth and show how they can be implemented in prekindergarten through second-grade classrooms.

Provide Explicit and Extended Vocabulary Instruction

While children learn many words through *incidental exposure*, they may not have enough rich exposure to academically important words in the context of everyday conversations to learn the words they need to succeed in school. Therefore, teachers must provide *explicit instruction* with *extended* opportunities for word learning to support children's word learning. Through explicit and extended instruction, teachers intentionally offer clear definitions, supportive contexts, and ample

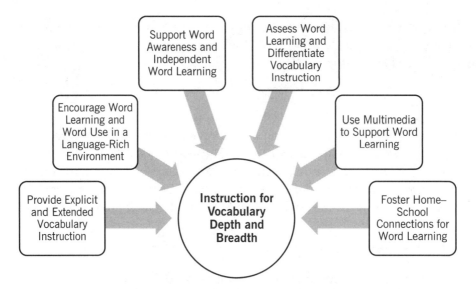

FIGURE 2.8. Principles of instruction for vocabulary breadth and depth.

opportunity to use words and receive feedback on word use so that children can learn words more quickly than if they were reliant on *incidental exposure* alone. While there are too many words for teachers to explicitly teach, instructing students on specific target words provides them with a foundation of word knowledge on which to build in future encounters; the more words children know, the easier it is for them to learn new words.

Research on explicit instruction shows how beneficial it can be. For example, Biemiller and Boote (2006), working with socioeconomically and linguistically diverse kindergarten, first-grade, and second-grade children in Canada, found that, of the new words they encountered during repeated readings of books by their teachers, children learned 12% through incidental exposure, 22% through explicit instruction, and 41% through explicit instruction plus review. Beck and McKeown (2007), working with kindergarteners and first graders from low-income families

Incidental exposure refers to children encountering new words without instruction.

Implicit instruction involves incidental teaching of vocabulary (e.g., providing brief definitions when words are encountered) during book reading or other activities.

Explicit instruction emphasizes intentional, direct, and sustained teaching of vocabulary through rich definitions and examples before, during, and after book reading or other activities.

Extended instruction includes explicit instruction *and* extension activities in which teachers review and reinforce word learning across book reading and other activities.

in the United States, found that children who received explicit instruction gained roughly 10–15% more in target word knowledge than children who did not receive explicit instruction, and children who received explicit instruction gained more than twice as much from *more* explicit instruction (i.e., approximately 28 minutes or 20 encounters with a word) compared with regular explicit instruction (i.e., approximately 7 minutes or 5 encounters with a word). Finally, Coyne et al. (2009), in a study with kindergarteners, found that, while children learned more through explicit instruction embedded in storybook reading than from incidental exposure to words, children learned even more, increasing their depth of word knowledge, through explicit instruction embedded in storybook reading plus extended instruction after storybook reading.

Research in preschool and prekindergarten classrooms has shown similar results. For example, Collins (2010), in a recent study conducted with preschool ELLs, compared children's word learning through incidental exposure with explicit instruction that included gesturing, defining, pointing to illustrations, providing synonyms, and using words across contexts. Children who received explicit instruction gained nearly 20% more in knowledge of words in the book than children who did not receive explicit instruction. Silverman et al. (2013), working in preschool classrooms with children from low socioeconomic and linguistically diverse backgrounds, compared children's word learning in a control ("business as usual") condition, an explicit instruction condition, and an extended instruction condition in which words were reinforced throughout the day. Findings revealed that children in the explicit instruction condition learned more words than children in the control condition, and children in the extended instruction condition learned more words than children in the explicit instruction condition.

The consistency of the finding that explicit and extended instruction supports word learning for all age and grade levels and for children from different backgrounds implies that teachers everywhere should be employing this form of instruction. In fact, Marulis and Neuman (2010), reviewing 67 studies on the effects of vocabulary intervention on prekindergarten and kindergarten children's word learning, found that children made significantly greater gains in vocabulary with interventions that included explicit or explicit plus implicit instruction rather than implicit instruction alone. Given the substantial body of research showing that explicit and extended instruction supports vocabulary breadth and depth, we feel confident recommending it as part of any curriculum aimed at supporting children's language and literacy. In Chapter 3, we provide recommendations for implementing such instruction in everyday classroom contexts.

Encourage Word Learning and Word Use in a Language-Rich Environment

In addition to providing explicit and extended vocabulary instruction, teachers should create opportunities for children to regularly hear and use new words in a language-rich environment. Research on how teachers use language in the classroom and how they question, prompt, and provide feedback during read-alouds and throughout the school day suggests that teachers can play a major role in promoting word learning and word use in early childhood and elementary school classrooms (e.g., Dickinson & Smith, 1994; Dickinson & Porche, 2011; Wasik et al., 2006). Furthermore, research on the classroom environment suggests that providing emotional support, instructional support, and organized materials and resources also serves to create a context wherein vocabulary learning flourishes (e.g., Burchinal et al., 2008; Cadima, Leal, & Burchinal, 2010; Connor, Son, Hindman, & Morrison, 2005).

An important line of research on encouraging word learning and word use in a language-rich environment focuses on reading books aloud to young children (i.e., read-alouds) and looks beyond explicit vocabulary instruction to teachers' questioning, feedback, and general interaction style. For example, Dickinson and Smith (1994) studied preschool teachers' book reading by looking at overall reading styles and examining specific kinds of teacher talk. These authors identified three distinct styles: (1) co-constructive, in which teachers fostered analytic conversation about the text during book reading (e.g., "Why do you think he is sad, Jake?"); (2) didactic-interactional, in which teachers asked questions about details in the text before, during, and after reading (e.g., "What was the male robin doing?"); and (3) performance-oriented, in which teachers engaged children in extended discussion of text before and after reading (e.g., after reading a book called *Never Talk to Strangers,* the teacher asks, "Why shouldn't we talk to strangers?"). These authors found that children in classrooms where teachers were more performance-oriented showed greater gains in vocabulary. Also, they found that analytic talk (i.e., talk about characters, plot, and vocabulary), seen mostly in the co-constructive and performance-oriented reading styles, was related to increased vocabulary in the classrooms studied. Overall, the research by Dickinson and Smith (1994) suggests that the more teachers foster rich language through extended conversations during book reading, the more children will grow in word knowledge.

One of the best-known read-aloud interventions for promoting language and literacy development in young children is called dialogic reading. In this approach, teachers read books with children and prompt them to say something about the book. Similar to the analytic talk in Dickinson and Smith's (1994) research, teachers' prompts in dialogic reading support literal and inferential thinking and use of contextualized and decontextualized talk. In one of the original studies on dialogic reading, Whitehurst et al. (1994) found positive effects of dialogic reading on preschoolers' expressive vocabulary. Subsequent studies on dialogic reading have replicated this finding. In fact, in a recent synthesis of read-aloud interventions on early reading outcomes among preschool through third-grade students at risk for reading difficulties, Swanson et al. (2011) found that "dialogic reading has the most causal evidence to support its effect on children's literacy outcomes," including "phonological awareness, print concepts, reading comprehension, and vocabulary" (p. 272). Other read-aloud interventions such as Text Talk (Beck & McKeown, 2001) and interventions that include read-alouds, such as vocabulary visits (Blachowiscz & Obrochta, 2005), have also been shown to foster language in general and vocabulary in particular. We discuss these interventions in detail in Chapter 4.

Along with book reading interventions, research suggests that other classroom activities throughout the day may also provide rich opportunities for language development in the classroom. For example, talking about words during morning meeting time, which is not usually a focus of vocabulary intervention, may support children's vocabulary learning (Hindman & Wasik, 2012; Silverman et al., 2013). Also, the Language Experience Approach, in which teachers guide children in talking about topics of interest and work with children to generate a written account of what was discussed, has shown promise as a context for promoting the language development of children from diverse backgrounds (Hoffman & Roser, 2012). Research also suggests that peer-based activities, which include having children use words and talk about words together, may be helpful for supporting word learning (Christ & Wang, 2012; Silverman, Martin-Beltran, Peercy, & Meyer, 2014). Also, infusing centers with activities to stimulate word learning and language use has been shown to be supportive of children's vocabulary (e.g., Bond & Wasik, 2009; Dockrell, Stuart, & King, 2010; Silverman et al., 2013). Finally, storytelling, story dictation, and even writing activities have been shown to yield positive effects on vocabulary development (Christ & Wang, 2011; Cooper, Capo, Mathes, & Grey, 2007; Tracy & Headley, 2013). We discuss each of these classroom activities in Chapter 4.

Support Word Awareness and Independent Word Learning

As well as supporting children in word learning by encouraging use of taught words and providing opportunities for children to encounter new words throughout the day, teachers can help children become aware of sophisticated words in their environment. The more children are aware of words, the more they will learn about words they are in the process of acquiring. Also, the more aware they are of words, the more likely they are to stop and think about a word that is new to them. To encourage word awareness, Beck et al. (2002, 2013) suggest providing positive reinforcement when children share that they noticed or used sophisticated words at school or at home. Graves and Watts-Taffe (2008) suggest promoting word play, fostering word awareness through writing, and involving students in investigations about words as ways to encourage word awareness. Lane and Allen (2010) suggest that teachers should model using sophisticated words in their own talk to help children develop word awareness. In fact, recent research by Dickinson and Porche (2011) indicates that teachers' use of sophisticated words in preschool has long-term positive effects on children's language and literacy.

As children develop word awareness and become interested in new words they encounter, they need strategies to be able to figure out words on their own. Research on teaching upper-elementary-grade students to use independent word learning strategies, such as using context clues and morphological word parts to figure out unknown words, has shown positive effects (Baumann et al., 2003), but less is known about teaching children independent word learning strategies in the earlier grades. For children in first and second grade who are readers, using these independent word learning strategies in the context of reading may be possible. However, given that children in these grades are often "glued to print," meaning that the decoding process is still laborious for them, support for word learning through oral instruction in the early childhood and elementary grades is needed.

Some research with young children shows that focusing on independent word learning strategies through oral activities may have positive effects. For example, Nash and Snowling (2006), working with 7- and 8-year-olds with poor vocabulary, found that teaching children to use "clue words" to figure out unknown words had positive effects on their expressive vocabulary and comprehension skills. Additionally, Apel, Brimo, Diehm, and Apel (2013) found that kindergarten, first-, and second-grade children who participated in a 9-week intervention that promoted morphemic analysis skills grew in their ability to define words based on their roots and affixes. More studies are needed on the extent to which supporting young children's use of context clues and morphological word parts to figure out the meaning of unknown words may benefit word learning, but the research to date suggests that attention to context clues and morphology in the early grades may be worthwhile for vocabulary development.

Young children can also be taught to use dictionaries and other resources to figure out unknown words, although many such resources are not accessible to them. There is little research on supporting children in using picture dictionaries, talking dictionaries, and other electronic resources to support word learning, but these may be helpful tools for children to learn to use. In general, the research base on supporting the word awareness and independent word learning of young children is thin. But, considering the importance of being aware of words and using strategies to figure out words for independent word learning throughout schooling and beyond, we believe that teachers should attend to these facets of

Morphemic analysis includes noticing meaningful word parts and using these word parts to understand words. In the early stages it includes, for example, recognizing the component words in compound words (e.g., *cupcake*); the plural -*s*; the past tense -*ed*; the present progressive -*ing*; the prefixes *un*-, *re*-, and *dis*-; and the suffixes -*er*/-*est*, -*ness*, and -*less*. If children recognize these word parts, they may have an easier time figuring out what inflected words (i.e., root words that have attached affixes) mean. For example, knowing *un*- and *help* and -*ful* will allow children to figure out *unhelpful* even if they have never heard that word before.

word learning in their early childhood and elementary school classrooms. We offer suggestions for how to foster word awareness and independent word learning in Chapter 5.

Assess and Differentiate Vocabulary Instruction to Meet Diverse Student Needs

Research by Leung et al. (2011) indicates that children in similar settings may have vastly different levels of word knowledge. In order to meet children's needs, teachers need to know where children are in terms of their vocabulary development. However, given the multiple facets of words and word learning, assessing vocabulary can be complicated (Pearson, Hiebert, & Kamil, 2007). Therefore, no one assessment of vocabulary can adequately measure children's word knowledge. And teachers may get very different kinds of results from different kinds of assessments (e.g., picture identification, sentence verification, or matching tasks). Knowing the purpose of assessment can guide teachers in choosing assessments to administer and/or in using assessment data to guide instruction (Walpole & McKenna, 2007). And, since vocabulary is often not measured systematically in school, teachers must be armed with their own assessments to evaluate students' vocabulary learning. Therefore, in Chapter 6, we discuss the purposes of assessment, different kinds of measures that can be used to assess vocabulary, and types of measures teachers can develop and implement in their own classrooms to understand children's vocabulary growth over time.

Since assessment and differentiation are intertwined, we propose these two principles together. Assessments can provide a general picture of the vocabulary level of the students in class, and teachers can use this information to plan vocabulary instruction during whole-class read-alouds. Assessments can also provide an indication of which children have more limited or advanced vocabulary for their age or grade, and this information can be used to differentiate instruction so children are optimally supported. For example, Silverman and Crandell (2010) found that instructional practices during read-aloud and non-read-aloud time differentially benefited children with more and less vocabulary. Specifically, whereas children with weaker vocabulary knowledge benefited more from teacher guidance to act out and illustrate words during read-aloud time, children with stronger vocabulary knowledge benefited more from teacher guidance to apply word knowledge across contexts beyond read aloud-time.

Given that children vary greatly in their word knowledge (Biemiller & Slonim, 2001), differentiated instruction is important in all classrooms. One model for differentiated instruction is Universal Design for Learning (UDL). According to the UDL framework, to address children's individual differences, teachers should provide multiple means of representation, action and expression, and engagement. In other words teachers should "present information and content in different ways," "differentiate the ways that students can express what they know," and "stimulate interest and motivation for learning" (*http://www.cast.org/udl*). Applying UDL to vocabulary instruction, teachers should present words in different ways, including verbal definitions and examples, visual pictures and video, and gestures and other actions. Teachers should encourage children to use words in speaking, writing, drawing, and gesturing. And teachers should engage children in word learning by making it fun, relevant, and personal. By using multiple means of representation, expression, and engagement in every vocabulary lesson, teachers can meet the needs of all students in their classroom. And, as teachers assess their students and monitor their progress over time, they can provide additional instructional supports for different learners as needed.

While differentiated instruction is meant to benefit all learners, it may be particularly important for meeting the needs of children who come to school with limited vocabulary compared to their peers. For children from low socioeconomic and ELL backgrounds and for children with SLI and SLD, teachers may need to offer more explicit and extended instruction and more opportunities to learn and use language so they can catch up to their peers in vocabulary. Specifically, the following instructional supports may be needed: elaborated instruction (Zipoli, Coyne, & McCoach, 2011), connections to children's cultural and linguistic background (Ortiz & Artiles, 2010), and use of nonverbal supports, including multimedia (Silverman & Hines, 2009). For example, Zipoli et al., in implementing instruction with kindergarteners from low socioeconomic backgrounds, found that enhancing instruction with attention to the semantic analysis of words supported children's word learning and helped them catch up to their peers in vocabulary. Similarly, Silverman (2007a) implemented an intervention with ELLs and non-ELLs in kindergarten that included explicit instruction on words plus added nonverbal support. All children gained in the intervention, but ELL children, who started out lower than their non-ELL peers in vocabulary, grew most, resulting in a narrowing of the vocabulary gap between ELL and non-ELL students in the study. Additionally, Munro, Lee, and Baker (2008) showed that preschool students with SLI benefit from small-group, differentiated instruction on semantic features of words within the context of oral and storybook narratives and related activities. Finally, Restrepo, Morgan, and Thompson (2013), working with preschool ELLs with SLI, found positive effects of intervention that included dialogic reading and hands-on vocabulary instruction in English or Spanish on children's word learning.

Recent studies show that differentiating the intensity of instruction may be an effective way of meeting the needs of different learners in the area of vocabulary. Specifically, researchers have applied the response-to-intervention (RTI) model to vocabulary instruction with promising results (Fien et al., 2011; Loftus & Coyne, 2013). According to the RTI model, all children receive high-quality core instruction (Tier 1) with some differentiation. Based on screening and progress monitoring data, children given Tier 1 instruction who do not show mastery of particular skills and/or are not showing progress in those skills receive supplemental instruction (Tier 2) and are monitored more regularly. Children who are unresponsive to supplemental instruction, based on progress-monitoring data, may receive intensive, more individualized instruction (Tier 3). The focus of Tier 3 intervention is often informed by information from diagnostic assessment. Loftus and Coyne (2013), working with kindergarteners, and Fien and colleagues (2011), working with first graders, have shown that using RTI to address vocabulary may help teachers support children with limited word knowledge in catching up with their peers over time. Much more research is needed in this area, but in Chapter 7 we discuss the promise of using UDL to differentiate vocabulary instruction for all learners and using RTI to provide intensified vocabulary support for children most in need.

Support Word Learning through the Use of Multimedia

In the digital age, the resources available to teachers and children to support word learning are vast—from audiobooks and electronic readers to videos and computer games. Multimedia that is aligned with UDL principles might show concepts visually and use voice-overs to explain them. Such multimedia may invite students to respond by touching or clicking or by speaking or typing. Finally, multimedia that embodies UDL principles might stimulate interest and engagement by giving students choices (e.g., click on your favorite word) and fostering student collaboration (e.g., add *weather* words to the class wiki on our study of *weather*). Using multimedia aligned with principles of UDL for supporting vocabulary has been shown to be effective in upper elementary school (e.g., Proctor et al., 2009), but more research is needed in early childhood and elementary classrooms.

Some research with younger children supports using multimedia with multiple means of representation to enhance vocabulary learning. This research has been founded on Paivio's (1986) dual coding theory, which suggests that children learn better when information is presented both verbally and nonverbally. Specifically, providing multiple modes of representation to show different facets of words in different contexts can support children in gaining deeper understanding of words and how they are used across contexts. For example, Silverman and Hines (2009), working in prekindergarten through second-grade classrooms, augmented read-aloud instruction focused on teaching words related to *habitats* with video. ELL children in particular benefited from the added video clips and made significant gains compared to children who did not receive the additional video support. Korat and Shamir (2012), working with prekindergarten and kindergarten children in Israel, found that electronic books that provide word explanations effectively promote children's word learning. And Segers and Verhoeven (2003), working with native and immigrant kindergarten children in the Netherlands, found positive effects of playing vocabulary-focused computer games on children's vocabulary learning. Such studies show the potential for using multimedia as a tool to support word learning in 21st-century classrooms.

However, not all multimedia resources are equally beneficial for children's vocabulary learning (Parish-Morris, Mahajan, Hirsch-Pasek, Golinkoff, & Collins, 2013; Silverman, 2009; Wood, 2001). With so many multimedia resources coming on the market every day, teachers must be ready to evaluate digital media to distinguish the good from the bad. Researchers who have studied the use of multimedia for educational purposes have proposed recommendations for evaluating different types of multimedia (e.g., Bishop & Santoro, 2006; Cahill & McGill-Franzen, 2013; Wood, 2001). We review these recommendations and offer some examples of how to evaluate multimedia resources to maximize the potential for student vocabulary learning in Chapter 8.

Support Word Learning through Home–School Connections

There is not enough time in the school day for teachers to address all of the words children need to know to understand what they hear and read in school. Thus, teachers need to support word learning beyond the classroom. While factors such as socioeconomic and language background may be related to lower levels of vocabulary knowledge, it is important to recognize that these factors can be overcome, and that families are rich resources of support with substantial funds of knowledge (Heath, 1983; Moll et al., 1992; Purcell-Gates, 2007). In fact, providing a connection between home and school language and literacy can serve as an important support for children, particularly children with limited vocabulary.

Studies show the promise of including home–school connections in a program to aid children's vocabulary breadth and depth. For example, Lonigan and Whitehurst (1998) investigated the effects of training teachers and parents to use dialogic reading using four conditions (e.g., no intervention, teacher-led intervention, parent-led intervention, and teacher- and parent-led intervention). Results showed significant gains in expressive vocabulary that were most pronounced for the two conditions that included parent involvement. Jordan, Snow, and Porche (2000) showed positive effects of a home–school connections program called Project EASE, in which parents of kindergarten students were taught to further children's language and literacy development by implementing such activities as talking during mealtime and retelling family narratives. Findings revealed that children whose families participated in the program made significantly greater gains in vocabulary than their peers whose families did not participate, and these effects were most pronounced for children who had low vocabulary knowledge at the start of the project. Saint-Laurent and Giasson (2005) implemented a similar program with families of children in first grade, many of whom were from low-income backgrounds, that included workshops on book reading, help with writing, and home activities that complemented in-class teaching. Specific discussion on supporting vocabulary was included. Results showed that children whose parents participated in the program used better vocabulary in their writing in school. Finally, Shanahan, Mulhern, and Rodriguez-Brown (1995) reported positive effects of Project FLAME, in which parents of ELL children ages 3–9 were instructed on how to support children's language and literacy development as well as English as a second language (ESL) instruction to improve their own English-language skills. Results from the project showed that children gained in language and literacy skills, including vocabulary, and parents grew in their confidence in being able to support their children in school.

All of these studies show that using home–school connections to support children's vocabulary had positive effects on children's word learning. More studies are needed on how to connect the home and classroom contexts. However, considering how influential home factors are on children's language development (e.g., Huttenlocher et al., 2010), focusing on the home literacy environment as a place where vocabulary can be learned and reinforced should be a priority for teachers concerned with optimally supporting children's vocabulary development. Therefore, in Chapter 9, we focus on various ways teachers can support vocabulary learning through home–school connections in prekindergarten through second grade.

Summary

In this chapter, we have outlined a road map for you to use to plan vocabulary instruction in your early-childhood or elementary classroom. Specifically, we have discussed choosing words to teach, balancing instruction for breadth versus depth, and determining which texts and materials to use to ground vocabulary instruction. We have also set forth our principles for effective vocabulary instruction and the research base from which we derived these principles. We know that this is a lot of information to absorb. Don't worry. In the chapters to come, we give specific recommendations for implementing these principles, illustrated with examples of how these principles can be readily applied in everyday prekindergarten through second-grade classrooms. And, in Chapter 10, we feature vignettes showing how all of these principles can be implemented in concert to most effectively foster children's vocabulary breadth and depth.

CHAPTER 3
· · · · · · · · · · ·
Explicit and Extended Vocabulary Instruction

GUIDING QUESTIONS

- What should be included in explicit vocabulary instruction?
- How should teachers implement instruction before, during, and after reading?
- How can teachers extend instruction throughout the day?

During read-aloud time, Ms. Adrisi read the book *Chugga, Chugga, Choo, Choo*, by Kevin Lewis (2001), to her kindergarten class. In the book, a toy train climbs up mountains, high and steep, and chugs through valleys, low and deep. Before, during, and after reading, Mrs. Adrisi focused on the words *steep, mountain, deep*, and *valley*. She defined the words and used pictures and gestures to illustrate them. She even had her students act out climbing up a steep mountain and chugging through a deep valley. Later, on the playground, Mrs. Adrisi couldn't help but smile when she heard one of her students say, "I'm gonna climb up the rock wall. It's so steep!"

When you think of explicit instruction, you may think of "skill drills." In fact, a lot of teachers we have talked with cringe when we use the term "explicit instruction" because it can be associated with boring and tedious scripted lesson delivery. However, explicit instruction, when done well, can be fun and engaging. It can also serve to support children as they develop independence. In this chapter, we focus on characteristics of explicit vocabulary instruction and describe ways you can incorporate explicit vocabulary instruction into your regular read-aloud routines. We also discuss the importance of extending instruction beyond read-alouds and reinforcing vocabulary throughout the day in prekindergarten through second-grade classrooms.

Characteristics of Explicit Vocabulary Instruction

The model of explicit instruction that provides ongoing support as students gain independence is called the gradual release of responsibility (Duke & Pearson, 2008). At first, teachers explain and model. Then, teachers provide students with highly supported guided practice. Once students begin to show proficiency with the instructional target, teachers begin to take away some of the support and allow students to become increasingly independent. The gradual release of responsibility model has been applied most widely in the area of comprehension, but it can be used in the area of vocabulary as well. (See Figure 3.1.)

At first, when teachers introduce new words, they provide definitions, explain the meaning of the words in context, and offer examples of how the words could be used in other contexts. They also focus on how words are pronounced or spelled.[1] This part of the explicit instruction process can be highly supportive and lots of fun if teachers use visuals and pantomimes to explain words and interesting examples to which children can relate. Next, they provide supported opportunities for children to use the words. For example, they might provide cloze sentences (i.e., fill-in-the-blank sentences) or ask closed questions (i.e., forced choice) about

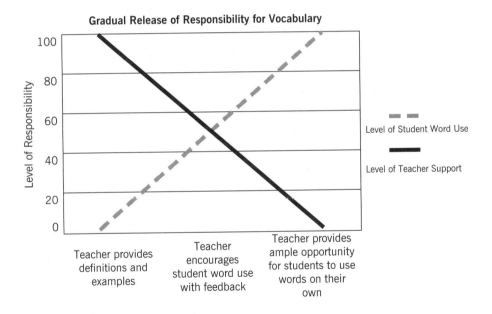

FIGURE 3.1. Gradual release of responsibility for vocabulary.

---

[1]Note, however, that vocabulary instruction should not be confused with spelling instruction. Knowing how to pronounce or spell words helps students remember them, but spelling instruction should be focused on letter–sound patterns and vocabulary instruction should be focused on meaning. The only time that spelling and vocabulary instruction should completely overlap is when the spelling of a word (i.e., including prefixes and suffixes) is related to its meaning.

word use in context so students can practice their word knowledge with support. Finally, teachers can provide opportunities for students to use the words themselves across contexts so they can gain independence in using the words on their own. At first, students may gain receptive knowledge of words and be able to understand them when they hear them, but over time they will gain expressive knowledge of the words and be able to use them productively. With lots of repeated practice, students' word knowledge gradually moves from shallow to deep, and the words become part of their personal vocabulary.

Research has converged on a set of practices that can be used throughout explicit instruction before, during, and after read-alouds and during instruction beyond read-alouds. These practices have been included for interventions shown to be effective at supporting children's vocabulary learning (e.g., Beck & McKeown, 2007; Coyne et al., 2009; Justice, Meier, & Walpole, 2005; Silverman, 2007b). Bringing together instructional practices used in explicit vocabulary instruction across studies, Silverman (2007a) developed and evaluated a multidimensional vocabulary program (MVP) that included instructional practices meant to call attention to various aspects of words and support children in engaging with words in different ways. The instructional practices we present in Figure 3.2 and discuss herein are based on the practices outlined in the MVP model. (Note that all children who participated in the MVP gained in word learning, and ELL children who participated in the program began to catch up to their peers in general vocabulary knowledge.) Next we describe each practice in more detail.

Say the Word for Students and Have Them Say It Back

Children need to make a connection between how a word sounds and what it means. They need to hear the correct pronunciation of the word, and then they need to practice saying it themselves. Hearing and saying the word will help

Say the word for students and have them say it back.	Provide a comprehensible definition of the word.	Provide examples of the word across contexts.
Show the printed word on a word card and have students attend to the letters and sounds in words.	**Multidimensional Vocabulary Instruction**	Guide children to analyze how the word is used in context and how it is related to other words.
Show actions, gestures, pictures, and props to illustrate the word.	Provide repeated exposure and review to reinforce word learning across contexts.	Encourage children to use the word in new contexts on their own.

FIGURE 3.2. Practices of multidimensional vocabulary instruction. Based on Silverman (2007b).

children remember the word over time, and it will give them a phonological representation of the word with which to associate the meaning of the word. First, teachers need to call attention to the words they are saying so children know which word is the target word they should be learning. To do this, teachers can call children's attention to their mouth with a hand signal that communicates, "look and listen." Having joint attention where the teacher and the children are focused on the same thing can help cue students in learning a new word. Next, teachers can say the word slowly (but not so slowly that the word becomes distorted) with clear articulation. For children who need extra time to process the sounds they hear, slowing down speech slightly when introducing a new word can help them hear all of the sounds in the word. Finally, teachers can have children say the word themselves. Choral response, when all of the children respond together, allows everyone to have a chance to participate. Teachers can look around the room to make sure everyone said the word and to make sure it looks like they said it correctly. If needed, teachers can repeat the word a couple more times and have children do the same. Through this process, teachers are supporting children as they establish a phonological representation of the word at hand, which will help them remember the word as they learn. Here's an example of how a teacher might introduce the word *vehicle,* which she is teaching in a unit on transportation:

TEACHER: The word we are going to learn today is (*pause*) *vehicle.* Look and listen as I say that word again: *vehicle.* Listen to me say it one more time: *vehicle.* Now your turn. Say *vehicle.*

STUDENTS: *Vehicle.*

TEACHER: Say it again.

STUDENTS: *Vehicle.*

TEACHER: One last time.

STUDENTS: *Vehicle.*

Show the Printed Word on a Word Card and Have Students Attend to the Letters and Sounds in Words

Even though many of the words teachers introduce to young children for vocabulary learning are beyond their decoding ability, displaying the written word helps children attend to the word and gives them an initial sense of how the word is printed in text. Children in kindergarten may be able to read some words and attend to the initial letters and sounds in the words on word cards. First and second graders may actually be able to read some of the words introduced. Regardless, even for prekindergarten children, showing the word on a word card can help them attend to the word and make the connection between words they hear and

FIGURE 3.3. Vehicle word card. Image Copyright 2013 by YenzHautArt. Used with permission.

words that are in the books their teachers are reading and they will, eventually, read themselves. Additionally, showing words on word cards helps children begin to establish an orthographic representation of the words they are learning, which will prime them to be able to read the words once their decoding skills have caught up with their vocabulary skills. The following is an example of how a teacher might explicitly introduce the word card, shown in Figure 3.3, for the target word, *vehicle*.

> TEACHER: Take a look at my word card. This word says, "*Vehicle.*" What letter does the word vehicle start with? [Or, depending on the children's level, teachers could say, "*Vehicle* starts with the letter *V.* What letter?"]
>
> STUDENTS: *V.*
>
> TEACHER: Yes, *vehicle* starts with /v/, /v/, V.

Display Pictures, Actions, Gestures, and Props to Illustrate the Word

Combined with the phonological and orthographic representation of the words, a visual representation of the word gives children an anchor on which to build their understanding of the word. For example, on the word card above, there is a prototypical example of a *vehicle*. While there are many other kinds of vehicles children can learn about and other uses of the word that children may encounter (i.e., air is a *vehicle* for sound, art is a *vehicle* for expression, and words are a *vehicle* for communication), the prototypical image is ideal for establishing a baseline for the word. Later, this image can jog students' memory and help them connect new examples and uses of the word when they hear or see them. Teachers can also use actions or gestures to help children comprehend and remember the word. For example, they can teach children sign language for the word *car* to help them remember the word vehicle. Finally, teachers can use props to provide concrete examples of words that will help children remember the word and what it means.

Provide a Comprehensible Definition of the Word

When children first learn words, they need comprehensible input about what a word means. Dictionary definitions are likely incomprehensible for young learners, offering definitions that often include words that are too complex to understand or so vague that it is impossible to figure out what the word actually means. For example, the *American Heritage Dictionary* (*www.ahdictionary.com*) defines *vehicle* as "(a) a device or structure for transporting persons or things; a conveyance: a space vehicle or (b) a self-propelled conveyance that runs on tires; a motor vehicle." For a child who doesn't know what *device, structure, transport, conveyance,* or *self-propelled* means, this definition does nothing to elucidate its meaning. However, by rephrasing definitions in terms young children can understand, comprising only words that they already know in the context of a full explanation, teachers can help children begin to develop a decontextualized understanding of a word on which they will build over time. Creating these definitions is not always easy. We have found a few resources that can be used to support coming up with comprehensible definitions, although the definitions in these resources sometimes need to be modified even further to use only known words or concepts. In Figure 3.4 we provide definitions of *vehicle* from some of these resources.

Provide Examples and Encourage Children to Use the Word across Contexts

When introducing a word through picture books, referencing how the word was used in the book supports children in thinking about word meaning in a familiar context. It also helps children connect the word to the bigger picture of the story or subject at hand. Beyond the context of the book, providing children with examples of how the word can be used in other contexts and connecting the word to examples in children's personal lives can help them develop a rich understanding of the word and how it is used across contexts. In the following example, the teacher connects the word to the context of the book, gives examples in additional contexts that might be relevant to children, and encourages children to connect the word to something in their personal lives. The teacher in this example is referencing *My Truck Is Stuck*, by Kevin Lewis and Daniel Kirk (2006). Although the

Definition of *Vehicle*	Source
Something used to carry and move people or things.	*kids.wordsmyth.net/wild*
Something used to transport persons or goods.	*www.wordcentral.com*
A machine with an engine that carries people or things from place to place.	*Collins COBUILD Student's Dictionary* (Sinclair, 2005)

FIGURE 3.4. Varying definitions for the word *vehicle*.

book doesn't specifically use the word *vehicle*, the teacher uses the book to teach the word *vehicle*. As we noted in Chapter 2, books can include target words or serve as jumping-off points for teaching target words in context.

> TEACHER: In the book, the truck driver had a problem. His *vehicle* broke down. Drivers in other *vehicles* tried to help. Some of the *vehicles* we saw were cars, buses, and, finally, a tow truck. This book reminds me of a time when my car broke down. Lots of *vehicles* passed by while I was waiting for the tow truck. I saw a motorcycle, a concrete mixer, and a garbage truck. What I needed was a tow truck. There are lots of *vehicles* in our neighborhood. What are some of the *vehicles* you saw on your way to school today?

Within this short explanation, the teacher connected the word to its immediate context (i.e., the truck in the story *My Truck Is Stuck*), encouraged use of the word in other contexts with which students are likely familiar (e.g., seeing cars trucks on the road), and prompted students to provide their own example of the target word (i.e., vehicles seen on the way to school).

While providing examples is an important way to help children generalize their word learning beyond the immediate context of the book, teachers should limit the amount of time spent simply listing examples, unless it is necessary to give lots of examples in order to highlight the nuances of a word's meaning. We have noticed that sometimes teachers stray or allow their students to stray too far off topic without coming back to the target word at hand. For instance, one teacher we observed teaching the word *delivery* used the example of a time when she had pizza delivered to her home. Then she asked children about things they had had *delivered* to their homes. Children got so focused on what kinds of foods or packages they had gotten in the past that they forgot all about the word *delivery*. Therefore, it is important to support children's use of the word so they use it appropriately in new contexts and do not stray. Some children may need more structure and assistance to use words effectively. Below are some ways teachers can scaffold children's use of words.

Providing Sentence Frames

Like an oral "fill in the blank" teachers can provide students with a sentence frame and students can fill in the rest with either a word or an example. For children who are readers, teachers can write the sentence stem on a sentence strip or on the board for children to use as they provide their examples. Asking children to restate the sentence frame and use the target word can help structure their word use. The following example of a sentence stem could support children in using the word *vehicle*.

TEACHER: Say, "A vehicle I saw this morning was a _____."

Offering Closed Choices

When children aren't sure how to use a word correctly, offering them choices can constrain the cognitive load required in figuring out when, where, and how to use words accurately. Here is an example of how a teacher might provide a closed choice for children to use the word *vehicle*.

> TEACHER: What kind of vehicle did you see this morning, Marcus? Did you see a car or a truck?
>
> STUDENT: Truck.
>
> TEACHER: Can you say, "A vehicle I saw was a truck"?
>
> STUDENT: A vehicle I saw was a truck.

Supporting Elaboration

To encourage children to think about how words can be used appropriately in context, teachers can support students in thinking beyond brief and general examples of using words by asking them to say more or explain their thinking. Here is an example of how a teacher might support elaboration in word use.

> TEACHER: You said the vehicle you saw was a truck, Marcus. What kind of truck? Was it a dump truck or a fire truck?
>
> STUDENT: A dump truck.
>
> TEACHER: So the vehicle you saw was a dump truck? Vehicles move things from one place to another. What did the dump truck move from one place to another?
>
> STUDENT: Dirt.
>
> TEACHER: Yes, dump trucks are vehicles that move dirt from one place to another.

Another issue that we have noticed is that sometimes, when children are still trying to figure out what a word means and how to appropriately use the word in different contexts, they give answers that are partially or totally incorrect. Teachers often don't know what to do in these cases. They don't want to discourage children from trying out the word, but they also don't want children to learn to use the word incorrectly. Thus, it is important for teachers to give timely, corrective feedback in a constructive and supportive way. Here are some feedback strategies for supporting word learning:

- *Clarifying.* If children use words incorrectly, it may be because they don't quite understand how to apply words. Providing additional explanation about when, where, and how to use words can help children figure out how to use words appropriately. Also, offering additional examples to demonstrate the correct way to use the word can be helpful.
- *Revoicing.* If children use words in a grammatically awkward way or if they need support to say more about a word, teachers can support them by simply revoicing what they said in a more accurate or elaborated way.
- *Affirming.* When children use words correctly, they benefit from an indication that they used the word correctly. Such affirmation will encourage them to use words in the same way in the future.

The following exchange between a teacher and a student about what vehicle the student saw on the way to school demonstrates how feedback can be helpful for supporting word use.

STUDENT: I saw a mailbox on the way to school today.

TEACHER: A mailbox? Is that a kind of vehicle? Let's think about that. A vehicle is something that is used to move people or things from one place to another. Can a mailbox move? [clarifying]

STUDENT: Uh, no.

TEACHER: Can you think of something that has to do with mail that does move? A mail _____. [scaffolding using a sentence frame]

STUDENT: Oh, a mail truck moves.

TEACHER: Yes, a mail truck is a vehicle because it is used to move mail from one place to another. [affirming and revoicing]

Supporting children in using words and providing feedback on their word use can be an invaluable way to help them adopt words into their own personal vocabularies for future use in listening, speaking, reading, and writing.

Guide Children to Analyze How the Word Is Used in Context and How It Is Related to Other Words

In order to go beyond understanding words at a surface level, children need to analyze words more deeply. By thinking about how words may or may not apply in given contexts and about how words are related to other words, children can begin to understand the finer nuances of what words mean. This analytic thinking about words helps children grow in depth of knowledge of the particular words under study and in depth of knowledge about how words work in general. There are at least three ways, which we discuss next, that teachers can support children in analyzing words. In all of these approaches, asking children to explain their thinking is a critical step in helping them be analytic about words. And, in all of these approaches, teacher feedback is critical to ensuring that children understand the underlying nuances about words.

Examples and Non-Examples

Teachers can give children examples and non-examples and have children decide which is which. In doing this, children have to think about what does and does not belong conceptually with the target word.

> TEACHER: We have been talking a lot about road vehicles. Now I want to ask you about some other things, and I want you to decide whether they are vehicles or not. Thumbs up if you think they are vehicles and thumbs down if you think they are not vehicles. An airplane?
>
> STUDENTS: (*Some have thumbs up and some have thumbs down.*)
>
> TEACHER: Maria, you had your thumb down. Why do you think an airplane is not a vehicle?
>
> STUDENT: 'Cause it's not like a car.
>
> TEACHER: Well, a vehicle is something that moves people or things from one place to another. Does an airplane do that?
>
> STUDENT: Yes, in the sky.
>
> TEACHER: That's right, an airplane is a vehicle because it moves people and things from one place to another in the sky. Cars and airplanes are both vehicles.

Context

Teachers can offer contexts and ask, "Does that make sense?" To respond, children have to consider the interaction between the meaning of the word and the given context.

> TEACHER: I am going to give you a sentence with the word *vehicles* in it. Then, I want you to decide whether it makes sense. Say "yes" if you think it makes sense and "no" if you think it does not make sense. I used my vehicle to cook pancakes this morning. Does that make sense: yes or no?
>
> STUDENTS: (*Some say yes and some say no.*)
>
> TEACHER: Daniel, you said yes. Why do you think that makes sense?
>
> STUDENTS: Maybe you cooked pancakes in an RV while you were driving to school?

TEACHER: Oh, I wasn't thinking of that. An RV is a kind of vehicle because it moves people from place to place. RVs are mobile homes and they have kitchens inside so you can cook while you are on the road. I don't have an RV, but I guess I could make pancakes in an RV while someone else was driving.

As shown in this example, sometimes children's answers make sense from their point of view. Asking them to explain and giving them feedback can help both the student and the teacher clarify their understanding.

Related Words

Thinking of other words that are related to target words can help children develop their semantic network. By building connections between words, children are able to strengthen their memory for words so that when they hear or read a word in the environment they will remember what it means in relation to other words in the context. In some cases, teachers can focus on antonyms and synonyms. In other cases, teachers can focus more generally on words related to the target word. For example, when children think of vehicles, they might think of *wheels*, *driving*, and *traffic*.

TEACHER: So, we are learning about vehicles. What other words do you think of when you think about vehicles?

STUDENT: Cars.

STUDENT: Wreck.

STUDENT: Tires.

STUDENT: Airplanes . . .

TEACHER: What a great brainstorm of vehicle words. Let's organize these vehicle words into a web. We can choose types of vehicles from our list and organize them by how they travel. For example, a car travels on a road. So, our first category is vehicles that travel by road.

Note that the chart in Figure 3.5 includes a finished word web in which words have been organized by the mode of travel the vehicle uses. This activity is productive because it elicits prior knowledge students may have about vehicles and provides a clear structure for organizing those discrete thoughts. In many instances, learning the organizational structure itself will be a key step in understanding the multiple facets of a single word. This chart can be posted after the initial brainstorming and used during other contexts to spark new ideas. (For instrance, during an independent writing activity, students could fill in a sentence stem with a vehicle

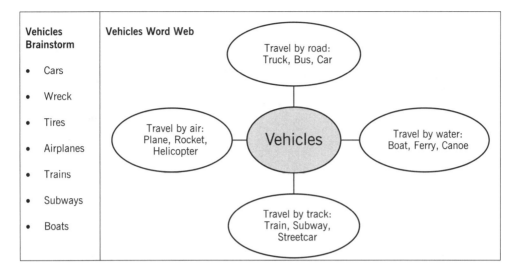

FIGURE 3.5. Example of brainstorming and word webbing for the word *vehicles*.

and the type of mode it uses to travel. "A vehicle that moves on _____ is a _____." "A vehicle that moves on water is a boat.")

Provide Repeated Exposure and Review to Reinforce Word Learning across Contexts

Given that word learning takes time, children need a lot of review and reinforcement to learn words. Teachers can accomplish this by doing repeated readings of the same book and reviewing those words in the book several times across a week, a month, or even a year. Teachers can also read other books to children that either contain the target word or offer contexts for using the target word. For example, after reading *My Truck Is Stuck*, teachers could read any of the books listed in Figure 3.6 (to name just a few). Each of these books features many different kinds of vehicles and could be used to reinforce children's learning of the word *vehicle*.

Teachers can also reinforce word learning by structuring opportunities for students to encounter and use the target words in activities throughout their day, week, and year. For example, prekindergarten and kindergarten teachers could add toy vehicles to the block, art, and dramatic play centers for children to use on their own. Or, first-grade and second-grade teachers could also implement more guided activities like a project in social studies about how vehicles can be used to get food from the farm to the grocery or to get mail from one part of the world to another to show how communities are interconnected. For students of any age, teachers could also extend instruction beyond the classroom by arranging a field

• *Bear on a Bike* (Blackstone, 1998)	• *Lightship* (Floca, 2007); *The Racecar Alphabet* (Floca, 2003); and *Moonshot* (Floca, 2009)
• *Chuck's Truck* (Anderson, 2006)	• *On the Go* (Morris, 1990)
• *Chugga-Chugga Choo-Choo* (Lewis, 1999)	• *Rush Hour* (Loomis, 1996)
• *Dig Dig Digging* (Mayo, 2002); *Choo Choo Clickety-Clack!* (Mayo, 2004); or *Zoom, Rocket, Zoom* (Mayo, 2012)	• *Trains* (Barton, 1986); *Planes* (Barton, 1998); or *Boats* (Barton, 1998)
• *Little Blue Truck Leads the Way* (Schertle, 2009)	• *Trains* (Gibbons, 1988); *The Bicycle Book* (Gibbons, 1995); *Trucks* (Gibbons, 1981); or *The Boat Book* (Gibbons, 1983)
• *The Trucker* (Weatherby, 2004)	
• *If I Built a Car* (Van Dusen, 2005)	

FIGURE 3.6. Sample reading list for a *vehicles* and *modes of transportation* unit.

trip to a museum where children can explore how *vehicles* have changed over time.

From small reminders to big projects, the main objective for teachers is to review words and reinforce word learning over time. To help teachers and students remember to use words, teachers can set up vocabulary word walls in their classrooms. While many teachers use word walls to support sight word learning, they can use picture word walls to support vocabulary learning by serving as a constant reminder to teachers and children to use target words on a regular basis.

Teachers can also make connections to target words in everyday routines. For example, the word *transportation* could be used on a classroom chart identifying the types of transportation children take to get home each afternoon. (See Figure 3.7.) It also serves a real purpose in the classroom (i.e., reminding teachers who goes to the bus line and who goes to the carpool line at the end of the day).

Our Modes of Transportation			
Car	Bus	Feet	Bike
Jacob Gabriella Ethan	Sophia Dylan Felipe Elizabeth	Ava Lorenzo Carla	Liam Elias Guadalupe

FIGURE 3.7. Example of a class transportation chart. Images Copyright 2013 by Yenz-HautArt. Used with permission.

Explicit Instruction through Read-Alouds and Beyond

Explicit instruction, including the practices we have noted, is most effective when it is connected to rich content and contexts and meaningful experiences. Read-alouds provide an ideal opportunity to introduce words to students because books have rich contexts and offer a shared experience in which to discuss words. Ideally, vocabulary can be introduced through prereading instruction that includes brief definitions and explanations. Then, when words are encountered in text, teachers can highlight words again and remind children of their meaning. After reading, teachers can help children expand their understanding of words by referring to them in the context of the book. Next teachers can help children deepen their knowledge by thinking about words in new and different contexts. Finally, teachers can provide opportunities for children to extend their knowledge of words through repeated readings and repeated practice of words as well as through activities in which children can apply their word knowledge independently. Extending word knowledge is especially practical in classrooms that use thematic units because students can apply their word knowledge across the day through interconnected lessons and activities beyond read-alouds. In the following sections, we outline how to implement the instructional practices we described before, during, and after read-alouds and through extension activities as well.

Vocabulary Instruction before Reading

While teachers may target as many as 8 to 12 words per week through repeated readings of books during read-aloud time, they should only focus on two or three key words during preteaching. We have noticed that when we have tried to teach any more than three words before reading, children get restless. They want to hear the book, so it is best to preteach essential words quickly and then get into the book. Good candidates for essential words are words that set up the theme for the book or words that are required for comprehension. These words can serve as anchors for other words that will be encountered as the book is read aloud. When teachers introduce words to students, they can provide rich information about the word so that it makes sense when encountered in context. However, such preteaching should be quick and to the point. If it is too drawn out, children will forget the words and the purpose for learning them before they even get to the book that they are reading. Brisk pacing when introducing words is a must. The five steps listed in Figure 3.8 can be done in a brief 2-minute overview.

   The following is an example of how the prereading vocabulary routine could be used to introduce the word *travel(s)(ed)(er)* from the book *What Do Wheels Do All Day?*, by April Jones Prince (2006), which shows how wheels are used in a wide variety of daily activities.

1. The teacher pronounces the word and has students say the word.
2. The teacher shows the word on a word card.
3. The teacher provides a picture or gesture representing the word.
4. The teacher provides a comprehensible definition of the word.
5. The teacher previews how the word will be used in context.

FIGURE 3.8. Vocabulary routine to be implemented before reading.

TEACHER: Today we are going to read a book called *What Do Wheels Do All Day?* In this book, we are going to read that "Wheels carry *travelers*." Put your thumbs up if you think you know what *travelers* are. Let's talk about the word *travelers*. Listen to me say the word (*pause*) *travelers*. Now you say the word *travelers*.

STUDENTS: *Travelers.*

TEACHER: Look at the word *traveler* on my word card. (*Holds up a card with a picture of a boat carrying travelers with the word* traveler *written on it.*) *Tr–, tr–, traveler.* Let me read the definition. *Travelers* are people who go from one place to another. Look at the picture on this word card. Do you see the people on the boat? They are *travelers*. In the book you will see that *travelers* are going from one place to another on a bus.

Note that the teacher asked children to put their thumbs up or down to show whether or not they thought they knew the word. Here the teacher is doing a quick check, based on self-report, of children's knowledge before she teaches the word. However, she does not ask children to share what they know about the word. Sometimes, when teachers start off by asking children what they know about a word, children say things that are off track. Unfortunately, when other children hear the off-track information, they can get off track too. In this case, teachers then have to unteach and then reteach the target word. For the purposes of pre-teaching, which should be quick and to the point, teachers should just give children the definitions of words and, by using the context of the book, model how to use the word appropriately.

Vocabulary Instruction during Reading

While teachers may not want to interrupt what they are reading the first time they read a text to children, when teachers read books again, they can stop to briefly define words in context while they are reading. In Figure 3.9 we list steps teachers can use to address words during reading, and in Figure 3.10 we show how teachers can build up over a 3-day period to deep discussions of words in context.

1. Teacher repeats the word, shows the word in the text, and refers to the pictures in the text if applicable.
2. Teacher repeats the child-friendly definition of the word.
3. Teacher explains and/or asks questions about how the word is used in context.

FIGURE 3.9. Vocabulary routine to be implemented during reading.

Discussing words in text affords children an opportunity to talk about words in the rich context of the book and helps children put the definitional and contextual information they are learning about words together. Sometimes teachers are concerned about other words besides target words that children may not know in a given text. If there are too many difficult words, the book might not be a good match for the audience, but in some cases there are a few words that children may not know that are not central to the theme or context of the book and, therefore, do not deserve to be target words. If these words are necessary for comprehension, teachers can very briefly define them without dwelling too much on the words that are not a priority. If the words are not necessary for comprehension and not target words, they can be skipped over altogether.

To address target words, teachers can call attention to words, offer definitions of words, and discuss words in context. Calling children's attention to words will help children notice them and think about what they might mean. Providing children with "just-in-time" information about words will help them understand the words as they are encountered. Briefly explaining how the words apply in the given context will help children see how the words are used and can build on their understanding of how to use the words across contexts for comprehension and communication. Here's an example of vocabulary instruction during reading with the target word *travelers*.

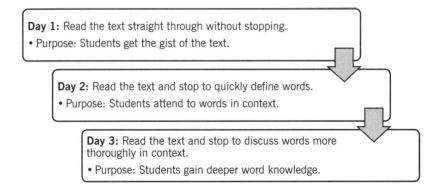

Day 1: Read the text straight through without stopping.
• Purpose: Students get the gist of the text.

Day 2: Read the text and stop to quickly define words.
• Purpose: Students attend to words in context.

Day 3: Read the text and stop to discuss words more thoroughly in context.
• Purpose: Students gain deeper word knowledge.

FIGURE 3.10. Sample progression of text reading across 3 days.

TEACHER: On this page it said, "Wheels carry *travelers*." Here is the word *travelers*. Say it with me. *Travelers*. These are the *travelers*. (*Points to the people on the bus in the picture*.) Remember that *travelers* are people who go from one place to another. How can you tell that these people are *travelers*?

STUDENT: 'Cause they're on the bus.

While discussing words during reading is important for supporting children's understanding in the context of the book at hand, it is important for teachers to keep during-reading vocabulary instruction brief and to the point. Even when children have heard books and been introduced to words previously, many children will lose focus if too much attention is paid to words during reading.

Vocabulary Instruction after Reading

Reminding children about the words that they are learning will help them solidify their word knowledge. Also, once they have heard the full context of the read-aloud book, children can get an even deeper understanding of how the word applies. Finally, discussing how all of the target words are related to the context can help children make connections between words, anchored in the content of the text they have been experiencing. In Figure 3.11 we list steps for vocabulary instruction after reading.

With every repetition, saying the word and showing a word card with a picture or using a gesture to illustrate the word will help children further develop a secure memory for the word. Repeating the definitions of the words over and over will help children remember the definitions later. Expanding children's understanding of a word by talking about how it was used in the specific context of the text that was just read and in new contexts that are related can help children get a more generalized sense of the word. And encouraging children to use words to think critically about how a word is related to other words and to think about

---

1. The teacher says the word and shows the word on a word card with a picture or gesture representing the word.

2. The teacher repeats the child-friendly definition of the word.

3. The teacher explains how words are used across a variety of contexts.

4. The teacher provides opportunities for children to critically think about words (compare and contrast).

5. The teacher provides opportunities for children to use words with lots of scaffolding.

FIGURE 3.11. Vocabulary routine to be implemented after reading.

other contexts when they can use the word will help them understand where and when and how to use it. Here is how a teacher might address the word *traveler* after reading *What Do Wheels Do All Day?*

> TEACHER: So, in our book today we read that "Wheels carry travelers." Say that word *travelers* with me. *Travelers.* Now look at the word on our word card again. I will put it up on our word wall. What do you see in the picture that shows travelers?
>
> STUDENTS: People on a boat.
>
> TEACHER: Remember, travelers are people that go from one place to another. In the book, people were traveling by bus. Maybe they were going to visit a new place. If I were a traveler right now, I would want to travel from here to the beach. Where would you like to travel to? Say, "If I were a *traveler*, I would travel to _____."
>
> STUDENT: If I were a traveler, I'd go to Disney World.
>
> TEACHER: Now I want you to think about some sentences with the word *traveler*. Thumbs up if my sentence makes sense and thumbs down if my sentence does not make sense.
>
> 1. Travelers get to see many places.
> 2. Travelers like to stay home.

Teachers should always ask a couple of children to explain their response. Note that for these analytic questions, there may not be a right answer. While the expected answers for the sentences above are thumbs up for (1) and thumbs down for (2), a child who puts thumbs down for (1) would be correct if he explains that some travelers travel to the same place over and over, and a child who puts thumbs up for (2) would be correct if she explains that some travelers don't really like to travel but they have to travel for work. The correct answer isn't as important as the depth of understanding children are developing through thinking analytically about words. Overall, the point of discussing words after reading is to dig deeper into word meaning and review words so that children can increase the breadth and depth of their word knowledge.

Extending Word Learning beyond Read-Alouds

Under natural circumstances, it could take a child a long time to encounter a taught word again. Children learn words incrementally over time, so they need repeated encounters with words to solidify their word knowledge and develop their ability to productively use words on their own when appropriate. Rather

1. The teacher provides ample opportunity for repeated exposure to words.
2. The teacher provides rich opportunities for children to use words across a variety of contexts.

FIGURE 3.12. Practices for extended vocabulary instruction.

than wait for this process to unfold organically, teachers can structure systematic opportunities for children to encounter words again after their initial exposure to words. Once teachers have taught words during read-alouds, they can choose other books to read that include the word. If words are chosen thematically, this is likely to be an easy task. For example, as discussed earlier, if target words such as *depart, arrive, vehicle, passenger, delayed*, and *rapid* are all taught in connection to the theme of *travel* or *transportation*, teachers can readily find or create books, pictures, props, activities, games, and videos that will allow children to review these words simultaneously. In Figure 3.12, we offer tips for extending instruction beyond read-alouds.

Children need sufficient repetition of specific words in different contexts to gain an understanding of how they are used. Beyond the initial introduction of words during read-alouds, children need to see that words can be used in other contexts and applied in different ways. Next we provide a sampling of the kinds of activities teachers can use to extend word learning beyond read-aloud time. We have clustered the activities according to whether they are whole-class, small-group, peer-based, or independent activities, though many of these activities can be used across these organizational structures. Throughout the activities, teachers should remind children of the target word and encourage children to use the target word on their own.

Whole-Class Projects

Whole-class projects can be a great way to extend vocabulary learning beyond read-aloud time. Projects can vary from basic to more elaborate depending on how much time teachers want to devote to given words and concepts. When teachers can reinforce words across the content areas and support word learning through connections in language arts, social studies, science, and/or math, then more elaborate activities may be warranted. Since a primary goal of extension activities is for children to actively use words, projects that involve expression through speech, writing, art, or movement can be particularly helpful. Here are some ideas for class projects that might be relevant for the transportation example we have used throughout this chapter.

A Class Book

Each child in the class can contribute a page to the book about a different kind of *vehicle*, which can be added to the classroom library for all of the children to read and share throughout the year. Class books do double duty in that they afford both an opportunity for children to express their understanding of words and a resource for reviewing words in the future.

A Class Presentation

Each child could research, prepare, and give a presentation about a different mode of transportation. Conducting research, planning what to say, and delivering a presentation to peers or even to another class are authentic ways that children can use the target word and practice language skills.

A Class Mural

Each child could add to a mural about *transportation* and *traveling* that would be displayed in the hallway as a showcase of all they have learned in the unit. Leveraging children's artistic skills and encouraging children to collaborate on a joint project afford many opportunities for children to use the target word to communicate to and with others.

Other Ideas

Some class projects will be particular to the theme and words chosen for the unit. For the transportation theme, having children use different kinds of materials to make vehicles is an example of a kind of activity that might be particular to this theme.

   In all these activities, teachers should make sure children attend to the target words (e.g., *vehicle* or *transportation*) and not just other related words that are not the academic words children need to learn for success in school (e.g., *bus, boat*). Also, teachers should make sure the activities don't take on a life of their own and become more elaborate and involved than necessary for vocabulary learning. Finally, teachers should plan activities that meet other instructional objectives as well as vocabulary so that children don't miss out on other important learning opportunities while doing vocabulary activities. It is hard for teachers to meet all of the objectives they need to address in early childhood and elementary classrooms, so strategic planning is incredibly important.

Small-Group Activities and Games

Small-group time provides an opportunity for teachers to work with a few children in a more personal way to support their skill development. While many teachers use small groups for phonemic awareness, phonics, and guided reading instruction, they often do not use small-group time to reinforce vocabulary. Given that in small groups children have more opportunities to talk and teachers can provide more focused guidance and feedback, teachers should consider small-group time as an ideal place to extend vocabulary learning. Here are some activities that can encourage word learning in the small-group setting.

Sorting Activities

Building on the word analysis portion of read-aloud lessons, teachers can support children in sorting words conceptually. Word sorting is a common activity for phonemic awareness and phonics, but comparing and contrasting words and placing words into categories can be supportive of vocabulary as well. For the transportation unit, teachers could have children sort pictures of *vehicles* and non-*vehicles* or objects that represent land, water, and air *vehicles*.

Word Webs

Relating words through semantic webs such as the one shown in Figure 3.5 can help children make connections among words. Having children explain how words are connected is an important part of word webbing. Teachers can have predetermined kinds of information for children to add to the web (e.g., a synonym, an example, and a non-example) or they can make it more open-ended. In a small group, all children should have the opportunity to contribute and add on to each others' ideas.

Small-Group Games

Children love to play games, and they often don't even realize they are learning when they play games in school. While games should never be used to introduce words to children, they are a great way to reinforce word learning. And it is optimal to use games during small-group time, when teachers can encourage children to use target words during the game and provide feedback as needed throughout the game. An example of a game that could be used for the transportation unit is a transportation board game. In this game, children have to choose a card from a pile. Cards include vehicles and non-vehicles. Vehicle cards include pictures of different types of vehicles that are slower or faster. If children pick a non-vehicle they lose their turn. If they pick a slow vehicle, they move one or two spaces (depending on the kind of vehicle). If they pick a fast vehicle, they move three or four spaces (depending on the kind of vehicle). As children choose words and try to get to the destination first, teachers can encourage children to use transportation words such as *depart, arrive, delayed*, and *rapid*.

Peer-Based Activities and Games

Many of the small-group activities and games can be done in pairs after teachers have shown children what to do or how to play. But there are other activities that children can do with partners to reinforce word learning. For example, peers can look through and talk about the book read in class or the class book together. They can look at the pictures in other books and read them to each other. And they can do centers activities, discussed next, together as well. Peers can provide a lot of encouragement and support to help each other talk and use words. (We say more about peer-based activities in the next chapter.)

Independent Centers Activities

Teachers can arrange activities and games in centers for children to play with peers or alone. And teachers can structure additional centers activities so that children have the tools to play with the words they are learning in a variety of contexts. If children interact with concepts in a variety of different centers, they will learn about different ways to use words across contexts. In this way, they will have the opportunity to deepen their knowledge of words taught in class.

Discovery Center

Placing objects and tools related to taught words for children to explore in a discovery center can be a way to encourage word learning. For example, teachers could put toy vehicles, an incline, and a timer in the discovery center, and children could discover which vehicles go fastest down the incline.

Block Area

Children can build intricate structures to represent their understanding of words and play with words with their hands. For example, teachers could encourage children to build roads and bridges and towns with blocks and demonstrate how vehicles could travel from one place to another.

Dramatic Play

Dramatic play in which children use props to act out words in real-life situations enables them to think about contexts in which target words apply. For example, placing a kid-size sit-and-ride car in dramatic play so children can act out traveling to new places with their pretend family would be a great way to encourage them to pretend to be travelers.

Art Center

Children can use all kinds of different media to express their understanding of words. They can use clay and paint to depict different types of vehicles or make collages with magazine cutouts to illustrate different places they would like to visit as they travel.

Library Center

Providing a resource for children to explore lots of books on the vocabulary topic so they can think about how words are used across contexts will enable them to generalize their word knowledge beyond the texts they have read in class. Placing some of these books in the library center for children to explore would be a great way to encourage word learning.

Writing Center

Prompting children to write their own narratives and reports having to do with the theme and target words is a great way to encourage children to use words on their own. Posting word cards in the writing center so children can use the words for reference and posting story starters or sentence stems in the center for children to use for support can help children use the words effectively on their own. Very young children or children with limited writing skills can draw their ideas about the given theme and words and dictate to teachers what they would like for teachers to write. Teachers can set aside time each day for a couple of children to share their writing so they have an audience for their work. This gives children an opportunity to see how they can use the words on their own to express their ideas to others.

Planning for Explicit and Extended Instruction
. . . .

Figure 3.13 is a lesson-planning checklist for before, during, and after reading as well as for extended vocabulary instruction. We have divided the checklist into steps for teachers' instruction and students' participation to clarify what teachers can do to provide explicit and extended instruction and how children should be actively engaged in explicit and extended instruction. Teachers can use this checklist to plan effective lessons with explicit and extended instruction to support children's acquisition of vocabulary breadth and depth.

Component	Steps for teacher instruction
Introduction	☐ Introduce the theme and activate prior knowledge.
Before reading	☐ Pronounce the target word and have students say the word.
	☐ Show the word on a word card.
	☐ Provide a picture or gesture representing the word.
	☐ Provide a comprehensible definition of the word.
	☐ Preview how the word will be used in context.
During reading	☐ Repeat the word, show the word in the text, and refer to the pictures in the text if applicable.
	☐ Repeat the child-friendly definition of the word.
	☐ Explain and/or ask questions about how the word is used in context.
After reading	☐ Say the word and show the word on a word card with a picture or gesture representing the word.
	☐ Repeat the child-friendly definition of the word.
	☐ Explain how the word is used across a variety of contexts.
	☐ Provide opportunities for children to think critically about words (compare and contrast).
	☐ Provide opportunities for children to use words with lots of scaffolding.
Extended	☐ Provide ample opportunity for repeated exposure to words.
	☐ Provide rich opportunities for children to use words across a variety of contexts.

FIGURE 3.13. Lesson planning checklist for explicit and extended vocabulary instruction.

Summary

Explicit and extended vocabulary instruction is an essential aspect of a comprehensive vocabulary program. For children to learn words they may not encounter or figure out on their own, explicit and extended instruction is invaluable. Also, by learning words through explicit and extended instruction, children will have a more substantial foundation of knowledge on which to build when they encounter unknown words on their own. In this chapter, we suggested instructional practices that you can use before, during, and after reading to support children's word learning. And we offered some suggestions for you to extend your vocabulary instruction beyond read-alouds. In the next chapter, we address how you can foster vocabulary development by creating a language-rich environment in which children are simultaneously exposed to words and encouraged to use words across classroom routines and activities.

CHAPTER 4

Word Learning and Word Use in a Language-Rich Environment

GUIDING QUESTIONS

- What are the characteristics of a language-rich classroom?
- Which routines and activities in the context of a language-rich environment most effectively support word learning and word use?
- How should these routines and activities be implemented to optimally support vocabulary development?

Mrs. Hunt's first graders are writing "All About Me" books. So far, her students have written their first drafts. Mrs. Hunt has read the drafts. Most of them are very repetitive (e.g., "I like biking. I like swimming. I like playing ball."). Today Mrs. Hunt is going to ask her students to "spice up" their writing with some interesting words. She has children brainstorm words they could use, and she suggests some too (e.g., *adore, cherish, treasure*). She wants to help her students see that word choice makes a difference and using interesting words can be fun!

Explicit instruction, discussed in the previous chapter, is necessary but insufficient for optimally supporting children's vocabulary development. Throughout every classroom activity, teachers should identify and take advantage of opportunities to foster children's word learning. With the strong focus on language in general and vocabulary in particular in the CCSS, teachers must focus more than ever before on promoting word learning and word use in a language-rich environment. Thus, teachers must evaluate their instruction and classroom environment to make sure they are doing all they can to support children's language development. In this chapter, we discuss characteristics of language-rich classrooms and suggest ways you can optimize the language environment in your classroom.

Although teachers use language throughout the day, many teachers don't realize that they are not fully leveraging classroom routines and activities to support children's vocabulary development. For instance, in most classrooms, teachers dominate the conversation. In fact, in most classrooms, 75% of the classroom talk is teacher talk. Therefore, 25% of the classroom talk is shared among roughly 25 children in the early childhood or elementary school classroom. That leaves little room for children to engage in dialogue and actively use words they are learning. This imbalance is a concern given that using words across contexts is important for developing vocabulary depth. Additionally, teachers who feel they need to "hold the floor" to maintain order and make sure curriculum content is covered often resort to the Initiate-Respond-Evaluate (IRE) method of questioning during classroom conversations. In this model, teachers ask students questions, call on a few children to respond, and quickly evaluate before moving on to other children and other questions. When it is their turn to talk, children typically give only very brief responses and aren't engaged in extended dialogue. The conversation below shows how IRE instruction can constrain children's opportunity to use their language and contribute to classroom conversation. The teacher asks a question that involves vocabulary knowledge, but she doesn't engage children in extended dialogue so that they can deepen their understanding of the concept under consideration.

> TEACHER: In the book *Officer Buckle and Gloria* [Rathmann, 1995] that we just read, Officer Buckle went to schools to tell students about safety tips. What are safety tips?
>
> ELI: Like how to be safe.
>
> TEACHER: Close. Does anyone else have an answer?
>
> KIERA: Tips to be safe?
>
> TEACHER: Right. But no one listened to Officer Buckle. He was what?
>
> GEOFF: Boring.
>
> TEACHER: Right, boring.

Given the new (or renewed) focus on language development to support reading, writing, speaking, and listening in the CCSS, teachers must find ways to balance their own verbal directions, explanations, and feedback with opportunities for students to practice their oral and written language. Teachers can provide more opportunities for children to use their words and support them in using more sophisticated and extended talk when they engage in conversation with others. Teachers can gradually infuse more opportunities for word learning and word use throughout routines and activities that are already in place, and they can eventually experiment with new routines and activities that provide fertile ground for vocabulary development. Understanding the characteristics of classrooms that embody a language-rich environment and the classroom routines and activities that are particularly fertile for encouraging children to use and extend their language is key. That is the focus of the rest of this chapter.

Characteristics of Language-Rich Classrooms

Classrooms that are language rich create a culture of conversation in which children are invited to be active participants in the ongoing dialogue in the classroom. Researchers, teachers, and administrators alike know when they walk into a language-rich classroom because they hear multiple voices and see children interacting and responding to each other's ideas in a positive and productive way. But what exactly is it that differentiates classrooms that are more or less language rich? Two groups of researchers have developed classroom observation systems, based on years of research, that offer indicators of classroom quality in early childhood and elementary school classrooms. The Early Language and Literacy Classroom Observation Tool (ELLCO) measures classroom structure, curriculum, language environment, books and reading, and print and writing in prekindergarten through third grade (Smith, Brady, & Anastasopoulos, 2008; Smith, Brady, & Clark-Chiarelli, 2008). The Classroom Assessment and Scoring System (CLASS) measures emotional support, classroom organization, and instructional support in prekindergarten through twelfth grade (Pianta, La Paro, & Hamre, 2008). In these two measures, there are several features of classroom environment and instructional quality that relate to supporting language. Some of these characteristics refer to how the classroom is structured, but most of them highlight aspects of quality teacher–child interactions, which research suggests are essential to supporting children's language and literacy in prekindergarten through second-grade classrooms (e.g., Burchinal, Peisner-Feinberg, Pianta, & Howes, 2002; Dickinson & Porche, 2011; Mashburn, et al., 2008). We now discuss characteristics of the classroom environment and instruction that are featured in these well-researched classroom observation tools and discuss why these characteristics are important in a language-rich classroom.

Positive Classroom Climate

A positive classroom climate is one in which teachers have positive affect, encouraging communication, and respect for children. Such a positive climate helps children to feel safe and secure. And when children feel safe and secure, they are more likely to share their thoughts and ideas with teachers and peers. Thus, development of expressive language skills is dependent on a positive classroom climate in school. As seen in the following example, teachers can foster a positive classroom climate by asking children to participate in classroom conversation and by acknowledging children's contributions.

TEACHER: Annie, what did you notice on our field trip to the arboretum yesterday?

STUDENT: Lots of trees.

TEACHER: Yes, there are lots of trees at the arboretum. What did you notice about the trees?

STUDENT: Some were the same and some were different.

TEACHER: That is a great observation, Annie. Some trees look the same and some look different. Let's talk about that some more. How did they look the same and how did they look different?

Teacher Language Modeling

Children need rich language input to develop their own language skills. When teachers model using sophisticated words and complex language, children will internalize these words and language structures. Such language modeling by teachers will support children's receptive language development over time. As in the following example, the words and phrases teachers use to provide feedback can serve as a model for the use of complex language in everyday situations.

TEACHER: Jacob! Your butterfly drawing is quite *impressive*. The details on the wings of your butterfly are so *similar* to the wings on the butterfly we *observed* outside yesterday. Great work *attending* to *details*!

Opportunities for Extended Conversation

Children also need opportunities for interaction and conversation to develop their language skills. Teachers can provide children with time to talk throughout the day. And teachers can ask open-ended questions about topics of interest to children so they will be motivated to talk in school. Finally, teachers can set aside time for children to talk with each other so they will have additional opportunities for extended conversation. For example, during read-alouds teachers can pause to allow students to share their thoughts with each other so they have more opportunity to talk before selecting a few students to share with the whole group. The following is an excerpt from a read-aloud of *Jamaica Louise James*, in which a little girl decides to paint pictures to hang in the subway station to make it more beautiful.

TEACHER: Turn to your elbow partner [i.e., the student sitting next to you] and tell your partner what you would paint for a picture to hang in the subway station. You have 3 minutes to share your ideas and then we will talk as a group.

Support for Student Expression

While some children may be chatterboxes when they start school, other children will need more encouragement and support to practice their language skills. Teachers can encourage and support student expression through questioning and scaffolding. For example, teachers can ask children to say more and provide sentence starters to help children use their words. And teachers can give ample wait time so they can collect their thoughts and find the words they need to communicate. When children respond with brief answers or comments, as in the following example, teachers can ask students follow-up questions to help them say more.

> TEACHER: Claudia, tell me about your idea. What would you paint to decorate the subway station? You would paint a _____.
>
> STUDENT: A garden.
>
> TEACHER: That sounds beautiful! Can you tell me more about that? What kinds of plants and flowers will you paint in your garden? What colors will you use?

Teacher Feedback and Responsiveness

For children to extend their language skills and use ever more sophisticated words and language structures, they need feedback on what they are saying and how they are saying it. When children try to use new words or sentence structures, their words may not be spoken correctly and their sentences may sound a little off. In a positive and supportive way, teachers can revoice what children say so they hear how it should sound. And teachers can provide additional prompting and encouragement for children to keep trying to use their language skills to the fullest. As shown in the next example, when a teacher overhears a student using a word incorrectly in the dramatic play center, she can affirm the idea while providing gentle feedback on language use.

> TEACHER: What are you doing, Adrian?
>
> STUDENT: I am *microscoping* the bug.
>
> TEACHER: You are *using the microscope* to investigate what the beetle looks like up close? What do you see?

Books and Materials

Children need content to discuss in a language-rich environment. Having lots of books of many genres on various topics available to children will give them something to talk about. Also, having pictures and props and other visual and tangible stimuli and manipulatives can support children's conversation. Having audio and video content available can provide conversation starters as well. In addition, giving children different materials with which to express themselves is important. For example, having writing and art supplies and e-mail and word processing programs allows children to use their language in lots of different ways.

Organization and Management

In order for children to have the freedom to talk a lot in class, teachers must maintain an organized classroom where children know the routines and expectations. For teachers to meet with children in small groups or one on one to provide additional language support, the other children in class must know what to do and how to do it. If teachers need to constantly stop to redirect children, they will not have time for instruction and feedback on language use. For example, teachers can set a nonverbal signal for asking permission to use the bathroom that doesn't disrupt the flow of conversation, such as holding up the sign-language symbol for bathroom.

This is more than just feel-good advice. It matters for children. Research shows that children in classrooms that have high ratings on the characteristics of instruction and environment above have higher vocabulary and language skills (e.g., Burchinal et al., 2002; Dickinson & Porche, 2011; Mashburn et al., 2008). Teachers can evaluate their own classrooms using tools such as the ELLCO and the CLASS and determine areas where they want to improve to optimally support children's language development. (Principals and coaches can also use these tools to provide feedback to teachers.) While teachers should strive to immerse children in a language-rich environment throughout the day every day, there are particular activities and routines that are ripe for infusing rich language. In the next section, we describe these routines and activities and discuss how they can be used to foster a language-rich environment in early childhood and elementary classrooms.

Instructional Routines and Activities in Language-Rich Classrooms

There are several activities and routines that teachers commonly implement in early childhood and elementary classrooms that, when implemented in alignment with the characteristics of high-quality classroom instruction and environment we have discussed, offer optimal opportunities for supporting children's vocabulary development. Since these routines are typically part of the school day anyway, we are not suggesting adding numerous new routines and activities. Instead, we suggest ways to enhance common routines and activities to foster children's vocabulary learning throughout the school day.

Whole-Class Activities

Whole-class activities give teachers opportunities to introduce themes and concepts that children will experience together. Introducing words in whole-class activities provides children with a common language, and supporting language use in these activities helps children to practice using that language in a group with support and feedback. The following whole-class activities can be used to support vocabulary learning.

Morning Meeting

Many early childhood and elementary school teachers hold morning meeting time in their classrooms. Kriete (2002) outlines the main activities that occur during this time of the day, which we describe in Figure 4.1.

Each of these morning meeting activities can be used to further vocabulary development in a language-rich classroom. Below are some ways to infuse language into each activity.

DURING THE MORNING MEETING

Teachers can encourage children to use their words as they greet each other. Teachers can connect the greeting to the class theme and ask children to use words they have been learning. For example, the following morning greeting would support word use during a unit on *space*:

TEACHER: Max flew to space today. What did he see along the way?

MAX: Meteors.

Component	Steps for Teachers
Greeting	☐ Prompt students to greet each other by name. • Additional activities include handshaking, clapping, or singing
Sharing	☐ Prompt students to share news of interest to the class and respond to each other. • Guide students to articulate their thoughts, feelings, and ideas in a positive manner
Group activity	☐ Lead a brief whole-class activity together. • Encourage class cohesion through active participation
Morning message	☐ Review daily message and introduce events of the day. • Provide opportunity for students to develop language skills by reading and discussing morning message

FIGURE 4.1. Components of morning meeting. Adapted from Kriete (2002). Copyright 2002 by Northeast Foundation for Children. Used with permission.

CLASS: Good morning, Max!

TEACHER: Maya flew to space today. What did she see along the way?

MAYA: Stars.

CLASS: Good morning, Maya!

To support students in this activity, teachers can refer students to the pictures and words on the vocabulary word wall to jog their memory for words they are learning in the unit on *space*.

DURING SHARING TIME

Teachers can ask children to tell about experiences they have had or are looking forward to in the future. Teachers can support children in using temporal words (e.g., first, then, last) and decontextualized language in talking about past and future events. Teachers can also encourage children to ask each other questions and make connections so everyone gets involved in the conversation. Teachers can also ask children to share their thoughts, opinions, and ideas about different topics. These sharing opportunities can be connected to class themes. For example, as described by Susan Lattanzi Roser (2012), during a unit on seasons, teachers can ask students to share about their favorite season and why it is their favorite.

DURING GROUP ACTIVITY TIME

Teachers can engage children in playful activities that stimulate language. These activities can serve to preview or review words and concepts learned in class. For example, teachers can have children play "Pass the Chicken," developed by Correa-Connolly (2004) to review words they have learned about *seasons*. Here is how Correa-Connolly (2004) describes the activity: "A student must name five things that belong in a specified category in the time it takes the others to pass a rubber chicken (or other item) all the way around their circle. The activity is fast-paced and students can play several rounds in five minutes. The activity provides an enjoyable way to review content and develop vocabulary. Everyone wants to beat the chicken!" (p. 70).

DURING THE MORNING MESSAGE TIME

Teachers typically use morning message as a way to introduce a class theme or announce a class activity. The morning message in Figure 4.2 might be typical in many early childhood or elementary school classrooms. Although teachers don't often use morning message time to increase vocabulary, they can take advantage of this time to focus on important concepts and words children are learning in

---

Dear Class,

Today we will be practicing for our class play. Let's have a great day!

FIGURE 4.2. Typical morning message.

school. Specifically, teachers can model using words that they want children to use themselves.

For example, the morning message in Figure 4.3 was based on a sample morning message included in *Morning Meeting Messages (K–6)* by Fisher, Henry, and Porter (2006). In this message, the teacher is reviewing the word *measurement* and previewing words such as *tool, ruler, scale,* and *timer.* The message gets children thinking about what they will learn and provides them with some language to enter the conversation when the math lesson begins.

Not all classrooms structure morning meeting in the same way, but even in classrooms that follow a different routine to review the calendar, the weather, and the schedule for the day, teachers can create lots of opportunities for children to hear, see, and use rich language. The trick is to be mindful that this is a chance for language development and to use language that the children would not yet use themselves.

Dialogic Reading

Of course, another common practice in early childhood and elementary classrooms is read-aloud time. In the last chapter we discussed how to use read-alouds as a vehicle for explicit instruction of specific vocabulary words. The good news here is that read-aloud time can be used to support children's language more broadly as well; it is a time of day when teachers can serve many masters at once. One well-researched approach to supporting general language development through read-alouds is dialogic reading (Zevenbergen & Whitehurst, 2003). Dialogic reading encourages children's active participation in the book reading experience. Teachers

---

Dear Class,

We've been learning about measuring in math. When you need to measure something, how do you decide which tool to use? What would you measure with: a ruler? a scale? a timer? Let's discuss what tools we can use to measure today in class.

FIGURE 4.3. Vocabulary-focused morning message.

engage children in talking about books as they read, using the context of the book to support dialogue and language use. In dialogic reading, teachers use the PEER method, described in Figure 4.4, to scaffold children's talk during book reading.

The following is an example of the PEER method in action during a book reading of *Harry the Dirty Dog*, by Gene Zion (2006):

> TEACHER: The book says, "Harry was a white dog with black spots who liked everything except . . . getting a bath." Why do you think Harry doesn't like getting a bath? [prompt]
>
> STUDENT: It's cold.
>
> TEACHER: Good thinking. [evaluation] Harry doesn't like getting a bath because he might get cold and start shivering like this. (*Hugs her body and demonstrates shivering.*) [expansion] Can you say, "Harry doesn't want to get cold and shiver"? [repetition]

During the prompting step in dialogic reading, teachers use CROWD (Completion, Recall, Open-ended, *Wh-*, and Distancing) prompts to support children's language use. A description of each kind of prompt and an example in the context of *Harry the Dirty Dog* are provided in Figure 4.5.

When teachers use the dialogic reading approach for multiple readings of the same text, children are able to increase their understanding of the content and extend their talk about the subject matter. And when teachers use the dialogic reading approach for multiple texts over time, children develop greater expressive language skills that they can apply more broadly across a variety of contexts. The dialogic reading approach has been developed through over two decades of research and has been used in many projects on building children's language and literacy development. Most of these projects have been set in early childhood classrooms, but the dialogic reading approach can be used in upper elementary classrooms as well. In using this approach with older children, teachers must ensure that they

Component	Steps for Teachers
Prompt	☐ Use a prompt to encourage student thought and verbalization about the book. (See Figure 4.5 for prompts.)
Evaluate	☐ Evaluate students' response to provide feedback on their verbalization.
Expand	☐ Expand on students' responses by rephrasing and adding information.
Repeat	☐ Repeat the original prompt to make sure students have learned from the expansion.

FIGURE 4.4. Components of the dialogic reading PEER approach. Based on Zevenbergen and Whitehurst (2003).

Prompt Type	Prompt Description	Prompt Example
Completion prompts	Similar to sentence starters, completion prompts are like oral fill in the blanks. Teachers ask students to provide the word or phrase that completes their sentence. In this way, teachers encourage children to use their words in the context of the read-aloud experience. Completion prompts are particularly useful when reading predictable books or during repeated reading of a book.	Harry was a white dog with _____.
Recall prompts	After reading a book or before or rereading of a book, teachers can prompt children to remember something specifically in the book. Teachers can scaffold children in telling the sequence of events or details from the text using completion prompts if needed. And teachers can encourage children to use words from the text as they retell so they can practice using those words in context.	Can you tell me what happened to Harry in this story?
Open-ended prompts	Open-ended prompts can be used in conjunction with pictures in a text. For example, teachers can ask, "What is happening in this picture?" or "What do you see in this picture?" These questions help children use their language in more open-ended ways.	What is Harry doing in this picture?
Wh- prompts	Wh- prompts start with the words *who, what, when, where, why,* and *how.* In the dialogic reading approach, they focus on the pictures just like open-ended questions do. But, they are more specific and focused on the content or concepts in the book. As with open-ended prompts, though wh-prompts are mostly focused on pictures in the dialogic reading approach, they can also be used to talk about what is happening in the book or what children are learning from the text beyond the pictures. The point of these questions is to have children use their expressive language skills to talk about text.	What is Harry carrying in his mouth? Why did Harry decide to go home? How did Harry feel when his family finally recognized him?
Distancing prompts	The purpose of distancing prompts is to have children think about how what they are reading is related to something in their personal lives. As Russell Whitehurst, one of the original researchers who developed and studied the dialogic reading approach, notes, "Distancing prompts help children form a bridge between books and the real world, as well as helping with verbal fluency, conversational abilities, and narrative skills." Although in the dialogic reading approach, distancing prompts are used mainly for making connections to personal experiences, teachers can use these prompts to encourage children to connect to other books they have read or content they have studied as well. The main objective of distancing prompts is to encourage children to use language from or related to the book in decontextualized ways.	How do you feel about baths? Have you ever tried to avoid something your mom or dad wanted you to do? Does Harry remind you of any other characters we have read about? How so?

FIGURE 4.5. Dialogic reading prompts. Based on Zevenbergen and Whitehurst (2003).

are asking sufficiently challenging questions and giving well-targeted feedback to encourage expressive language use at this more advanced level. Overall, dialogic reading can be a useful routine for helping children become active participants in the reading experience, which is crucial to their acquiring expressive vocabulary and general language skills in early childhood and elementary school.

Text Talk

Another language-based program that supports vocabulary learning through book reading is Text Talk, developed by Beck and McKeown (2001). As with dialogic reading, purposeful teacher questioning is central to the Text Talk approach, which we describe in Figure 4.6.

When teachers read books in a Text Talk lesson, they ask questions that require children to describe and explain rather than just recall and retrieve ideas in the text. Teachers also ask follow-up questions to encourage elaboration of thoughts and ideas. To encourage children to listen to the text and to think about the words, Beck and McKeown (2001) suggest showing pictures only after book reading, connecting to background knowledge only sparingly to avoid tangents, and attending to vocabulary words explicitly as needed to help children comprehend text. The following are examples of initiating questions that could be used in a Text Talk lesson with the book *Abiyoyo* (Seeger, 1986). (This book is about a father and son who quiet the giant named Abiyoyo.)

"Why were the father and son ostracized?"
"Who was Abiyoyo?"

Components	Steps for Teachers
Select text	☐ Choose texts that provide grist for children to build meaning.
Ask initial questions	☐ Ask open-ended questions that require children to describe and explain text ideas rather than just recall what was in the text.
Ask follow-up questions	☐ Ask questions to extend children's thinking. Encourage elaboration and development of ideas.
Show pictures after reading	☐ Show pictures after children have listened to the text.
Activate background knowledge	☐ Invite children to consider background knowledge, but use this judiciously so children do not go off on tangents.
Attend to vocabulary	☐ Focus on sophisticated words from the text after story discussion.

FIGURE 4.6. Components of Text Talk. Adapted from Beck and McKeown (2001). Copyright 2001 by the International Reading Association. Used with permission.

"Why were the women screaming and the men fainting when Abiyoyo came to town?"

"How did the father and son make Abiyoyo disappear?"

"Why did the people in town let the father and son move back to town?"

> Dialogic reading and text talk can foster children's expressive language skills and help children meet the CCSS, which require them to ask and answer questions about key details in a text (CCSS.ELA–Literacy.RL.K.1, CCSS.ELA–Literacy.RL.1.1, CCSS.ELA–Literacy.RL.2.1).

Teachers can also ask generic questions throughout read-alouds such as "What's that all about?" or "What does that mean?" When children respond to teachers' initiating questions, teachers can repeat and rephrase to encourage children to say more. As teachers come across new words in text during Text Talk lessons, they can teach them explicitly by using the context of the text and helping children comprehend the words beyond the context of the text. After reading the book, teachers can ask children to summarize and think about the book as a whole. For example, after reading *Abiyoyo*, teachers could say, "Let's see if we can tell the whole story by thinking of cause and effect." Teachers can provide prompts as needed. For example, they could ask, "What happened in the end and why did that happen?" Supporting children in understanding the text and talking about text helps them navigate the language of the text and, thereby, provides children with an opportunity to develop their receptive and expressive language skills.

The Language Experience Approach

In many early childhood classrooms, teachers engage students in language experiences. Language experiences are rich opportunities for children to use language with teacher scaffolding and support and can be conducted one on one or in small or whole groups. Essentially, in language experiences, teachers encourage children to talk about a personal experience, a book, a picture, or a topic or event about which they are interested. Teachers support conversation generation by asking questions and using key words or phrases that might support children in discussing the subject. Once children have expressed some initial ideas about the subject, teachers ask them to help create a written account of what they have discussed. Teachers write down what children say and encourage them to say more. Once the written text is complete, they can read the text to the children or have children read the text. To further vocabulary learning and oral language development, teachers can then use this text to talk about words and phrases that help make the text rich and interesting, thereby encouraging children's use of sophisticated language. In Figure 4.7, we outline the steps of the Language Experience Approach, adapted from Meyerson and Kulesza (2006, pp. 32–33).

Here's an example of how the Language Experience Approach might be used in a unit on *plant life*.

Activity	Steps for Teachers
Select a topic	☐ Choose a common experience from either home life or class activity.
Brainstorm	☐ Generate vocabulary related to the topic.
Dictate	☐ Record students' dictation in a large format visible to all (i.e., overhead projector or chart paper).
Read aloud	☐ Read the text aloud. Model fluency and connect speech and print. ☐ Prompt students to read and reread the text orally and silently.
Manipulate the text	☐ Focus on components of the text such as sentences, words, and letters. ☐ Guide students to manipulate text using sentence strips and word or letter cards.

FIGURE 4.7. Steps in the Language Experience Approach. Adapted from Meyerson and Kulesza (2006). Copyright 2006 by Pearson Education, Inc. Adapted by permission.

> TEACHER: We are going to be studying about different kinds of plant life in our class over the next few weeks. Our first topic will be vegetables. Vegetables grow on different kinds of plant. Yesterday we visited the school vegetable garden. And Ms. Smith, who is in charge of the garden, told us about the vegetables she is growing there. What are some of the things you saw and learned on our trip to the vegetable garden?
>
> STUDENT: Vegetables grow on the plants.

During this activity, children are given an opportunity to talk about what they learned using the words that they heard on the field trip to the school vegetable garden. Children assumed the roles of author, reporter, and expert, and through the process they were able to internalize key words related to vegetables that they can build on as they learn more about the topic in school. Accordingly, the Language Experience Approach can become one piece of the puzzle for building children's expressive language skills in school.

Vocabulary Visits

The CCSS state that students should participate in shared writing projects, such as the Language Experience Approach, as they develop research, writing, and presentation skills (e.g., CCSS.ELA–Literacy.W.1.7).

Combining aspects of reading aloud and writing together to immerse children in a rich language experience, Blachowicz and Obrochta (2005) developed a virtual field trip program to foster children's vocabulary development. They implemented the program, which we review in Figure 4.8, with first graders in a multiethnic urban school. The goal of the program was to

Activity	Steps for Teachers
Jump Start	☐ Introduce the topic and ask students what they know about it.
First Write	☐ Ask students to write words they think of that connect to the topic.
Group Talk	☐ Display a poster with thematic pictures to stimulate discussion. Ask students, "What do you see?" Record student contributions on sticky notes and post these on the poster. Ask questions and suggest vocabulary as students talk.
Reading and Thumbs Up	☐ Read a series of books on the thematic topic. Ask students to put their thumbs up when they hear new words related to the theme. After reading, add words and comments to the poster using sticky notes.
Follow-Up	☐ Hang the poster on the wall and encourage students to use the poster in other reading, writing, and vocabulary activities (e.g., sorting words conceptually).
Final Write	☐ After the series of books has been read, ask students to list all of the words they think of that connect to the topic. (Students will see they know more words after the vocabulary visit than before.) Ask students to write a report on the topic of the vocabulary visit to show what they learned.

FIGURE 4.8. Steps for conducting a vocabulary visit. Adapted from Blachowicz and Obrochta (2005). Copyright 2005 by the International Reading Association. Used with permission.

provide children with active and engaging word learning opportunities. The field trips began with the teacher introducing the topic and having children write down words they could think of related to the topic. This assignment served to activate children's background knowledge and to inform the teacher about what students already knew. Next, the class engaged in group talk. The teacher brought out a poster with pictures of the content under investigation and asked children, "What do you see?" Teachers wrote down children's ideas and mediated as needed. Next teachers read a related book and asked children to listen for target words. After reading, teachers facilitated a discussion of what the children read and encouraged children to add more words to the list of words they had developed during group talk. This process was continued over the course of several books on the topic, and children continued to add new words to the list. At the end of a five-book sequence, children wrote about what they learned and wrote down a list of as many words they could think of about the topic.

After the series of vocabulary visits, children in the study by Blachowicz and Obrochta (2005) were able to identify significantly more words than before the vocabulary visits. For children who have less opportunity to go on field trips and develop vocabulary through such rich real-life experiences, vocabulary visits can provide an alternative. Teachers

Virtual field trips align with the CCSS, which require children to recall information from experiences or gather information from provided sources to answer questions about topics of interest (e.g., CCSS.ELA–Literacy.W.1.8).

can make words come alive through pictures, books, discussions, and writing so children can develop conceptual knowledge and learn academic vocabulary. If children cannot get out into the world to experience new concepts and words firsthand, teachers can bring the world to them in their language-rich classroom environment.

Peer-Mediated Activities

In addition to whole-class activities to support student language development, encouraging children to talk to their peers is another way to support their language use. In language-rich classrooms, small groups and pairs of children work together and are encouraged to talk while they work. We describe some programs that support peer-mediated learning in a language-rich environment.

Buddy Reading

Christ and Wang (2012) implemented a buddy reading program in Head Start preschool classrooms as part of a comprehensive vocabulary program. In the buddy reading portion of the program, buddies got together to "read" a text that had been read repeatedly by the teacher. The children were emergent readers; thus, they weren't able (nor were they expected to) actually read the text. Instead, they were expected to retell the text as best as they could using the pictures and what they remembered from the teacher's read-aloud. Before the buddy session began, teachers modeled buddy reading and reviewed the rules of buddy reading. According to Christ and Wang, "The rules included placing the book in the middle, taking turns to 'read' and turn the pages, listening to each other, and helping each other" (p. 277). When children first started participating in the program, teachers scaffolded and supported students, but they allowed children to become gradually more independent over time.

Christ and Wang found that buddies used different types of interaction styles with each other. When they worked together but did not collaborate, they called this a parallel reading style. In this style, children took turns "reading" but they did not integrate each other's ideas or work together to co-construct the text. When one child took the lead and another child followed, they called this the tutor–tutee style. They found that children had lots of opportunities for language exposure in this style, but children didn't seem to deepen their word knowledge or extend their word use using this style of buddy "reading." The most productive style of buddy "reading" was collaborative. In dyads that showed this "reading" style, there were lots of opportunities to discuss words and clarify meaning as children co-constructed the text together. The following exchange from Christ and Wang's (2012) study on buddy "reading," excerpted with permission, shows how children clarified understandings and supported word learning in the collaborative learning style.

KALVIN: The bird is on the wall and this bird is on this (*referring to an illustration of bats*).

PATRICK: Those are, those are bats (*referring to the illustration of bats*). They're not birds. These are bats.

KALVIN: Bats?

PATRICK: They'll take your blood.

KALVIN: That's—this bat (*pointing now to an owl in an illustration on another page*).

PATRICK: No, those are owls (*referring to illustration of an owl*). Owls are little— owls are bigger than bats. (p. 281)

Overall, Christ and Wang found buddy reading to be highly successful and encourage more use of this format in schools. While the buddy reading approach used in the Christ and Wang study targeted preschool-age children, same-age buddy reading could be done in kindergarten, first, and second grade as well. Children could take turns reading and talk about the text as they read together. Teachers would need to prepare children to work together to read and discuss texts, but children at all grade levels could benefit from this same-age partner reading model.

Reading Buddies

Over the past few years, we have been working with our colleagues Melinda Martin-Beltran and Megan Peercy at the University of Maryland and partners at WGBH Boston to develop a cross-age reading buddies program to promote vocabulary and comprehension in the classroom (Silverman, Martin-Beltran, Peercy, & Meyer, 2014). Similar to the approach that Christ and Wang took, reading buddies sessions follow teacher-led lessons on vocabulary and comprehension so that students have background knowledge to draw on when they work together. Our program includes specific supports for ELLs but includes children who are ELLs and non-ELLs alike. In our program, we partner kindergarten little buddies with fourth-grade big buddies who are trained to be language models and support children's language learning.

The program is hosted by Martha, the talking dog from the book *Martha Speaks* (Meddaugh, 1995) and the television show by the same name (*http://pbskids.org/martha*). The content of the program includes texts from Martha's True Stories (*http://pbskids.org/martha/stories/truestories*), which focus on science, technology, engineering, and math topics. The program was based on a previous reading buddies program developed by WGBH Boston (*www.pbs.org/parents/martha/readingbuddies*). Before reading buddies lessons, children are taught to cooperate and collaborate. While big buddies read the texts, review the words, and go over a checklist that they can use as a guide during the reading buddies lesson, little buddies are only given a preview of the words and the text so they get to experience it for the first time with their big buddies. Big buddies are taught

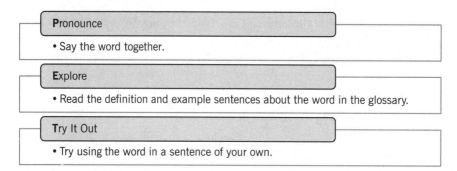

FIGURE 4.9. The PET vocabulary strategy from the reading buddies program. Adapted from Silverman, Martin-Beltran, Peercy, and Meyer (2014). Copyright 2014 by Silverman et al. Adapted by permission.

to use the PET strategy, shown in Figure 4.9, to foster vocabulary and the PAWs strategy, shown in Figure 4.10, to support comprehension. See *pbslearningmedia. org/collection/msts* for access to all materials for the reading buddies program we developed.

The activities the buddies engaged in were as follows:

- *Read and PAWs.* Big buddies read to little buddies and guided little buddies through the steps of the PAWs strategy.
- *PET your words.* Big buddies reviewed the vocabulary words with little buddies by guiding them through the steps of the PET strategy.
- *Play your learning game together.* Big and little buddies played a game together to review words and concepts from the text.

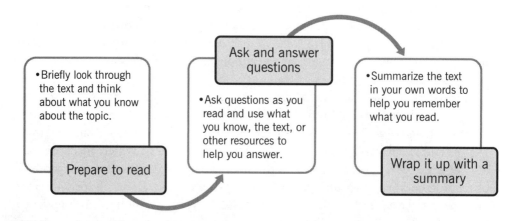

FIGURE 4.10. The PAWs comprehension strategy from the reading buddies program. Adapted from Silverman, Martin-Beltran, Peercy, and Meyer (2014). Copyright 2014 by Silverman et al. Adapted by permission.

Big buddies provided cognitive, linguistic, and socioemotional support to little buddies to help them use their language (Martin-Beltran, Daniel, Peercy, & Silverman, 2013). These types of support are described in Figure 4.11; the same concepts apply to teacher–child dyads and classroom interactions as well as to our program.

Overall, big and little buddies had rich conversations about new information. Big buddies served as models for the little buddies, and the little buddies were incredibly excited to meet with their big buddies each week. Little buddies also had support and "air time" to talk about the words and content covered in class. This type of structured opportunity to use words in a supportive environment is priceless for building vocabulary and language. The exchange between the big and little buddy in the following excerpt shows how reading buddies can be invaluable in providing opportunities to use language.

BIG BUDDY: So the house in the book was gigantic. Do you know what *gigantic* means?

LITTLE BUDDY: Uh, no.

BIG BUDDY: *Gigantic* means really, really big. (*Uses his hands to show gigantic.*) Gigantic.

LITTLE BUDDY: (*Points to pictures in book.*) This one is big and this one is little.

BIG BUDDY: (*Points to picture in book.*) This one is big. It is gigantic. Can you say *gigantic*?

LITTLE BUDDY: *Gigantic.*

BIG BUDDY: Yeah, you got it!

Support Types	Description of Discursive Supports
Cognitive	Encourages the use of background knowledge to understand words. Guides integrating information about words across contexts. Supports monitoring and strategy use when new words are encountered.
Linguistic	Provides comprehensible input (e.g., definitions and examples). Supports word learning (e.g., gestures, visuals, use of home language). Provides support for using words (e.g., options, sentence starters, revoicing, home language support).
Socioemotional	Develops relationships (e.g., smiling, joking, talking about personal experiences). Provides positive reinforcement (e.g., high-fives, compliments, encouragement). Supports attention and provides redirection when needed.

FIGURE 4.11. Support types and description of discursive supports during the reading buddies program. Adapted from Martin-Beltran, Daniel, Peercy, and Silverman (2013). Copyright 2013 by Martin-Beltran et al. Adapted by permission.

Although we have been working with kindergarten and fourth grade in our research project, this approach could easily be adapted for use by first- or second-grade big buddies and prekindergarten or kindergarten little buddies, especially if teachers use digital texts, as we do in our program, that can be heard rather than read. If first- and second-grade children are to serve as big buddies, teachers may need to additionally train and support big buddies and carefully monitor student pairs to make sure they have the support they need to succeed. Our reading buddies approach can be adapted for use with same-age peers as well.

Collaborative Reading Groups

In some classrooms, children read books and meet together in collaborative learning groups to discuss books together. There are different formats for such collaborative reading groups. While there is little research on how participation in collaborative reading groups supports vocabulary, we see the potential for children to increase their vocabulary and language skill through this common classroom activity. Book clubs are one manifestation of collaborative book reading that has shown promise as a context for vocabulary development (Kong & Fitch, 2002/2003). The book club approach includes four components: reading, writing, discussion, and instruction (Murphy, Wilkinson, Soter, Hennessey, & Alexander, 2009). First, children read a text that could be connected to the unit theme. Then, they write responses to the text in the journal. They use their journal entry to support discussion in the book club. Finally, the teacher facilitates a whole-class meeting in which children can share what was discussed in their book club. Teachers can instruct how to model and encourage strategy use and heighten children's awareness of text structure and elements of text throughout the book club session. To support vocabulary learning and word use, teachers can encourage children to discuss interesting words and use those words to talk about the text. They can also encourage the use of word learning strategies, to be discussed in the next chapter, during book club time.

Another format for collaborative reading is called Literature Circles. In the Literature Circle approach, children choose a text to read and teachers group students by text choice. Children are encouraged to take notes as they read. When the group meets, children discuss what they read. Children are given specific roles to facilitate the group discussion. Figure 4.12 shows possible roles for children in Literature Circles.

As can be seen, there is a specific job called *Vocabulary Enricher*, which teachers can rotate to different students over time. Teachers could add to this role the job of finding interesting words to bring up for discussion by the group. After children participate in Literature Circles, teachers can encourage different student groups to report to the whole class about words they found so they can share their experiences beyond their group. Making vocabulary an important part of Literature

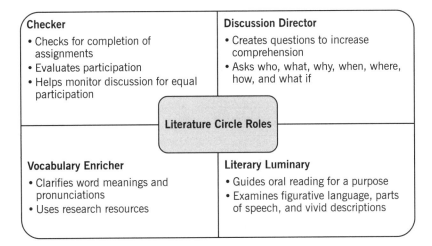

FIGURE 4.12. Literature Circle roles from the Read/Write/Think program. Adapted from *ReadWriteThink.org* (2014). Copyright 2014 by the International Reading Association and the National Council of Teachers of English. Adapted by permission.

Circles is bound to encourage children to notice, learn, and use the words in the texts they are reading. In a study on Literature Circles in grade 4, Davis, Resta, Davis, and Camacho (2001) report positive outcomes with regard to language and literacy skills. While more research is needed, this discussion format could be successful with younger learners as well.

The CCSS include a focus on participating in collaborative conversations with diverse learners (e.g., CCSS.ELA–Literacy.SL.2.1). Buddy reading, reading buddies, and collaborative reading groups are all activities that teachers could use to foster children's collaborative conversation skills.

Regardless of the specific collaborative reading format teachers employ, having children meet in groups to discuss text is likely to promote children's receptive and expressive language skills. The key is making vocabulary learning and use an expected practice in collaborative reading groups so children know to point out and use interesting words as they talk about reading. In general, encouraging children to talk about reading, either with teachers, with buddies, or in small groups, is a promising way to foster vocabulary development in a language-rich classroom.

Centers Activities

In centers activities children can explore their environment and use language in the process. Teachers can structure centers to maximize children's language use as they play and learn. Here are some centers activities to consider.

Talking Time Centers

To increase time for language development, teachers in early childhood and elementary classrooms can structure centers time to provide opportunities for children to use language and extend their vocabulary. Dockrell et al. (2010) used the structured centers approach to promote language in their program called Talking Time, which they implemented with preschoolers from low socioeconomic and ELL backgrounds in England. In the Talking Time program, small groups of children participated in three centers activities with adult supervision, modeling, and support. These centers activities and the language objectives they meet are described in Figure 4.13.

Dockrell et al. (2010) found that children who participated in the program for 15 minutes twice a week for 15 weeks showed growth in vocabulary and comprehension over the course of the intervention. Their growth in these areas was greater than that of peers who were not in the intervention. Dockrell et al.'s study shows that providing even brief, structured opportunities to use language in a language-rich environment can produce meaningful gains for children's language and literacy.

Conversation Stations

Another approach to supporting language development during centers time was implemented by Bond and Wasik (2009) in Head Start classrooms. The purpose

Activity	Objective	Description	Example
Acting Out	Children develop vocabulary on specific themes.	Teachers present a situation and ask children to act it out using props.	During a unit on travel, children could be guided to act out planning, packing, departing, arriving, and traveling to different places.
Story Talk	Children use language to predict and infer in the context of picture books.	Teachers use books as starting points for conversation.	Teachers could read *If You Give a Mouse a Cookie* (Numeroff, 2010) and ask children to predict what the mouse will want next and why.
Hexagon Game	Children describe pictures and use pictures to produce connected narratives.	Teachers present children with pictures and ask them open-ended questions about the pictures and the links between the pictures. Then teachers have children retell the story to a doll who missed the story.	Teachers could present a series of pictures of a chef making pasta during a unit on cooking. Children can talk about what is happening in the pictures and then retell the story in sequence.

FIGURE 4.13. Description of the structured centers in the Talking Time program. Adapted from Dockrell, Stuart, and King (2010). Copyright 2010 by the British Psychological Society. Used with permission.

of Conversation Stations is to develop children's "thoughtful listening" skills. Thoughtful listening teaches children to listen carefully to the speaker so they can respond appropriately, and it enables children to practice new vocabulary and discuss concepts related to the current class theme. In the Conversation Stations approach, teachers set up a special area of the room for the Conversation Station center. Children rotate through the Conversation Station center just as they do in other centers in class; the primary difference is that there is always an adult at the Conversation Station. The role of the teacher, specialist, aide, or volunteer is to model and support meaningful conversation. Bond and Wasik recommend that no more than two or three children be allowed at the Conversation Station center at a time to ensure that children have ample time to talk and teachers can effectively support and respond. The steps for introducing children to Conversation Stations and guidelines for structuring Conversation Station sessions are listed in Figure 4.14.

A Conversation Station enables children to initiate the conversation. When children have something off topic to say in class, teachers can tell children to hold their thoughts and express their ideas in the Conversation Station later in the day. Teachers can write the names of students who have something to share in the Conversation Station sign-up so they know they will have a chance to talk later. However, teachers need to be sure to give reticent children a chance to talk too. For these children, having conversation starters such as "Let's talk about . . ." with reference

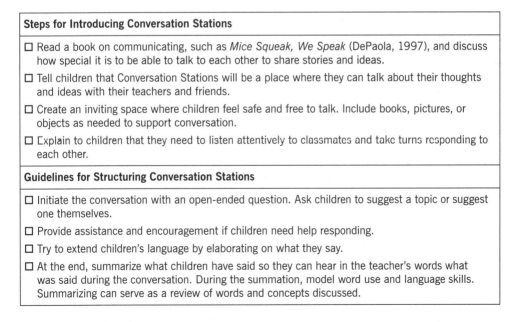

Steps for Introducing Conversation Stations

☐ Read a book on communicating, such as *Mice Squeak, We Speak* (DePaola, 1997), and discuss how special it is to be able to talk to each other to share stories and ideas.

☐ Tell children that Conversation Stations will be a place where they can talk about their thoughts and ideas with their teachers and friends.

☐ Create an inviting space where children feel safe and free to talk. Include books, pictures, or objects as needed to support conversation.

☐ Explain to children that they need to listen attentively to classmates and take turns responding to each other.

Guidelines for Structuring Conversation Stations

☐ Initiate the conversation with an open-ended question. Ask children to suggest a topic or suggest one themselves.

☐ Provide assistance and encouragement if children need help responding.

☐ Try to extend children's language by elaborating on what they say.

☐ At the end, summarize what children have said so they can hear in the teacher's words what was said during the conversation. During the summation, model word use and language skills. Summarizing can serve as a review of words and concepts discussed.

FIGURE 4.14. Recommendations for implementing Conversation Stations. Adapted from Bond and Wasik (2009). Copyright 2009 by Springer Science + Business Media. Used with permission.

The CCSS focus on speaking clearly; describing familiar people, places, things, and events; and recounting experiences with appropriate detail (e.g., CCSS.ELA–Literacy.SL.K.4 and CCSS.ELA–Literacy.SL.K.6). Talking Time and Conversation Stations are both activities that could support students in meeting these standards.

to the unit theme might help. Teachers can use books, pictures, props, and so forth to help children in talking. Teachers can ask children open-ended questions about what they have been learning in class or how what they have been learning in class connects to their personal lives. Teachers can also encourage a positive relationship with students in the Conversation Station by asking children how they are feeling and what they are thinking about various topics of interest. Bond and Wasik (2009) note that Conversation Stations helped even the most quiet and reluctant children share their thoughts and ideas in the classroom.

Individual Activities

Engaging with children individually helps teachers provide focused support for and feedback on language use. The following activities enable teachers to work one on one with students to support their vocabulary learning.

Storytelling and Story Acting

The idea behind the storytelling and story acting yes approach originated with Vivian Gussin Paley (1981) and has been further developed by Patsy Cooper (2005). In a recent study by Cooper et al. (2007), the authors describe the two main components of the approach as follows:

> The first is the dictated story, in which the teacher—or scribe—is an active participant, freely asking questions that help clarify the child's intention. . . . The second component is the dramatization of the story by the author and his or her chosen classmates. In this part, the teacher acts as director, while the remaining children constitute the audience. (p. 256)

During the storytelling or story dictation part of the approach, teachers meet one on one with children during centers time and ask them what they would like to write about. If a child doesn't have any ideas, the teacher can offer suggestions. Teachers write down what children say and read it out loud as they write. They make comments or ask questions to help children expand their ideas. Teachers can also call attention to words, letters, or sounds as they write. We observed the following exchange during storytelling time with one teacher and student in a prekindergarten classroom:

TEACHER: What do you want your story to be about?

STUDENT: The jungle.

TEACHER: Wow! That is a great setting for your story. Is it a pretend story? Do you want to start with "Once upon a time"?

STUDENT: Once upon a time I was in a jungle.

TEACHER: Great. And what happened?

STUDENT: I was swinged from a vine.

TEACHER: You were swinging from a vine. *Vine* is a great word. That was in our book the other day. Then what happened?

STUDENT: I fell on an alligator.

TEACHER: Oh no! Was he a scary alligator?

STUDENT: He was a nice alligator.

TEACHER: Was he kind and gentle?

STUDENT: Yeah, he was kind and gentle. I rided on his back to go home.

TEACHER: You rode on his back all the way home? Is that the end of the story?

STUDENT: Yep. Will you read it to me?

Once children are done dictating their story, teachers read the whole story back to them and ask if the retelling sounds right. Finally, teachers and children discuss how the story could be dramatized, what the different roles would be, and which children could act them out.

When it comes time to act out the story, the teacher serves as the director. No rehearsals, props, or costumes are needed. First, teachers read the story to the class. Then, teachers call on children in the class to serve as actors for the story. Next, teachers guide children to act out the story as it is read again. Teachers can give stage directions during the performance and add pauses for children to use dialogue to act out the story. If children can't remember the dialogue, teachers can read the dialogue and the children can echo. At the end of the dramatization, the children take a bow and the audience claps. While children love seeing their own stories brought to life, they also enjoy acting out adult-authored stories from books that teachers have read aloud to them. Teachers can use the dramatization approach for acting out those stories as well.

Cooper et al. (2007) studied the effects of the story acting approach with prekindergarten and kindergarten children, including low-income and ELL children, over the course of a year. They found that, compared to children of the same age, from similar backgrounds, and from similar school settings, children who participated in storytelling and story acting had significantly higher vocabulary and literacy scores on standardized, norm-referenced measures. This study showed the promise of the story-acting and storytelling approach for supporting language development in young children.

Story Dictation

Often teachers use story dictation even if they do not use the full storytelling and story-acting approach. Recently, Christ, Wang, and Chiu (2011) implemented a multicomponent vocabulary intervention that included read-alouds with explicit instruction of vocabulary and story dictation in preschool classrooms. In their approach, story dictation occurred during centers time. One child at a time dictated a story. The purpose was to contribute to a class anthology on the topic they were studying, and anthologies were shared during circle time.

When the teacher worked with a child, she asked a broad question related to the unit theme. The example the authors include in their paper is "Tell me a story about birds in the rainforest." The teacher served as a scribe while the children dictated their story. During the dictation, the teacher employed a number of instructional strategies to support students. She used repetitions such as rereading for accuracy and repeating the child's dictation while scribing. She asked questions to encourage students in providing details, using words, clarifying their thoughts, and recounting accurate information about the topic at hand. The teacher used prompts for children to repeat words they said and recall information that was presented in the read-aloud. She also offered sentence starters as needed to scaffold children's dictation. The teacher modeled use of specific words and reviewed content information. She also offered feedback to help children learn how to state their ideas most effectively. Finally, she affirmed and praised children throughout the process to encourage their efforts. After the dictation was over, children were prompted to illustrate their story. The teacher discussed their illustration with them and offered to label parts of the picture. Teachers then assembled children's stories in a binder and read the anthology of stories to children during circle time.

Results from the study indicated that children learned and used target words during story dictation time. And children's use of target words in their writing increased in quantity and quality over time, suggesting that story dictation supported children's breadth and depth of word knowledge. Hearing and seeing their words in print likely helped them own the words and internalize them more readily than they would have without the story dictation experience.

Writing Workshop

In writing workshop, which is used often across the elementary school grades, children repeatedly engage in the writing process (i.e., brainstorming, drafting, revising, editing, and publishing) as they gain fluency and independence in writing. Teachers provide modeling and guidance through mini-lessons on various aspects of the writing process. During these mini-lessons, teachers can support children in vocabulary and oral language use by showing them how writers use specific words and phrases to say what they want to say in clear language and in an interesting way. In individual conferences about students writing, teachers can encourage children to use words and phrases as tools to make their writing clearer and more exciting for their readers. Teachers can also encourage individual children who try to use language in more interesting ways in their writing so that they will be motivated to continue taking risks and using advanced language. Writing is a great way for children to use words in different syntactical constructs.

> The CCSS focus heavily on using drawing, dictating, and writing across genres to communicate ideas and information to others (e.g., CCSS.ELA–Literacy.W.K1–3; CCSS.ELA–Literacy.W.K2–3; CCSS.ELA–Literacy.W.K2–3). Story dictation, storytelling/storyacting, and writing workshop are all instructional activities that could serve to support students in developing these essential writing skills from an early age.

A recent study by Tracy and Headley (2013) investigated the use of writing workshop with children in fourth grade. Although these authors did not set out to study vocabulary in the context of writing workshop, they discuss how children in their study developed a shared vocabulary during writing workshop about such topics as genre and qualities of good writing. Specifically, the researchers participated in and observed a writing workshop series that focused on nonfiction genres such as memoirs, letters, opinion pieces, how-to guides, feature articles, and research reports. For each genre, the teacher provided mentor texts and reviewed various features of the genre. She also encouraged children to try using the various genres in their own writing. Consequently, children internalized vocabulary such as *details, heading, persuasive, organization,* and *voice.* While the researchers did not mention it, it is likely that children learned and used other words related to the content of the writing as well. Although the study by Tracy and Headley (2013) focused on writing workshop in fourth grade, it is likely, given the positive relationship between vocabulary and writing across grades (e.g., Coker, 2006; Kim et al., 2011), that the effects on vocabulary would be consistent across the early childhood and elementary grades. Thus, while writing workshop is not typically perceived as a vocabulary-building activity, it may contribute to the overall language-rich environment of the classroom, even though research is needed to determine how best to support vocabulary in the writing workshop context in the early grades.

Summary

There are innumerable ways in which you can establish a language-rich classroom environment that optimizes students' potential to acquire and apply new language. In this chapter, we discussed characteristics of a language-rich environment, and we provided examples of how these characteristics manifest in common routines and activities in early childhood and elementary school classrooms. Given the emphasis on vocabulary in the CCSS, teachers must rethink their instructional routines and activities to focus more on language development. Change doesn't always come easy, but you can take it one step at a time. First, you can ensure that the routines and activities you have already established adhere to the characteristics of effective instruction and language-rich environments outlined at the beginning of this chapter. Then, you can experiment with new activities and routines that create rich opportunities for vocabulary learning and language use. In the next chapter, we discuss how, within the language-rich environment of your classrooms, you can foster children's word awareness and provide children with independent word learning strategies so they can acquire words on their own as they become more fluent and autonomous readers over time.

CHAPTER 5

Word Awareness and Independent Word Learning

- What is word awareness, and why is it important?
- What are instructional routines and activities that can be used to support children's development of word awareness?
- How can young children engage in independent word learning?
- What are instructional routines and activities that can be used to support young children's development of independent word learning?

Every morning, Mr. Jackson's second graders settle in to their desks and take out their journals. On Mondays, their assignment is to write a list of Wonderful Weekend Words. These are interesting words they heard over the weekend. After taking attendance on Mondays, Mr. Jackson calls on a couple of students to share their Wonderful Weekend Words with the class. He asks students to use the words in context, he calls attention to meaningful word parts, and he models looking up words in the dictionary. Mr. Jackson is teaching his students to be aware of words they hear or read in their environment and use resources to learn words independently.

To acquire the sheer number of words they need to know to make sense of the texts they will encounter throughout schooling, children need to be able to figure out some words on their own. If they know enough words in a text, recognize which words they don't know, and have strategies they can use to figure out unknown words, children can become fairly efficient independent word learners. However, without prior instruction, many children will not even notice that they

don't know certain words much less employ effective strategies to figure those words out. By ignoring new words, children are missing out on opportunities to add to their own vocabulary knowledge. But we can change that.

By fostering word awareness, teachers can encourage students' appreciation of new words so they are excited to stop and think about new words independently. As Graves and Watts-Taffe (2008) point out, "The advantage of word consciousness activities is that they are enticing and enjoyable, build on students' existing vocabularies be they large or small, and help students with small vocabularies without limiting those with larger ones" (p. 186). Teachers can also help children develop independent word learning strategies so they can figure out what new words mean when they encounter them on their own. As Graves (2006) notes, "Teaching students word learning strategies—strategies such as using context and word parts to unlock the meanings of words they don't know—is tremendously important. With tens of thousands of words to learn, anything we can do to help students become more proficient independent word learners is an absolute necessity. Fortunately, we can do a lot to sharpen students' skills at learning words on their own" (p. 91).

While young children may not be able to engage in independent word learning in the context of reading text until they become fluent readers, teachers can introduce them to word learning strategies through oral language activities such as read-alouds. They can also support children in practicing word learning skills right from the start so that they will be ready to fully deploy independent word learning strategies once they can read extensively on their own. In this chapter, we describe ways you can promote word awareness and independent word learning in your classroom through a wide range of instructional routines and activities appropriate for prekindergarten through second-grade children.

Developing Word Awareness

Word awareness involves both metacognition (i.e., knowing what one does or does not know) and interest in or excitement about words and word learning. Children who have word awareness notice when they hear a word they don't know and are interested in finding out the meaning of that word. A constant refrain from children with word awareness is "What's that mean?" Whether this curiosity stems from an innate interest in words or adult modeling of word interest, children who notice and ask what words mean likely have more opportunity to learn words when they encounter them and, more often than not, try to use them on their own. What do teachers do with children who don't arrive in school with word awareness? Teachers model word awareness, encourage word awareness, and provide opportunities for children to demonstrate word

> Students who have **word awareness** tend to notice words in the environment, recognize when they do or do not know a word, and exhibit excitement about and interest in word learning.

awareness in school. In classrooms where word awareness is fostered and valued, children will likely catch on and catch up quickly.

Unfortunately, as mentioned in Chapter 2, the research base on promoting word awareness in young children is not substantial. Thus, we have drawn our recommendations from our own work and the work of others in which attention to word awareness has been part of a larger vocabulary program to foster vocabulary breadth and depth. In fact, many of the recommendations we discuss in this section are based on activities for explicit and extended instruction discussed in Chapter 3 and language-rich classrooms described in Chapter 4. It is important to note that attention to word awareness can target words children already know or words that children are encountering for the first time. For words children already know, providing opportunities to become aware of how, when, and why to use those words in relation to other words can foster vocabulary depth. And for words children are encountering for the first time, supporting discovery and exploration of those words can support vocabulary breadth and, in time and over multiple reencounters with the words, vocabulary depth. The more aware children are of words in their environment, the more likely they are to add to their existing word knowledge and seek out opportunities to learn words on their own. So, supporting word awareness is, perhaps, one of the most generative principles in our model for promoting breadth and depth of vocabulary in prekindergarten through second-grade classrooms.

Attending to Word Choice in Reading

One way to develop word awareness in young children is to guide them to notice words in the books they hear and read in school and beyond. In addition to teaching words explicitly and providing a language-rich environment in the classroom, teachers can call children's attention to the kinds of words authors choose to convey meaning. Asking children what words authors use to describe or explain what they are writing about can help children see the importance of word choice. And paying attention to the words authors use to express themselves also requires children to monitor their understanding of the words they hear and read.

Noticing new words allows children to ask about them or, as we discuss later, use independent word learning strategies to figure them out. So, how can teachers support children in attending to word choice in reading? Next we describe a few ways to raise children's awareness of the words authors use in text. Many of the activities are extensions of ideas presented in Chapter 4 on promoting a language-rich environment.

> Guiding children to notice word choice in reading helps them develop word awareness and supports them in meeting the CCSS that call for children to describe how words and phrases supply rhythm and meaning in literature (CCSS.ELA–Literacy.RL.K.4, CCSS.ELA–Literacy.RL.1.4, CCSS.ELA–Literacy.RL.2.4).

Word Wall Connections

Teachers can have children listen to a book and guide them to create a word wall of all of the words they hear having to do with the theme of the book. For example, teachers could read the book *Listen to the Rain* (1988), by Bill Martin and John Archambault, which describes the rhythm of rain. Teachers could ask children to brainstorm all of the words the authors use to describe rain and write those words on a "Sounds of Rain" word wall. Teachers can invite children to use these words whenever they talk about rain in school or at home. This kind of activity helps children see how words are related and yet subtly different. Recognizing the nuanced similarities and differences between words and developing rich semantic networks of related words helps children develop a broad and deep vocabulary knowledge.

Word Swap

Teachers can read a book to students and guide them to think of other words the authors could have used to say the same thing. For example, teachers could read the book *Brown Bear, Brown Bear, What Do You See?* (1992), written by Bill Martin and illustrated by Eric Carle, and ask children to suggest other words the authors could have used to describe bears, cats, and fish. Instead of *brown* bear, *purple* cat, and *gold* fish, children could say *fierce* bear, *gentle* cat, or *wet* fish. These kinds of activities help children see how different words have different meanings and how choosing words carefully can be important to conveying the intended message.

Word Comparison

Teachers can have children read a book (or listen to the teacher read a book) and underline or highlight (or have teachers underline or highlight) all of the words that describe the main character or the setting in narrative texts or the topic under investigation in information texts. For example, teachers could read the book *Charlotte's Web* (1952), by E. B. White, and prompt students to list character traits of Charlotte and Wilbur. At the end of the story, teachers could compare the traits chronologically to investigate how a particular character developed in the story.

Attending to Word Choice in Writing

Just as helping children attend to words in reading can help them be more aware of words, so too can helping them attend to words in writing. When children are taught that the words they use themselves can make a difference in how well they convey their message, they begin to see the importance of the words around them. And they start to think about how to choose the most appropriate words to get across their meaning. Thus, having children think about word choice in their own writing is a powerful way to develop their word awareness. Next we describe a few

ways to support children's word awareness in the context of their own writing.
As in the previous section, these activities are extensions of ideas discussed
in the previous chapter on promoting a
language-rich environment.

Having children attend to word choice
in writing can help them become more
aware of words and meet the CCSS that
call for children to use acquired words
in writing (CCSS.ELA–Literacy.L.K.6,
CCSS.ELA–Literacy.L.1.6, CCSS.ELA–
Literacy.L.2.6).

Picture Captioning

Teachers can have children draw pictures and then guide them to caption their
pictures using interesting words. Children could dictate their caption to the teacher
or write it down themselves. Teachers could prompt children to think of the most
poignant words to describe their picture. For example, during a unit about sea
creatures, Ms. Jacobs asked her students to draw an underwater scene. Daniel
drew an octopus and said he wanted his caption to read, "This is an octopus, and
this is a shark." After the teacher questioned Daniel about what was happening in
his picture, Daniel revised what he wanted his caption to say and asked his teacher
to write, "The giant octopus is hiding behind the coral so the shark won't attack."
Ms. Jacobs helped Daniel use words effectively in his writing to get his message
across.

Writing and Revising

Teachers can have children write stories or reports and then model the revision
process to find more specific or more interesting words to fit their stories. For
example, teachers can ask children to highlight words in their writing that are kind
of boring and replace these words with words that are more exciting. Teachers can
even work with students to make a list of kind of boring words or phrases that
appear frequently in their writing and words or phrases to use instead. Then they
can write these on chart paper and hang the chart paper on the wall so everyone
in class can refer to it when revising. In Figure 5.1, Andrew had written a report
about skateboarding, highlighted words he thought were kind of boring, and then
replaced these words with more interesting words in his second draft.

First Draft	Second Draft
The Skateboard	The Skateboard
The skateboard is a great **thing.** It has four wheels and a **big** board. You have to **have** a helmet and pads when you ride. One **thing** you can do is a 180. If you are **really good,** you can do a kickflip. I really **like** to skateboard!	The skateboard is a great **invention.** It has four wheels and a **long** board. You have to **wear** a helmet and pads when you ride. One **trick** you can do is a 180. If you are **experienced,** you can do a kickflip. I really **treasure** my skateboard!

FIGURE 5.1. Sample student writing showing revision for word choice.

Collecting Words

Words are fun, funny, and funtabulous! If children don't already know this, their teachers can make them aware that knowing words can be enjoyable. A great way of introducing word awareness to young children is reading books to them about kids who love words. Three great books that can help are *Max's Words* (2006), by Kate Banks; *The Boy Who Loved Words* (2006), by Roni Schotter; and *Donavan's Word Jar* (1998), by Monalisa DeGross. In each of these books, the main character is a boy who learns the joy of recognizing and collecting interesting words and sharing those words with others. Once the concept of collecting and sharing words is introduced, teachers can institute a classroom word collection routine. As part of the daily morning routine, children can be encouraged to add words to their word collection journal. Even if they can't write the word (invented spelling is, of course, encouraged), children can draw a picture to remind them of the word. Teachers could encourage children to think of words they heard in books, on television, or just out and about with their family and friends. If children hear interesting words during the school day, teachers can remind them that they may want to add that word in their word journal. Then, once a week, teachers can call on a few children to choose words to add to the class word collection.

The class word collection could be a word wall, a word book that can be found in the classroom library throughout the week, or a word jar (like the one in *Donavan's Word Jar*). Teachers can help children define the word and provide an example of how the word is used in context. Throughout the following week, teachers can encourage children to use the new words they added as well as the words from the previous weeks. Teachers should make sure all children get a turn to contribute to the class word collection. And teachers should let children know that all kinds of words are welcome so they don't feel self-conscious about the word they pick. Teachers can also enlist parents to remind children about adding words to their word journal when they hear new words outside the classroom. Finally, each week, children can vote on their favorite word, which, of course, they will be encouraged to use all week, so all children feel like they are part of the word collection process. The main goal here is to promote children's awareness of the words around them and an excitement for learning new words or even just more about words they already know.

Playing with Words

Word play can be a great way to support children in becoming aware of words and excited about words. Once a week, teachers can hold word play sessions in which children get into groups to play word games facilitated by the teacher. Some days, teachers can facilitate more generic word games such as I Spy Preschool Game, Pictionary Junior, or Scrabble Junior, where children need to find, draw, or spell words to win the game. (These games are great for indoor recess!) Other days, teachers can moderate more specific word games that attend to different aspects of words. These word games can be preceded by mini-lessons on a certain aspect of words, and then children can play with words using what they have learned. Here are some examples of mini-lessons and related games that teachers can use in the classroom.

Act It Out!

Teachers can lead a mini-lesson on what action verbs are and how they are used in sentences. Then, children can play a charades-type game in which they have to act out different action words for their teammates to guess. (A child can act out running, and her teammates have to guess that she is *sprinting*.)

Synonym Bingo

Teachers can lead a mini-lesson on synonyms and how thinking of synonyms can help them use bigger words when they speak or write. Then, children can play a bingo-style game in which they have to match synonyms. (When the teacher says the word *grin*, children can put a marker on the word *smile* with a picture of a smiley face on their game card.)

Double Jeopardy

Teachers can lead a mini-lesson on multiple-meaning words and how it is important to think of which meaning is used in specific contexts. Then, children can play a Jeopardy-like game in which they have to come up with two meanings for the same word. (Answer: A word that means an animal with wings and something you can use to hit a ball. Question: What is a bat?)

Other published word games for older children such as Hedbanz, Apples to Apples, and Mad Libs can be adapted for younger children as well. Once children have played these games with their teachers in whole-class settings, teachers can include these games in centers and children can play them in small groups or pairs during centers time each day for added reinforcement.

In addition to formal games, teachers can use a variety of word play activities that focus on having fun with words. Attention to multiple meanings, puns, idioms, and similes and metaphors, described in detail in Figure 5.2, can call children's attention to the wonder of words. Teachers can have a pun of the day or an idiom of the week that children can laugh over and talk about together. For example, perhaps during a unit on animals and adaptation, the pun of the week could be "I tried to buy some camouflage pants but couldn't find any." Or the idiom of the week could be "A leopard can't change his spots." Or the simile of the week could be "as blind as a bat." Teachers can engage children in talking about why a pun is

Term	Definition	Example
Multiple-meaning words	Multiple-meaning words have more than one meaning. They can sound alike (e.g., homonyms) or different (e.g., heteronyms).	*Ant* and *aunt* are homonyms while *wind* (i.e., the wind blows) and *wind* (i.e., a wind-up toy) are heteronyms.
Puns	Puns are jokes that play on the multiple meanings of words.	I wondered why the baseball was getting bigger . . . then it hit me.
Idioms	Idioms are expressions that are not meant literally and are understood by people of the same language and culture.	It's raining cats and dogs.
Similes	Similes are figures of speech that compare one thing with another using *like* or *as*.	His feet are as big as boats.
Metaphors	Metaphors are figures of speech that compare one thing with another without using *like* or *as*.	Her hair is silk.

FIGURE 5.2. Features of words to address through word play.

funny or what the idiom might mean in different situations. By playing with words like this, children can come to understand how words can be used in different and interesting ways to convey meaning.

Investigating Words

Yet another way to encourage word awareness in the classroom is to hold weekly word investigations. Teachers can choose words from the classroom word collection or words from the class theme, school activities, or interests of the children in the class to investigate. In a word investigation, teachers can steer children through the process of looking up the definition, synonyms and antonyms, and etymology of a word. Teachers can guide children to use word parts and context clues to figure out words, a strategy that will be discussed later in this chapter. They can also support children in investigating different contexts when they might hear or use the word and can help children look up examples of how the word is used on the Internet. (In this case, teachers must ensure that safe surfing protections, restrictions, and/or software are applied and/or installed on the classroom computers.) Teachers can encourage children to interview parents, teachers, and friends about what they know about the word and how they use it. After collecting lots of sources of information about a word throughout a week, children can help teachers make a word investigation collage or complete a word investigation graphic organizer that will show all they learned about the word that week.

In one first-grade classroom we observed conducting a word investigation, teachers introduced the word *astronaut* since many children in the class were interested in space at the time. Using the overhead projector connected to her computer so all the children could see, the teacher looked up the word on Word Central and read the definition: "A traveler in a spacecraft." Then she read the etymology of the word. She introduced children to other words with *astro-* and *–naut*, such as

> *Astronaut.* From *astro-* "star, heavens" (derived from Greek *astron*, "star") and *-naut* (derived from Greek *nautēs*, "sailor," from naus "ship").

astronomy and *nautical*. Then she guided students as they looked up "astronaut" on the Internet. She explored with them a few Internet websites that discussed astronauts, such as *www.nasa.gov/astronauts*, *http://kids.nationalgeographic. com*, and *http://kids.discovery.com*. Finally, she told children to interview their parents, teachers, and friends about what they knew about astronauts. At the end of the investigation, the class made a book about the word *astronaut* to put in their school library so other children could learn about the word just like they did. Engaging children in researching words, where they come from, and how they are used is a great way to get kids aware of, excited about, and interested in words.

Summary

Classroom activities focused on helping children notice and become interested in words are a powerful way to sensitize them to the power of words and encourage them to think about when, where, why, and how to use words most effectively. Through noticing words in reading, using words in writing, collecting words, playing with words, and investigating words, children add to their breadth and depth of word knowledge and develop an awareness of words that will serve them well as they become more independent word learners. In the next section of this chapter, we turn to the word learning strategies children can use to help them learn about words in their environments once they become more aware of the words around them.

Fostering Independent Word Learning Strategies

Once children begin to notice that there are words they don't know, they need strategies to help them figure out what they mean. This is tricky for young children because most prekindergarten and kindergarten children do not know how to read, and many first- and second-grade children are not yet fluent or independent readers. So children need to be taught strategies they can use that are not dependent on being able to read fluently. In the previous chapter, we described the PET strategy we taught

> In the CCSS, children are expected to determine or clarify word meaning using context clues, word parts, and reference sources even in kindergarten through second grade (e.g., CCSS.ELA–Literacy.L.K.4, CCSS.ELA–Literacy.L.1.4, CCSS.ELA–Literacy.L.2.4).

children in our reading buddies program. The PET strategy encourages children to Pronounce, Explore, and Try It Out. We envision this strategy as one that children can use with buddies or on their own to review words taught by their teachers or learn new words they encounter independently. To explore words, children can think about the context and about word parts, and use reference sources that are accessible for emerging and beginning readers. Being able to figure out a word independently can be a powerful experience for children. In this next sections, we discuss how teachers can teach children how to use context, word parts, and reference sources to learn word meanings independently.

Think about the Context

Though most young children are not reading, or at least not reading advanced texts with fluency, children can be taught to use context clues through read-alouds and oral instruction. A great way to start teaching children about using context clues is to guide children to use the pictures and words in read-aloud books to figure out the meaning of unknown words. (However, we do not advocate that children use pictures to figure out how to *read* unknown words. This takes their attention away from the letter–sound correspondences they should be using to figure out how to decode.) Context is not always helpful for figuring out unknown words, but children can be taught to ask themselves, "Does that make sense?" to check their understanding of what words mean. Teachers can provide explicit instruction on using context clues to figure out what words mean by following the gradual release of responsibility model we discussed in Chapter 3. Teachers can model how to use context clues, guide children in using context clues, and then provide children with lots of opportunities to practice.

In their work with upper-elementary-age children, Baumann and colleagues (2003, 2007) taught children to look for five different kinds of clues in text. These are reviewed in Figure 5.3. The authors suggest encouraging children to look for clues before and after a word and explaining to children that (1) sometimes clues will be closer and sometimes they will be farther from the word in question and (2) sometimes clues will be obvious and sometimes they will be less obvious. Children need to learn to be somewhat flexible in using context clues and to always check for whether the meaning makes sense.

Young children can be taught to use these clues too, and picture clues can be added to the list. Let's think about how this might play out with these students. Consider the book *Alexander and the Terrible, Horrible, No Good, Very Bad Day* (1972), by Judith Viorst. On the first page of this book, the text reads, "I went to sleep with gum in my mouth and now there's gum in my hair and when I got out of bed this morning I tripped on the skateboard and by mistake I dropped my sweater in the sink while the water was running and I could tell it was going to be a terrible, horrible, no good, very bad day." There is a picture on this page of Alexander standing with arms crossed and a frown on his face. If children didn't know the word *terrible*, the teacher could talk her students through the process of identifying clues as follows:

"If I didn't know what *terrible* meant, I would look for clues in the text."

"First, let's look for a definition of the word *terrible*. I think 'no good' and 'very bad' are definitions the author included in the text."

"Next, let's look for possible synonyms of the word *terrible*. If we know what *horrible* means, it is a synonym we can use to figure out what *terrible* means."

"Now, let's look for examples in the text. The boy got gum in his hair, tripped on a skateboard, and got his sweater wet. These are examples of what he means by *terrible*."

"Last, let's look for other clues. How does the boy look? He is frowning and he looks unhappy."

"Putting all of these clues together helps me figure out that *terrible* means very bad. Does that make sense? Yes, that makes sense because if he got gum in his hair, tripped on a skateboard, and got his sweater wet, he is probably having a very bad day."

Type	Explanation	Example in Text
Definition	The author explains the meaning of the word right in the sentence or selection.	"It's long feelers, or *antennae*, help it find food." From *Sea Creatures* (Malyan, 2005)
Synonym	The author uses a word similar in meaning.	"The mole didn't think there was room for both of them, but when he saw the rabbit's *big kickers* he moved over." From *The Mitten* (Brett, 1989)
Antonym	The author uses a word nearly opposite in meaning.	"Left foot, *Left* foot/*Right* foot, Right./Feet in the *morning./* Feet at *night.* From *The Foot Book* (Seuss, 1968)
Example	The author provides one or more example words or ideas.	"Whether it is *a nest, a den,* or *a lodge,* river creatures are clever at using plant materials to build their *homes.*" From *Rivers and Lakes* (Holland & Lofthouse, 2003)
General	The author provides several words or statements that give clues to the word's meaning.	"Sometimes she went to the *conservatory* in the middle of the park. When she stepped inside on a wintry day, the warm moist air wrapped itself around her, and the sweet smell of jasmine filled her nose. 'This is almost like a tropical isle,' said Miss Rumphius. 'But not quite.'" From *Miss Rumphius* (Cooney, 1982)

FIGURE 5.3. Context clues and explanations with examples from children's texts. Adapted from Baumann, Edwards, Boland, and Olejnik (2003). Copyright 2003 by Sage Publications. Used with permission.

Of course, this example is very obvious, but obvious examples are good for demonstrating the process. After modeling with more obvious examples, teachers can show children how to find and use context clues in less obvious examples. Consider the book *The Snowy Day* (1962), by Ezra Jack Keats. In this book, a little boy went out to play in the snow. When he got home, "He told his mother all about his *adventures* while she took off his wet socks." In this sentence, there are few direct clues to support children in figuring out what the word *adventures* means if they don't already know it. Teachers can talk through what to do when clues are less obvious by saying the following:

> "Sometimes when you hear a new word, you have to really think through the clues. In this book, I would have to think hard about the word *adventures* if I didn't know what it means. There are no definitions or synonyms or antonyms for the word in this book. The clues won't be easy to find so I have to think hard about them, and I have to be careful not to get tricked."
>
> "To figure out the word *adventures* in this book, I might look at the picture. But, in the picture, the little boys' mother is taking off his socks. Does *adventures* mean getting undressed? Would that make sense? Would the little boy tell his mom about getting undressed? No, I don't think so. So, sometimes the pictures won't help. In fact, they might even trick me."
>
> "Instead, I am going to think about what happened in the book so far. What would the little boy tell his mother? Maybe he would tell her about making tracks, making snow angles, and climbing the snow mountain. Maybe those are *adventures*. Maybe his *adventures* are the exciting things he did in the snow. Maybe *adventures* are things you do that are exciting. Does that make sense? Yes, I think so because he probably wants to tell his mother all of the exciting things he did in that day."

Using think-alouds to make the process of using context clues transparent is an important part of teaching children how to use these clues to figure out unknown words. Beck et al. (2002, 2013) caution that teacher think-alouds require a lot of teacher talk, rendering children more passive in the learning process. Thus, think-alouds should always be followed by guided and independent practice so that children can be more active learners. Only by trying the strategy out on their own will children internalize it and learn to use the strategy when needed.

Teachers can provide practice in using context clues through a game called "Guess My Word!" or "Guess What My Word Means." Teachers can present children with a picture and a sentence or multiple sentences, either made up or from a book, with a covered-up word and one or more embedded clues to figure out the word. Teachers can ask children to try to identify what the covered-up word is (if it is a word they likely already know) and/or what it means using the clues and to explain the clue they used. And they can ask children to ask each other or themselves if their answer makes sense. Then, teachers can uncover the hidden word and give its definition. Children can discuss whether they were able to identify the word and/or what the word means or if they got tricked. This practice can be a fun way for children to practice figuring out what words mean using context clues, especially when they begin to encounter new words on their own, which they will do more and more as they develop fluency.

While young children will not be able to use context clues completely independently until they learn to read fluently, they can practice independent word learning when they hear words in their daily lives. For example, if they hear a word they don't know on television, they can think about whether there are any clues they could use to help them figure out what the word means. For example, in an episode of the children's television program *Arthur,* there is a *blackout.* Although the word *blackout* is never defined, children could use context clues such as the lights going out, the electricity not being on, and the characters using flashlights to see to figure out the meaning of the word *blackout.* If they are encouraged to try to use context clues both as they listen to and read text, children can begin to develop the independent word learning skills they need to build on their word knowledge throughout schooling and beyond.

Think about Word Parts

In addition to using context clues, children can learn to use word parts as clues to figuring out words they don't know. Even before children learn to read, they can be taught simple prefixes and suffixes that might help them figure out what words mean. Introducing children to prefixes and suffixes using the books *If You Were a Prefix* (2008) and *If You Were a Suffix* (2008) written by Marcie Aboff, or *Happy Endings* (2011), by Robin Pulver, can add fun and excitement to learning about word parts. Baumann and colleagues' (2003) work with upper-elementary-school students also included attention to word parts and taught children the following procedure for using "word part clues" to figure out unknown words (p. 114). We think that this makes sense for younger children too. In Figure 5.4, we provide an overview of word part clues from Baumann et al. (2003). Baumann et al. (2007) taught children how to use over 40 word parts to figure out unknown words. Some of these word parts may be too advanced for children in prekindergarten through second grade, but many others are easy for young children to grasp.

Apel and colleagues (2013), in a recent study with kindergarten through second-grade students, developed lessons with lots of oral activities to support children in identifying and using word parts in the early grades. These authors focused on 12 word parts: plural *-s* and third-person *-s, -ing, -ed, un-, re-, dis-, -er, -ly, -ness, -y, -er,* and *-est.* Each week of their 12-week intervention, teachers explicitly taught one word part by explaining what it means or how it changes words and giving examples of how the word part could be used. Then they encouraged children to be word detectives and listen for meaningful word parts in words. They even distributed magnifying glasses to help make the act of finding word

Word Part Clues	Examples
1. **Look for the root**: the basic part of the word	• A whole word (e.g., *happy*) • A meaningful part of a word (e.g., *vis-, vid-*)
2. **Look for a prefix**: a word part added to the beginning of a word that changes its meaning	• *Un-, in-* = "not" • *Re-* = "again"
3. **Look for a suffix**: a word part added to the end of a word that changes its meaning	• *-ness* = "state or quality of" • *-ible, -able* = "capable of"
4. **Put the meanings of the root and any prefix or suffix together** and see if you can build the meaning of the word.	• *Un*happy, happ*iness, un*happ*iness, vi*sion, visible, invisible, televi*sion, vid*eotape, vi*vid, evi*dent.

FIGURE 5.4. Word part clues. Adapted from Baumann, Ware, and Edwards (2007). Copyright 2007 by the International Reading Association. Adapted by permission.

parts more concrete. Over the course of four 25-minute lessons per week, they engaged children in a series of activities to help them become aware of how these word parts change the meaning (and, for first and second graders, the spelling) of words. Figure 5.5 shows some of the activities that these authors included in their lessons.

All of these activities call children's attention to how word parts can be used to make words and to figure out what they mean. In addition, all of these activities can be done through listening and speaking with or without picture support for emergent and beginning readers. The word parts Apel and colleagues (2013) introduce are particularly important because children will encounter them often in what they hear and read in school. The following example illustrates how the activities in the work of Apel and colleagues (2013) could be used to support children in learning about the suffix *-est*.

- First, the teacher introduces the *-est* word part on a word card, has children pronounce it, and explains that *-est* means *most*. She then has children listen for the *-est* sound in words she reads (i.e., *softest, loudest, yummiest*). When children hear the *-est* sound, they raise their magnifying glasses.
- Then, the teacher introduces a sorting activity. Given three pictures, children can choose the one that is the most (e.g., the *biggest, smallest,* or *longest*) and sort that picture into the "*-est* " pile and the other two pictures into the "not *-est*" pile. For example, given the word *big* and three pictures of cats (e.g., a house cat, a lynx, and a lion), they would put the picture of the biggest cat (i.e., the lion) into the "*-est* " pile.
- Next, the teacher plays the "Say It Another Way" game with the children. She asks them to say, for example, the *most strong* or the *most funny* in another way (i.e., strongest or funniest).
- Then, the teacher tells the children to listen for *-est* as she reads the book *Things That Are Most in the World* (2001), by Judi Barrett. In this book, children will hear about the *wiggliest, silliest,* and *quietest* things in the

world. Every time they hear -*est*, they can raise their magnifying glass to indicate they detected the word part of the day.

- In a follow-up activity, children can construct words by combining words with -*est* to make new words. Emergent readers can connect blocks with pictures (e.g., a block with a smiley face and a block with -*est* to make *happiest*), while beginning readers can connect a block with a smiley face and the word *happy* with a block with -*est* to make *happiest*. Teachers can call attention to the fact that sometimes when you add endings to words, the spelling changes.
- The teacher can further develop this activity by having children look for words with -*est* in writing and writing their own affix book about -*est* words. These activities will help children see how -*est* changes the spelling of some words but not others, and they will allow children to generate their own -*est* words.
- Finally, the teacher can review the -*est* suffix and some of the words that the children learned. Making connections between words (e.g., *big, bigger,* and *biggest*) in a final "word relatives" activity (i.e., an activity that highlights how words are related) will help children see how word parts can influence the meanings of related words and how using knowledge of word relations can help them figure out words on their own.

Activity	Description
Listening Activity	Students listen for the word part and raise their magnifying glass when they hear it.
Word Sorting	Students sort picture or words into two categories: pictures/words with the word part or pictures/words without the word part.
Say It Another Way	Teachers ask students how they could say something another way and children respond with a word that includes the targeted word part (e.g., "How do you say . . . more than one stick . . . another way?" p. 167).
Story Activity	Students listen to a story and put a thumb up every time they hear a word with the target word part.
Add-On	Students use blocks with words and word parts written on them and connect words and word parts to make new words.
Written Activity	Students circle the target word part in a list of words, some of which contain the word part and some of which do not.
Affix Book	Students define a word part and write sample words or paste pictures of sample words that include that word part.
Wrap-Up	Students review the word part, its meaning, and "word relatives," which are words that are related in meaning (e.g., *eat* and *eating*).

FIGURE 5.5. Activities to support word part learning. Adapted from Apel, Brimo, Diehm, and Apel (2013). Copyright 2013 by the American Speech–Language–Hearing Association. Adapted by permission.

There are many other activities that have not necessarily been evaluated as part of a research study that may support children in identifying and using word parts to figure out what words mean. Here are a few of them that could be used in prekindergarten through second-grade classrooms to support using word parts.

Compound Word Game

In this matching game, children match two pictures or two words to make a compound word. For example, they could match a picture of *fire* and a picture of a *fly* to make the word *firefly*. Other examples include: *applesauce, bedroom, cupcake, drumstick,* and *eyelid.*

Build a Word Game

In this game, children are given word cards with prefixes in one color, root words in another color, and suffixes in yet another color (e.g., green, yellow, and red). For beginning readers, pictures can accompany root words. Children are also given a mat with two or three columns. Children place word cards down in their corresponding word part columns to try to make real words. As shown in Figure 5.6, children could make words like *un-help-ful, re-build-ing,* and *pre-view-ed.* To reduce the complexity of the task, the activity can be done with only prefixes and root words before adding suffixes.

Prefix/Suffix Flip Book

In this activity, children read a book in which the prefix or suffix is fixed, but the root word changes to make new words. Children can also make their own flip books to practice using the same word part to figure out the meaning of lots of different words (e.g., *uni-* with *unicycle, uniform,* and *unicorn*). Pictures next to the root words can help beginning readers figure out the words as they flip through the book.

In addition to these twists on classic matching and sorting games, there are many games that can be played on the computer or on tablet devices that similarly support word learning. We discuss these more in Chapter 8 on multimedia, but

Prefix	Root	Suffix
un	help	ful
re	build	ing
pre	view	ed

FIGURE 5.6. Sample chart with word parts for *build a word* game.

suffice it to say that the interactive nature of these games can be a great way to support children's learning of how to use word parts to figure out words and make new words independently.

Use Reference Materials and Other Resources

While dictionary definitions can be tricky, children should be taught to use dictionaries and other resources to figure out words on their own. Though traditional dictionaries rely on rather well-developed literacy skills to find a word in alphabetical order and then discern the meaning of an often abstract definition, children can use picture dictionaries, children's dictionaries, or online dictionaries to aid them in figuring out unknown words. Picture dictionaries show pictures of concepts; children's dictionaries are written for beginning reading levels; and online dictionaries have text-to-speech options that enable children to hear a definition aloud. As children get more accustomed to using dictionaries, they should be encouraged to cross-reference definitions in multiple dictionaries to see how words are defined. This can be an eye-opening experience for children as they see that dictionaries don't always agree on how to define a word!

Before children are able to fluently use a dictionary, they need to be taught several skills:

- First, they have to be taught how to look words up either alphabetically or through a search bar electronically. To build alphabetic knowledge, teachers can have children play games in which they have to practice putting things in alphabetical order using the alphabet song and alphabet strips (i.e., word cards with the alphabet written on them). To build digital literacy skills, teachers can model how to find the search bar and type in the unknown word.
- Second, children need to be taught the parts of a dictionary definition. Teachers can explicitly teach the pronunciation guide, the parts of speech, and the enumeration of multiple definitions in the dictionary.
- Third, children need to be taught a strategy for figuring out which definition to use. Regardless of whether they are using a paper or computer-based dictionary, children need to learn that different definitions are appropriate for different contexts. Children can try out the definition in context to see if it makes sense before they decide that they have the right definition for the sense they mean.

One way to teach use of dictionaries is a "Let's look it up!" lesson like the one that follows, in which the teacher models the steps in the process of looking up a word. Teachers can either do this kind of lesson one on one, in small groups, or on an overhead projector with a whole class. In this lesson, the children watch a video clip on wild animals in the jungle as part of the unit they are studying on habitats.

> **Carnivore**—(1) a flesh-eating animal or (2) a plant that traps and digests insects (Word Central, n.d.)
>
> **Carnivore**—an animal that eats the flesh of other animals (Wordsmyth, n.d.).

After the video clip is over, one little boy raises his hand and asks, "What does *carnivore* mean?" The teacher responds, "Oh, in the video they said that jaguars are fierce carnivores and you are wondering what *carnivore* means. Let's look it up!" The teacher goes to her computer, which is connected to the overhead projector and pulls up the Internet. She models looking up the word *carnivore* on Word Central and Wordsmyth and reads the definitions above.

The teacher asks whether the meaning they are looking for refers to a plant or an animal. The children choose *animal* since the video was talking about a jaguar. She asks her students to compare the two definitions. One little boy says, "They both talk about flesh. What's that?" So, the teacher looks up flesh in the same way in Word Central and Wordsmyth.

The teacher again asks whether they should look at the definition for an animal or a fruit or vegetable and the children choose *animal* again. She asks the students what they think *flesh* means based on these definitions. One little girl replies, "The part of animals we eat." The teacher responds, "OK, so flesh is like meat. And a jaguar is a flesh-eating animal. So that means he eats _____." The children respond, *meat*. Finally, the teacher says, "OK, so a carnivore is an animal that _____." And the children respond, *eats meat*. To support children in checking their response, the teacher says, "So does that make sense? Does it make sense that a jaguar eats meat?" And the children respond, emphatically, "*Yes!*" Together with their teacher, the children have practiced looking up a word in an authentic context, and, over time, they will internalize this experience and be able to look words up on their own. Because this is a natural routine, it takes very little instructional time: the teacher has the Internet and projector at the ready for a teachable moment.

> **Flesh**—(1a) the soft parts of the body of an animal and especially the muscular parts, (1b) sleek plump condition of body, (2) parts of an animal used as food, (3) the physical being of a person as distinguished from the soul, or (4) a fleshy plant part (Word Central, n.d.).
>
> **Flesh**—(1) the soft parts of the human or animal body that lie between the skin and the bones or (2) the soft part under the skin of a fruit or vegetable (Wordsmyth, n.d.).

A thesaurus is another reference source children can consult when they are trying to figure out words. Again, there are paper-based and computer-based thesauri, and children need to be taught how to use them. Teachers can help children discover how to use a thesaurus by looking up common words like *hot* to see all of the other ways they can say *hot*. Children can then discuss how these words are similar but not exactly the same. Teaching about how to use a thesaurus in the context of writing can be helpful, because children can use the thesaurus to find other words to say what they are trying to say in even more sophisticated and precise ways.

In the following example, the teacher models how to use the thesaurus to find interesting words to use in a class report about their field trip to the farm. When the teacher asks children to talk about what they saw at the farm, one girl raises her hand and says, "We saw the horses running around." The teacher says, "That's true. We did see horses running around. I wonder if there is another word we could use to say what the horses are doing. Does anyone have another word to use here?" When she gets blank stares from the children in her class, the teacher says, "Well, let's look it up!" The teacher pulls out the thesaurus, demonstrates how to look up the word *run*, and reads the entries. She writes the words on the board after she reads them: *dash, gallop, jog, scamper, sprint, trip, trot*. Then she says, "Do any of these words fit with what we are saying and make what we are saying sound even better?" The teacher then walks the children through each word and asks if it makes sense. "Do horses *jog*?" Once children settle on the words that go best with horses, the teacher asks, "So, were the horses *trotting* or *galloping*? What is the difference?" After discussing that *galloping* is faster than *trotting*, the teacher asks the children to vote on which word should go in their sentence. The children decide that *galloping* makes more sense because the horses were *running* around very fast. So, the teacher replaces the word *running* with the word *galloping* in the report. Like looking up words in the dictionary, choosing just the right word in the thesaurus is a skill that children will internalize over time and, eventually, be able to use on their own to figure out which words say just what they want to communicate.

Using Multiple Sources Together

Children need to be taught that none of these ways of figuring out words by themselves may be perfect. They may get only partial information from many sources they consult. So, children should learn to try to use multiple sources of information about words together. Baumann and colleagues (2003) taught children in their study what they called the vocabulary rule:

- First, try to identify context clues before or after the word to try to figure it out.
- Second, try to find word part clues that can be used to figure out the meaning.
- Third, use the context clues again to try to see if the meaning makes sense.

In Figure 5.7, we show an extension of this rule that teachers could use to teach children to become independent word learners.

Children can be taught that if their definition doesn't make sense, they can try again until they feel like they have a definition that does. Between prekindergarten and kindergarten, children may need a lot of support to engage in any one of these

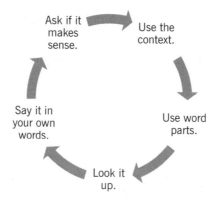

FIGURE 5.7. Using multiple sources to understand vocabulary.

processes, much less all of them together, but teachers can help them build an early foundation for independent word learning by modeling, guiding, and providing independent practice on these skills at their level from the early grades in school. By the time children are reading fluently, they should be ready to activate the skills they have been learning with their teachers on their own to acquire more and more words as they encounter them in their independent reading texts.

Ask a Peer or Teacher

Sometimes, no matter how much children try to figure out a word on their own, they may need some help. Children can be taught that if they need to know a definition and really can't figure it out on their own, they can ask a peer or a teacher. Teachers should create a classroom where asking questions about what you don't know is praised and children are rewarded for identifying the need for help and seeking it out. Many teachers have rules such as "ask three before you ask me," which requires children to ask their peers before they ask a teacher. This is a great way to position all children in the classroom as experts and collaborators. Sometimes children can find out what they need from a peer, and the interchange between peers helps both of them deepen their understanding of word meaning. As mentioned in the previous chapter, peer collaboration can be a powerful way of supporting children's vocabulary and language development.

Try It Out

As children develop their own sense of what a word means through the process of using context clues, word parts, and reference resources, they need to be encouraged to try out using words. By trying out words, children get the feedback they need to see if their use of the word makes sense and to refine their understanding of the word. Thus, children need to know that using big words in school is valued, and making fun of using big words in an awkward way is not acceptable. Children should feel free to try out their word knowledge and see how words fit in different contexts. The classroom needs to be a safe space for word learning to take place. And teachers can encourage children to try using words they are learning in their storytelling, in their writing, and in their conversations with others throughout the day.

Summary

Since teachers cannot possibly teach all of the words children need to know to succeed in school, they must support children in becoming aware of words in their environment and becoming aware of when they do and do not know particular words. They must also help children develop independent word learning skills to figure out words on their own. Although young children may not be able to be completely independent in looking up and exploring words, teachers can support them in these independent word learning strategies so they will develop these skills over time and, by the time they are reading fluently on their own, become expert independent word learners. In this chapter we reviewed ways you can encourage your students to be aware of words and support the development of their independent word learning skills. In the next chapter, we turn to the topic of assessing word knowledge and word learning skills to inform instruction in prekindergarten through second-grade classrooms.

CHAPTER 6

· · · · · · · · · · ·

Assessing Vocabulary
Knowledge

GUIDING QUESTIONS

· ·

- Why should teachers assess vocabulary knowledge?
- How can teachers assess vocabulary knowledge to effectively inform instruction?

Ms. Rodriguez is concerned about Eddie. Eddie has been in Ms. Rodriguez's prekindergarten class since the beginning of the year, but it is now almost November and he is still exceptionally quiet. Furthermore, Eddie scored far below his same-age peers on the vocabulary screening measure she administered at the beginning of the year. Ms. Rodriguez consults with specialists in her school. The specialists administer some diagnostic language assessments to identify Eddie's strengths and needs. These assessments indicate that Eddie has limited expressive vocabulary. Together, Ms. Rodriguez and the specialists develop an intervention and progress monitoring plan to make sure that Eddie receives the support he needs to increase his expressive vocabulary and speak up more in class.

In order to plan vocabulary instruction to meet students' needs, it is important to know children's initial level of vocabulary knowledge. And, in order to adjust instruction to meet students' needs across a school year, it is important to monitor children's progress over time. While most teachers would agree that assessment is important to drive instruction, many teachers don't have access to robust data on the vocabulary breadth and depth of their students in order to make informed decisions about their strengths and needs. Teachers may have a general sense of children's understanding and use of vocabulary, but they typically don't have the same kind of systematic data for vocabulary as they do for other skills like phonics and fluency. The lack of data on vocabulary likely stems from the fact that assessing breadth and depth of vocabulary is a complicated endeavor. We begin with an overview of what it is about vocabulary that makes it so hard to assess. Then we delve into the purposes of assessment and the various kinds of assessments that are available to measure children's vocabulary. Finally, we offer suggestions about ways you can assess children in your class on the vocabulary you are teaching so you can plan instruction to best meet their needs.

The Complexity Involved in Assessing Vocabulary

First, vocabulary develops along multiple dimensions. Children acquire breadth of vocabulary (i.e., at least surface-level knowledge of a wide range of words) and depth of vocabulary (i.e., rich and robust knowledge of many different facets of words) simultaneously. As we noted in Chapter 1, vocabulary depth includes knowledge of phonology, orthography, morphology, syntax, semantics, and pragmatics. Thus, to measure children's knowledge of a word like *print*, an assessment would need to capture whether children can say the word, recognize its spelling, understand how *print*, *printed*, and *printing* are related, know how to use *print* in a sentence, relate *print* to other words such as *write* and *type*, and recognize what print means in different situations (e.g., "*print* your name on your paper" versus "download and *print* out a copy of your word list at home"). Second, word knowledge may be receptive (words can be understood when they are heard or read) or expressive (words can be used in speech or writing), and word knowledge may differ in the domains of listening and speaking (oral communication) and reading and writing (written communication) (Pearson et al., 2007). (See Figure 6.1.) As children learn words, their word knowledge along these dimensions will be out of sync. For example, children may understand the word *print* before they can use it or they may be able to read the word *print* before they can write it. It would be impossible for any one assessment to measure all of these different aspects of word knowledge at once.

To complicate matters further, children's development is incremental within each dimension and domain (Nagy & Scott, 2000). For example, children may be able to fully understand the word *print* when they hear it (e.g., "please *print* your

	Oral Communication	Written Communication
Receptive language	Listening	Reading
Expressive language	Speaking	Writing

FIGURE 6.1. The intersections between the modes of communication and language processes.

name at the top of the page"). But, when they need to use the word in speech, they may be able to give only a partially correct sentence using the word *print* (e.g., "I will *print* a picture of a dog on my paper"). Also, children are at various points of word knowledge for a vast number of words at any given time. So they know some words with more depth than others even though those words don't seem that different in level of difficulty (e.g., *write* and *print*). The extent to which children know particular words depends, in large part, on their interests and experiences and their exposure to words. Assessing the depth with which children know individual words is incredibly time consuming. Therefore, teachers can only assess depth of word knowledge for a few critical words at a time.

Finally, since young children can't read passages and answer multiple-choice or written response questions on their own, assessments are usually conducted one on one. Thus, assessing children on multiple occasions on multiple measures, which would provide the most robust picture of children's vocabulary knowledge, would be impossible. Therefore, teachers must be judicious in their use of vocabulary assessment. To do so, teachers will need to determine the best type of vocabulary assessment to meet their needs, and, since they likely can only administer a couple of vocabulary assessments at any given time, they will need to be cautious in generalizing information from a small set of vocabulary assessments too broadly. Despite the difficulties in assessing vocabulary, if teachers recognize the strengths and limitations of various assessment methods, they can choose measures wisely and use them effectively to plan instruction. Even a little information on students' vocabulary knowledge can go a long way in helping teachers implement responsive instruction.

Purposes for Conducting Vocabulary Assessment

With the wide range of considerations that come into play when deciding on what and how to assess, it is, first and foremost, important to consider the different reasons that a teacher might want to assess children's vocabulary knowledge. Specifically, as shown in Figure 6.2, teachers might want to assess students for the purposes of (1) screening, (2) diagnosis, (3) progress monitoring, or (4) outcome measurement (Walpole & McKenna, 2007).

Screening assessment is used to determine whether children may need additional support in a particular area. Teachers may give screening measures to all children in a class at the beginning of the year to identify which children may be at risk for experiencing difficulty. Vocabulary screening measures can be used to ascertain which children have limited vocabulary knowledge or limited skill in specific strategies. Although screening measures help determine which children are at risk, they do not provide detail on what, exactly, should be addressed through additional instruction.

If children are identified as needing support, diagnostic assessment can be used to determine specific areas to target. In vocabulary, broad measures of receptive

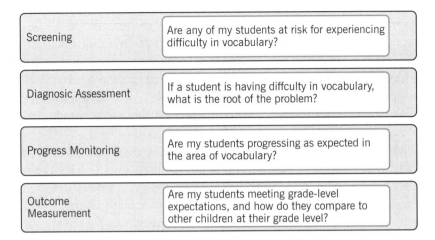

Screening	Are any of my students at risk for experiencing difficulty in vocabulary?
Diagnosic Assessment	If a student is having diffculty in vocabulary, what is the root of the problem?
Progress Monitoring	Are my students progressing as expected in the area of vocabulary?
Outcome Measurement	Are my students meeting grade-level expectations, and how do they compare to other children at their grade level?

FIGURE 6.2. The purposes for assessment. Adapted from Walpole and McKenna (2007). Copyright 2007 by The Guilford Press. Adapted by permission.

versus expressive or oral versus written vocabulary can be used. Moreover, assessments that provide age and grade-level norms offer information on the general level of word knowledge children possess. Since vocabulary does not progress as neatly as phonemic awareness or phonics ability, vocabulary measures may be imprecise, but they can be used along with ongoing progressing monitoring to determine children's instructional needs in the area of vocabulary.

Progress monitoring determines whether children are responding to instruction. In other words, are students growing in their vocabulary knowledge over time, and are they learning the words and skills that are being taught? Teaching without testing whether children have learned what has been taught is like cooking a meal without tasting it or asking others how it tastes. In vocabulary, teachers can assess whether children have learned specific words or skills that they have taught and adjust their instruction accordingly.

Finally, outcome assessment can be used to determine (1) how much children's vocabulary knowledge grew and (2) where they ended up in relation to their peers in a given area. Did children make gains? Did they begin to catch up with their peers or get closer to grade level? For vocabulary, teachers can evaluate whether children made gains in their knowledge of words specifically taught in class and how children compare in the extent to which they learned these taught words. To do this, teachers can sample a set of specific words they taught over the year or ask students to demonstrate what they have learned. Teachers can also assess how much children grew in general word knowledge (i.e., words not specifically taught in class) and how children compare overall in vocabulary. To do this, teachers can readminister screening, diagnostic, or progress monitoring measures or assess children using more global measures of vocabulary to determine the grade and skill level of students at the end of the year. In addition to informing future instruction for children since such assessments are passed on to teachers in the next grade level, outcome assessments can also help teachers to understand, overall, how well their vocabulary program or curriculum or approach to instruction is working. If most children in the class are making expected gains, then the program, curriculum, or approach to instruction is working well. If most children in the class are not making expected gains, then teachers can try to identify how to make changes to better support children's vocabulary growth in the future.

Given that assessing vocabulary knowledge is a tricky business, the published measures teachers can choose from for screening, diagnostic, progress monitoring, and outcome assessment are somewhat limited. However, since these assessments provide some information that can be useful for planning instruction, we next describe a few available vocabulary measures. In addition, since we encourage teachers to develop and use their own assessments to evaluate children's learning of the specific words and strategies they are teaching, we discuss these types of assessments later in the chapter.

Published Measures of Vocabulary

Published measures of vocabulary may be curriculum-based measures, criterion-referenced measures, or norm-referenced measures. Curriculum-based measures (CBMs) are brief assessments that are aligned with general grade-level curricular expectations and used for screening or progress monitoring to determine whether students are at risk for experiencing difficulties and whether students are progressing in specific skills. Some CBMs provide information about student performance in comparison to grade-level benchmarks or criteria. Such CBMs are considered criterion-referenced measures. Norm-referenced measures are more comprehensive measures that can be used for diagnostic and outcome assessment. They evaluate students on a range of skills and provide indications of their performance compared to that of other children at their age and grade level. See Figure 6.3 for how these different types of assessments can be used for different purposes. We will refer to these terms as we describe several published assessments available for measuring vocabulary knowledge.

Assessment Type	Assessment Purpose			
	Screening	Diagnosis	Progress Monitoring	Outcome Measurement
Curriculum-based measures	✓		✓	
Criterion-referenced measures	✓	✓	✓	✓
Norm-referenced measures		✓		✓

FIGURE 6.3. The suitability of assessment types for each assessment purpose.

Vocabulary Assessments for Screening and Progress Monitoring

There are a few different types of published assessments for screening and progress monitoring. The three criterion-referenced measures we describe below vary somewhat in the targeted grade, age level, and format used to assess vocabulary. (See Figure 6.4.)

Individual Growth and Development Indicators

One CBM for use in screening and progress monitoring in prekindergarten is the Picture Naming measure of the Individual Growth and Development Indicators (IGDIs; Carta, Greenwood, Walker, & Buzhardt, 2010). In this assessment, children are shown a series of pictures and asked to name them. Teachers ask, "Do you know what that is?" or "What's that?" The objects in the assessment are common in everyday environments, including home (e.g., cake, sink), classroom (e.g., glue, book), and community (e.g., rabbit, train) (Missall & McConnell, 2004). Children name as many pictures as they can in 1 minute. If children are unable to name a certain number of pictures within 1 minute, they may be considered at risk for difficulty in vocabulary. The IGDIs Picture Naming task is available for purchase at *www.myigdis.com/why-myigdis/assessments/early-literacy*.

Dynamic Indicators of Basic Early Literacy Skills

A CBM tool for use in kindergarten through third grade is Word Use Fluency (WUF; Good & Kaminski, 2002), an experimental task developed and currently being revised as part of the Dynamic Indicators of Basic Early Literacy Skills (DIBELS) battery of assessments. Students are asked to listen to words that range in difficulty (e.g., from *nap* to *decision*) and use them in sentences as best they can. If students use the target word correctly in a sentence, one point is given for each word children say in their response. For example, if a child responds to the word *going* by saying, "The fireman is going to the fire" the student's score is 7. In the

Assessment	Age/Grade Range	Administration	Testing Time	Skill(s) Assessed
IGDIs: Picture Naming	3–5 years old	Individual	1 minute	Oral expressive vocabulary
DIBELS WUF-R	Grades K–3	Individual	3 minutes	Oral expressive vocabulary
CORE Vocabulary Screening	Grades 1–8	Individual	10–20 minutes	Written receptive vocabulary

FIGURE 6.4. Screening and progress-monitoring assessments for vocabulary.

revised version of the DIBELS WUF measure, responses that demonstrate under-standing of the meaning of a word but are grammatically incorrect will receive partial credit (i.e., half a point for each word children say in their response). For example, if a child responds to the word *going* by saying, "Going to the park," the child gets 2 points for saying four words in a partially correct response. If children score below a certain level (e.g., the bottom 20th percentile), they may be consid-ered at risk for difficulty in vocabulary. Once validation is complete, the revised version of the WUF will be available at *https://dibels.org/next/wufr.php*.

Consortium on Reading Excellence Vocabulary Screening

A CBM measure that can be used with children in grades 1–8 is the Vocabulary Screening measure in *Assessing Reading: Multiple Measures* (Diamond, 2008), published by the Consortium on Reading Excellence (CORE) and available for purchase at *www.corelearn.com*. Students are provided with target words and then prompted to choose one of three words that means the same or about the same as the target word. For the word *gift,* for example, students would be pre-sented with the choices *hair, present,* and *spring*. Obviously, *gift* and *present* mean the same or about the same thing. In total, students are presented with 30 target words. As with the IGDIs and DIBELS measures, if students score below a certain benchmark for their grade, they are considered at risk for difficulty in vocabulary.

Strengths and Limitations of Screening and Progress Monitoring Measures

Each of these three measures has strengths and limitations. A major strength of these assessments is that they are not time intensive, so teachers can assess a whole class of students in a relatively short amount of time. Another strength is that they evaluate, at least at a cursory level, words that are likely to appear in grade-level texts. If teachers use these measures to provide initial information about children's vocabulary and how their vocabulary compares with that of their peers, these assessments can be useful. These measures can also be useful for indicating which children may need extra support for vocabulary in school. However, there are sev-eral limitations inherent in each of these measures. First, vocabulary knowledge is confounded with other skills in each of these measures. For example, fluency is needed on the Picture Naming task; semantics and syntax are both tapped on the WUF; and decoding ability is needed for the Vocabulary Screening measure. Thus, if children do not do well on these assessments, it could be because they are having difficulty with other aspects of the assessments besides vocabulary. Second, each measure alone captures only a narrow slice of what children know about words. So, children could be over- or underidentified as having a problem with vocabu-lary based on an assessment that captures a fairly limited amount of their word knowledge. Despite these limitations, these screening measures are one source of information that teachers can supplement with others to determine which children to monitor or further assess. If teachers deem children at risk for experiencing difficulties in vocabulary, further assessment should be conducted to determine how far behind their peers they are in vocabulary and what aspects of vocabulary are most problematic for them.

Diagnostic Assessments for Measuring Vocabulary Knowledge

Diagnostic assessments can be used to determine how far behind children are in vocabulary compared to their peers and which aspects of vocabulary are the most troublesome for them. Using diagnostic assessments that tap different aspects of vocabulary to determine children's strengths and needs in this area can inform instruction for struggling students. Therefore, using data from multiple assessments or subtests of assessments when trying to understand children's strengths and needs in the area of vocabulary is optimal. Several published criterion-referenced and norm-referenced measures that are widely used in schools across the country provide age or grade equivalents and standard scores based on norming samples. These assessments are available for purchase from their respective publishers, but they are rather costly. Typically, specialists such as speech–language pathologists rather than classroom teachers administer these assessments, but classroom teachers can ask for data from the assessments and seek advice from specialists to determine how to intervene for children struggling in vocabulary in school. Note that some of these measures are available in Spanish, which can be useful in determining whether bilingual children have difficulties in both languages. The assessments we review here vary on whether they assess vocabulary through listening, speaking, reading, or writing. (See Figure 6.5.)

Peabody Picture Vocabulary Test and Expressive Vocabulary Test

The Peabody Picture Vocabulary Test (PPVT, now in version IV; Dunn & Dunn, 2007) measures oral receptive vocabulary. In this assessment, children are asked to point to one of four pictures that best represents the target word, spoken orally by the administrator. The test is appropriate for children above 2 years and 6 months of age and can be administered through adulthood. Word difficulty increases over the course of the assessment from words as simple as *ball, dog,* and *spoon* to words as complex as *deciduous, expunging,* and *conflagration.* Administrators discontinue the assessment if and when children incorrectly identify 8 or more words in a set of 12. Note that the Spanish version of the PPVT is the Test de Vocabulario en Imagenes Peabody (TVIP; Dunn, Lugo, Padilla, & Dunn, 1981).

Assessment	Age Range	Administration	Testing Time	Skill(s) Assessed
PPVT	2.6–90+ years	Individual	10–15 minutes	Oral Receptive Vocabulary
EVT	2.6–90+ years	Individual	10–20 minutes	Oral Expressive Vocabulary
CELF Formulated Sentences	5–21 years	Individual	5–15 minutes	Oral Expressive Vocabulary (Semantics and syntax)
CELF Word Classes	5–21 years	Individual	5–10 minutes	Oral Receptive Vocabulary (Semantics)
CASL Basic Concepts	3–7 years	Individual	5–10 minutes	Oral Receptive Vocabulary (Semantics)
CASL Syntax Construction	3–21 years	Individual	5–10 minutes	Oral Expressive Vocabulary (Syntax)
CASL Pragmatic Judgment	3–21 years	Individual	5–10 minutes	Oral Receptive and Expressive Vocabulary (Pragmatics)

FIGURE 6.5. Diagnostic assessments for vocabulary.

The Expressive Vocabulary Test (EVT, now in version II; Williams, 2007), which parallels the PPVT, requires children to name what they see in a given picture. Administrators are provided with directions for scoring answers to limit subjectivity in interpreting results. Simple questions include items such as "What color is this?" (*green*) and "What shape is this?" (*heart*). More complex questions include items like "Tell me another word for *quickly*, as in 'He went quickly'" (*swiftly, rapidly*). After the student answers five consecutive items incorrectly, the examiner discontinues the test.

Clinical Evaluation of Language Fundamentals

The Clinical Evaluation of Language Fundamentals (CELF, now in its fifth version; Semel, Wiig, & Secord, 2013) has several tests relevant to vocabulary. (There is a Spanish version of the CELF as well.) In our work, we have found Formulated Sentences and Word Classes to be useful indicators of the depth of children's word knowledge. Specifically, these measures tap aspects of children's semantic and syntactic knowledge. In Formulated Sentences, children are given a word or phrase and, in most cases, a picture. Children are then asked to create a sentence to describe the prompt using the target word or phrase. For example, children are given the target word *forgot* accompanied by a picture of three children dressed for cold weather who are missing some warm articles of clothing. A typical response to this prompt is the sentence "The girl forgot her boots." Responses are scored on a scale of 0–2. A score of 1 represents a complete sentence that contains the word and two or fewer semantic or syntactical errors. A score of 2 represents a semantically and syntactically correct sentence that contains the target word. The Word Classes subtest measures a student's ability to identify relationships between words. Children are asked to identify two semantically related words, orally presented by the administrator, from sets of four words (e.g., *fence, window, glass, rug*). For the earlier items on this subtest, the verbal directions are also paired with pictures for the student to reference for the target words.

Comprehensive Assessment of Spoken Language

The Comprehensive Assessment of Spoken Language (CASL; Carrow-Woolfolk, 1999) has multiple subtests that can help assess the nature of receptive or expressive language difficulty in young children. Recommended "core" subtests include the Basic Concepts, Syntax Construction, and Pragmatic Judgment measures. The Basic Concepts subtest assesses children's expressive semantics skills. As with the PPVT, The examiner prompts the student, "Show me *(target word)*" while the student looks at a quadrant of drawn pictures for each question. For example, on one of the earlier items, the examiner says, "Point to the one that is *round*," and the student is given choices between an *orange, kite, window,* and *carton of milk*. The Syntax Construction subtest measures students' expressive syntax skills by asking them to respond to sentence prompts from the examiner. For example, the examiner would read, "Here the boy is standing *(examiner points to the standing boy)*. Here *(examiner points to the sitting boy)* the boy is _____ *(sitting)*." The student is expected to generate a word that correctly describes the picture and follows the syntactic construction of the sentence. Finally, the Pragmatic Judgment subtest measures children's pragmatic awareness, including their knowledge of how to use words and phrases appropriately in various contexts. For example, the examiner would ask the student, "Suppose the telephone rings. You pick it up. What do you say?" The student would be expected to state an acceptable greeting, such as "Hello" or an extended statement like "Hi, this is the Smucker family, who's calling please?"

Strengths and Limitations of Diagnostic Assessments

Diagnostic assessments can be useful in determining which specific language skills may be impacting children's vocabulary. They enable teachers to get a sense of whether a vocabulary problem is primarily receptive or expressive or specific to semantics, syntax, or pragmatics. Using multiple subtests allows teachers to determine if children have difficulties in specific areas or general difficulties across all areas of vocabulary. For example, comparing results on the PPVT and EVT could reveal that a student has a relative weakness in expressive but not receptive vocabulary that could be addressed through instruction. This information can help teachers target their instruction to better support children in their areas of need. A caution in using these assessments is that there are not large numbers of non–English speakers in the norming-samples of these measures, and they may have some cultural bias (e.g., what children may say when answering the phone, if they are even allowed to do so, may differ across cultures). So teachers should be mindful of children's linguistic and cultural background and take that into consideration when interpreting results from these assessments.

Outcome Assessments
for Measuring Vocabulary Knowledge

Teachers often want to determine how an entire class or group of students compares to their peers for the purpose of outcome assessment. Statewide assessments (e.g., the Partnership for Assessment of Readiness for College and Careers [PARCC] assessments and the Smarter Balanced assessments) typically include items related to vocabulary, but these assessments are not administered to young children. Assessing Comprehension and Communication in English State-to-State (ACCESS for ELLs), created by World-Class Instructional Design and Assessment (WIDA), is administered to all ELLs in kindergarten through twelfth grade. The assessment includes items related to vocabulary, but the results of this measure do not disaggregate vocabulary from other language skills. So teachers must use other measures for vocabulary outcome assessment. A wide range of vocabulary outcome measures has been used over the years. We describe only three of these measures that can be purchased by districts and schools for outcome measurement purposes. All of these assessments offer standardized scores (e.g., percentile ranks, standard scores, grade equivalents, stanines) for a variety of analytic purposes. (See Figure 6.6 for an overview.)

Stanford Achievement Test

The Stanford Achievement Test Series, now in its tenth edition (SAT-10; Pearson, 2009), includes two vocabulary subtests. On the Listening Vocabulary subtest, the examiner reads a sentence out loud and then students independently determine the meaning of a target vocabulary word from the sentence. On the Reading Vocabulary subtest, students are either given a sentence or asked to complete it with a target word, or they are given a short passage and asked to determine the meaning of the target word in the sentence. Students select from multiple choice responses to finish the sentence or choose the correct meaning of the word.

Gates–MacGinitie Reading Test

The Gates–MacGinitie Reading Test (GMRT; MacGinitie, MacGinitie, Maria, & Dreyer, 2000) also includes two subtests that measure vocabulary. For

Assessment	Grade Range	Administration	Testing Time	Skill(s) Assessed
SAT-10 Listening Vocabulary	Grades K–9	Group or individual	15–30 minutes	Oral and Written Receptive Vocabulary
SAT-10 Reading Vocabulary	Grades 2–adulthood	Group or individual	15–30 minutes	Written Receptive Vocabulary
GMRT Basic Story Words	Grades K–1	Group or individual	15–30 minutes	Written Receptive Vocabulary
GMRT Word Knowledge	Grade 2	Group or individual	15–30 minutes	Written Receptive Vocabulary
GRADE Verbal Concepts Picture Categories	Grades preK–K	Group or individual	15–30 minutes	Receptive Vocabulary (Semantics)
GRADE Word Meaning	Grades 1–2	Group or individual	15–30 minutes	Written Receptive Vocabulary

FIGURE 6.6. Outcome assessments for vocabulary.

kindergarteners and first graders, the Basic Story Words assessment evaluates students' ability to identify frequent words from written text. The examiner reads the questions aloud, and the students independently select the correct picture and/ or word from several choices. For second-grade students, the Word Knowledge subtest measures students' level of beginning reading vocabulary knowledge by prompting them to select the correct meaning from among multiple choices.

Group Reading Assessment and Diagnostic Evaluation

Finally, the Group Reading Assessment and Diagnostic Evaluation (GRADE; Williams, 2002) includes a Verbal Concepts subtest and a Picture Categories subtest for prereaders. In the Verbal Concepts subtest, students are asked to identify which picture matches the description presented by the administrator. Descriptions refer to size, shape, and position. In the Picture Categories subtest, students are asked to choose which picture out of four does not fit conceptually with the other pictures (e.g., a *barn* does not fit with a *tree*, a *bush*, and a *flower*). The Word Meaning subtest is appropriate for beginning readers. This subtest requires students to match written words with pictures that represent the target word.

Strengths and Limitations of Outcome Assessments

A strength of these measures, like most outcome assessment measures used at the state or district level, is that they can be administered in a group setting so teachers can simultaneously evaluate multiple children at once. Additionally, these standardized measures are norm-referenced, which means that teachers can compare individual students' levels to their same-age or grade-level peers nationwide. These assessments are best used to pass on general information about students' vocabulary level from teacher to teacher and to evaluate general trends in the data that suggest how well the vocabulary curriculum is functioning overall. However, teachers should be advised when using these data that these measures give only limited information about students' vocabulary strengths and needs, and often children do not perform optimally in group settings. So if children perform poorly on these outcome measures, additional information about their linguistic profile, educational history, and background will be needed to determine how best to support their vocabulary development in school.

Formats Teachers Can Use to Assess Vocabulary Learning

Published measures are useful for providing indications of children's vocabulary-related strengths and needs. But teachers want to know whether children learned the words and strategies they taught and how well they know them. To meet this need, teachers can develop their own assessments and focus on the particular words and strategies they have introduced in instruction. Teachers can use data from these assessments to determine whether children have mastered the words and skills they have taught or whether reteaching is necessary. Assessments matched to instruction, when used regularly, can be invaluable in helping teachers hone their teaching to meet students' needs. Next we describe some formats teachers can use to assess vocabulary they have taught in class. Teachers can administer these assessments after instruction to see what children learned; or, better yet, they can administer these assessments before *and* after instruction to see what children know before instruction takes place and what they learn over the course of instruction.

Picture Task

Teachers can develop their own picture test, similar to the PPVT discussed earlier, by drawing images representing the target words or using images available online to test children's knowledge of words they have taught. This method has been used in several vocabulary studies in preschool and early elementary school to capture children's receptive vocabulary knowledge (e.g., Leung et al., 2011; Silverman, 2007a, 2007b; Silverman et al., 2013). Figure 6.7 shows a picture test item used to assess children's knowledge of the word *mask* in the Leung et al. (2011) study.

For this study, an art student drew pictures to match the words of interest. In other studies, we have used clip art from computer programs or the Internet. Note that we use open-source clip art or purchase copyrights through clip-art programs on the web. The Appendix provides a list of websites where you can find great clip art for picture tasks. In our studies, we have tried to keep the style of the clip-art

FIGURE 6.7. Sample item from a picture vocabulary task for the word *mask*. From Leung et al. (2011). Copyright 2011 by the American Educational Research Association. Reprinted by permission.

pictures we choose to use consistent (e.g., we have used animated clip art and photo clip art separately). While picture tasks are most appropriate for asking students about nouns (i.e., people, places, and things), we have also used them to ask about verbs, adverbs, and adjectives as well. For example, we have asked, "Which picture shows *decomposing?*" and shown pictures of (1) fresh strawberries growing on plants, (2) fresh strawberries on a plate, (3) fresh strawberries in cereal, and (4) decomposing strawberries on the ground.

For the target picture, we typically look for one that clearly shows something related to the target word. For the distractor pictures (i.e., pictures other than the picture of the target word), we typically include pictures of some objects that are not at all similar to the target word and others that are somewhat similar to it but would not be confused with it by someone who clearly knows what the target word means. For example, in the item for *mask* above, a hat is worn on the head as a mask is worn on the face, which could confuse children who don't clearly know what a mask is. But children who have a solid understanding that a mask is worn on the face would not be tricked. While this assessment is usually given individually, teachers could adapt this measure for group administration by having children circle the picture or fill in the bubble by the picture that goes with the word that they would say aloud.

The strengths of this assessment are that (1) it does not require students to say anything if they are reluctant to respond or have limited expressive language skills, (2) it uses pictures for support, and (3) it requires children to think analytically about the target word to get the right answer because they have to choose which among four pictures best represents the target word. Its limitations are that (1) it assesses only receptive vocabulary; (2) it is not easy to create or find picture task items for less imageable words, and sometimes children just don't understand the connection between the picture and the word even though they know what the word means; and (3) it could allow children to guess more than they would on other tasks because all they have to do is point to a picture to move on to the next word or complete the task. This last point can be addressed if teachers ask children to explain their guesses, but that turns the task into a receptive/expressive task rather than simply a receptive task, which could make it more difficult for children who have trouble with expressive language skills.

Yes/No Task

Several researchers (Beck & McKeown, 2007; Coyne et al., 2009; Kearns & Biemiller, 2010/2011; Silverman & Hines, 2009) have used the yes/no method to assess children's vocabulary. In this method, teachers ask students questions using target words and children are expected to respond with *yes* or *no*. Teachers can ask four questions per word (two *yes* and two *no*). For example, for the word *habitat*, teachers could ask: (1) "Does *habitat* mean a place where an animal lives?" (2) "Does *habitat* mean food that an animal eats?" (3) "Is a rainforest a *habitat*?" and (4) "Is an elephant a *habitat*?" Teachers could give a point for each correct answer so children can get up to four points for each word. The more points children get for each word, the more likely it is that they know the word and have not just guessed the right answer. This assessment could be given individually and students could orally respond *yes* or *no*. Or it could be administered in groups (Kearns & Biemiller, 2010/2011). Teachers could read the questions and students could circle *yes* or *no* or a "smiley face" for *yes* and a "frowny face" for *no*.

The strengths of this approach are that (1) items can be administered relatively quickly, (2) it assesses children's knowledge of words in context, and (3) it is relatively nonthreatening to children who may be reluctant to talk. Its limitations are that (1) it requires a lot of attention to and comprehension of what teachers say, (2) it requires teachers to ask a lot of questions before they can be sure children know the word in question, and (3) it requires that children have background knowledge and general understanding of the context in addition to the target word to answer correctly. As with the picture task, teachers could expand on the task by asking children to explain their answers, though this increases the difficulty of the task.

Matching Task

Espin, Busch, Shin, and Kruschwitz (2001) have developed and effectively used vocabulary matching tasks as a way to monitor progress in vocabulary learning. While Espin et al.'s (2001) work was conducted with older students, their method could be used with younger students as well. To develop this kind of task, teachers can create a pool of words they plan to teach over a year or unit or week. These words can be taken from the core materials, content-area lessons, or read-aloud books the teachers plan to use in their lessons. Teachers can line these up on one side of a piece of paper, and then choose pictures that represent the words and place those on the opposite side. To administer the assessment, teachers can read the words to children and have them draw lines between the pictures and the corresponding words. As mentioned earlier, the pictures can show verbs, adverbs, and adjectives and not just nouns. For example, teachers could say, "Put your finger on the first word. This word is *humongous*. Draw a line from the word *humongous* to the picture that shows something *humongous*." Teachers can administer this measure individually or, by using an overhead projector and pointing to the words as they read them, in groups for older or beginning readers.

One strength of this task is that it provides children with options to choose from, so their choice is somewhat limited and supported. A limitation is that children may get mixed up once they have given one incorrect answer and end up getting more answers incorrect inadvertently. Comparing and contrasting multiple options draws on children's cognitive processing and analytic reasoning abilities, which can be an advantage or a disadvantage of using this kind of task depending on what kinds of skills teachers want to capture when they assess.

Word Relations Task

In this task, as in the CELF Word Relations task , teachers can ask students to say or circle the word or picture that is similar to the target word. For example, children can be asked which word has a meaning that is similar to (kind of the same as) the word *accelerate: climb, speed,* or *stop.* In selecting options for children to choose from in this task, it is important to make sure all of the choices are words children likely know and to choose words that are the same part of speech as the target word so they are all plausible answers.

The strengths of this task are that it is closed choice so children have some support for providing a response and it gives teachers a sense of how well children can differentiate the meaning of a word from among other meanings, which requires some level of depth of knowledge. Its limitations include the fact that children have to remember the answers while they think about which one goes best with the target word, which may tax memory, language, and processing ability. For older or beginning readers, having a visual cue and/or the written word to support children's memory and processing ability may help. For example, based on an assessment described by Graves, August, and Mancilla-Martinez (2012), we have used the format shown in Figure 6.8, which includes a stoplight and each word printed to support children in remembering their choices as we say them out loud. In this example, the teacher says, "Which word is similar to vacant? *Full, bright,* or *empty?*" On an overhead projector, teachers can point to each word and the color of the stoplight while reading the options. This modification may help some children who need visual support, but the additional stimuli could overwhelm others. Teachers can modify the word relations task as needed to support their students.

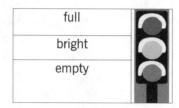

FIGURE 6.8. Sample item for a word relations task.

Definition Task

A traditional measure used frequently in research and classroom practice to measure children's expressive vocabulary knowledge is the definition task (e.g., Coyne et al., 2009; Silverman, 2007a, 2007b, 2013). In a definition task, teachers simply ask children to tell them what a target word means. For example, a teacher might say, "Tell me what the word *adventure* means. Tell me everything you know about the word *adventure*." Teachers can score answers children give in one of two ways. On the one hand, teachers could simply score answers as correct and incorrect. Correct answers would be close approximations of the definition of the target word teachers provided in explicit instruction. Scoring definitions in this way allows teachers to see whether children acquired the definition they had been taught. On the other hand, teachers can score definitions using a scale that allows partial credit and captures incremental knowledge of words. (We provide examples of how we have scored definitions in Figure 6.9.) We have used this approach in our research and sometimes found that even though some children may not have shown progress from no knowledge to full knowledge of a word we taught, they may have shown progress from no knowledge to partial knowledge of the word. Teachers may want to capture this incremental word learning in order to have a fuller picture of the knowledge children acquire from vocabulary instruction in school.

Although the definition task is traditionally administered individually and orally, it could be adapted for administration in groups and through writing for older children by having children write definitions of words. Of course, involving writing in the assessment introduces greater cognitive demand as children need to recognize what words mean, produce definitions for words, and coordinate the handwriting and spelling skills needed to express their definitions in writing. Thus, this more advanced version of the definitions task should be used with caution as it may not fully capture young children's word knowledge. However, for children who are older or who have more advanced reading and writing ability, involving writing in the definition task may provide an appropriate level of challenge. As always, teachers should modify these kinds of assessments based on the levels of the children they teach.

The strengths of the definition task are that it is fairly easy to administer (i.e., all teachers have to do is ask children what words mean and record their answers),

Score	0	1	2	3
Description Student Responses	No knowledge of the word exhibited.	Connotative knowledge of the word exhibited.	Contextual knowledge of the word exhibited.	Full knowledge of the word exhibited.
Student examples for **compare**	*That you eat a pear with your teeth and your teeth get off.*	*Observing something and studying something.*	*Compare means to compare something flat and something up (gestures different heights).*	*Compare means to see what's the same and what's not the same.*
Student examples for **exact**	*Exact means you going to be someone's friend.*	*Exact means both the same.*	*Exact is when you say something right in school.*	*Exact means to be just right like just right temperature or just right size.*

FIGURE 6.9. Examples of how we have scored a definition task using a rubric.

it gets to the core question of whether children know what target words mean, and it is well aligned with explicit instruction in which teachers provide clear, child-friendly definitions of words. However, the definition task has limitations as well. It can be hard to score when children give answers that are ambiguous (e.g., "Original means like me. I am original."). Although a child may provide a true statement, if it lacks context, the examiner cannot say with confidence whether the student truly knows the target word. Prompting can be used to encourage students to explain what they mean or say more, but sometimes they aren't able to move beyond this kind of general definition. In fact, the definition task requires a rather high level of cognitive skill because definitions, which are context-free, are fairly abstract. And it depends on children's expressive vocabulary knowledge and general verbal ability. In other words, children who have difficulty with expressive language in general will have a hard time conveying their understanding of a word through the definition task. Thus, the definition task may be more appropriate for some children and less appropriate for others depending on their level of language competence.

Sentence Construction Task

Another tried-and-true method for assessing vocabulary is the sentence construction task. While this method is often used with older children, who are asked to write their own sentences with the words they have been taught in class, young children can simply be asked to use target words in sentences orally. This task is similar to the WUF assessment previously described, but, as we show in Figure 6.10, teachers can score student responses according to the degree to which the responses show understanding of and ability to use the target word in context.

Score	0	1	2	3
Description / Student Responses	No knowledge of the word exhibited.	Connotative knowledge of the word exhibited.	Contextual knowledge of the word exhibited.	Full knowledge of the word exhibited.
Student examples for **efficient**	*I get efficient in my report card.*	*Efficient is good.*	*I'm efficient at multiplication.*	*I'm an efficient student because I am on task.*
Student examples for **confirm**	*They are to confirm the ruler.*	*She is confirming what she wants.*	*He confirms it's really windy.*	*The man confirmed the length of the sandwich with a ruler.*

FIGURE 6.10. Examples of how we have scored responses on a sentence construction task.

Like the definition task, the sentence construction task can be scored as correct or incorrect depending on whether children show the meaning taught in class, or the task can be scored on a scale of 0–3 depending on the extent to which the target word is used correctly in a sentence and shows depth of word knowledge.

The strengths and limitations of this task are also similar to those of the definition task. The strengths are that the assessment is easy to administer (i.e., all teachers have to do is ask children to use a word in a sentence) and aligned with explicit instruction that includes using the word across contexts. Asking children to use the word in context rather than provide an abstract definition makes the task somewhat easier for most children, since it is often easier to come up with an example of a word rather than a definition of a word. But children may not convey what they know about a word if they give short and unelaborated sentences. For example, for the word *decide*, a child could say, "There is a girl deciding," which is a complete sentence that uses the target word (or a derivation of the target word) but does not show whether or not the child knows the word at all. Like the definition task, the sentence construction task can be hard to score because children often may provide ambiguous sentences (e.g., an ambiguous sentence for *destroy*: "That's because when you're destroying something, like you're destroying the world."). It also depends on expressive vocabulary, general language skills, and background knowledge about various contexts in which words could be used, which could make the task particularly difficult for some children.

Cloze Sentence Task

The cloze sentence task, also known as fill-in-the-blank, is somewhat more supportive than the sentence construction task, since it is not open-ended and requires children to simply provide the word that fits in the sentence. Giving children options to choose from to fill in the blank reduces the cognitive load of the task so that children are not searching for the target word from memory without any direction. The cloze task provides context that supports children in demonstrating their word knowledge. To help children in completing this task, teachers can place the "blank" at the end of the sentence so children do not have to remember back to the beginning of the sentence when they are trying to figure out which word goes in the blank. A sample test item would be: *I went to the doctor because I felt _____. Which word fits best? Glad, proud, or ill.* Notice that when choices are provided, the options should be the same part of speech and level of difficulty.

The strengths of this task are that it provides support to students who may not be able to come up with contexts on their own, and it encourages children to think analytically about which word would best fit in a given context. However, if children do not understand the context, they will not be able to show their knowledge of the target word, even if they have some understanding of the word. It is also challenging for teachers to come up with contexts that will be comprehensible to students. If teachers use contexts taught directly in class, they may not know whether children can transfer their knowledge beyond the taught context. But if teachers present new contexts, there is more likelihood that their assessment of children's word knowledge will be confounded by the children's understanding of the specific context presented. These are all factors teachers can weigh in choosing this type of task for vocabulary assessment.

Morphology Tasks

Given the importance of independent word learning strategies, evaluating children's ability to use word parts to figure out unknown words is essential. Several strategies can be used to assess morphology skills. Here are a few that could be used to assess various aspects of morphological awareness in young children.

Compound Morphology Task

Teachers can give children two words and ask them to put the words together to make a new word. Teachers can also give children a compound word and ask them to break it up into two words. In both cases, teachers can follow up by asking children to explain what the words mean together and separately. For example, a teacher could ask children what *head* means and what *ache* means. Then she could ask them to put those two words together to make *headache*. Finally, she could ask them what *headache* means.

Inflectional Morphology Task

Teachers can give children a root word and ask them to change the root word to fit in a sentence that requires inflection. For example, teachers could tell children to change the word *skip* so that it fits in the following sentence: "Yesterday, Max

_____ to the front of the line." In this way, teachers can evaluate children's use of inflectional endings such as *-ed, -ing,* and *-s.*

Derivational Morphology Task

Teachers can give children a derived word and ask them to transform the derived word to fit in a sentence. Sample items on the Extract the Base assessment by the Center for Applied Linguistics (August et al., 2001), which is intended for older students, provide good examples. Figure 6.11 has three practice items that would be appropriate for young children. Teachers could choose items in the assessment to align with the specific morphological word parts focused on in classroom instruction to assess whether children learned those word parts and can use them productively on their own.

Morphological Comprehension Task

While these tasks focus mainly on whether children can use morphology to make new words, equally important is whether they can use morphology to comprehend new words. This is addressed in the morphological comprehension task, in which teachers can provide children with a morphologically complex word or nonword (i.e., made-up word) in or out of the context of a sentence and ask them to decide what the word means based on word part clues. For example, a teacher could give children the sentence "I am *unwugful.*" She could then ask them what *unwugful* means. She could provide choices: (1) not full of wug, (2) under wug, (3) full of wug, or (4) over wug. Using nonwords adds complexity to the task and taps children's knowledge of the word part beyond their knowledge of the root word, but it could prove too confusing and abstract for some children. The point of this assessment is to evaluate children's understanding of word parts and ability to use word parts to figure out unknown words. Children may need more or less support for this task depending on their language ability.

While we presented each of the morphology tasks as oral and individual tasks, they could be used as written and group tasks for older students or beginning readers, especially if teachers read while students follow along on their own copies. The strength of these tasks are that they isolate children's knowledge and use of word

farmer	My uncle works on a _____ .
careful	Handle those glasses with _____ .
happiness	My pet dog makes me very _____ .

FIGURE 6.11. Sample items from a derivational morphology assessment.

parts to figure out and produce words, but their limitation is that they are not conducted in authentic contexts, which is when children will really need to be able to activate their morphological awareness to figure out words We will have more to say about this when we discuss the strategy use task, which assesses children's use of word parts in a more authentic context.

Context Clue Task

To evaluate children's use of context clues, teachers can read sentences to students with new or even nonsense words and ask them to identify (or choose from provided choices) what words mean based on the context. Teachers can assess the various context types discussed in the previous chapter. For example, teachers could read the following sentences to students: "The mouse *scampered* across the floor. He ran so quickly that the cat didn't even see him." Teachers could then ask students to use the definition clue in the second sentence to figure out what *scampered* means. She could provide choices by asking, "Does *scampered* mean *looked quickly, ran fast,* or *hid carefully?*" All of these would be plausible answers, but children need to use the context clues to figure out the word if they don't already know it. Teachers can ask these questions individually and orally or they could, for older children or beginning readers, administer these questions in groups using printed sentences and multiple-choice or written responses, though even beginning readers will likely need teachers to read the items on the task.

Just as the contrived nature of the task was a limitation of the morphology tasks presented above, so too is the contrived nature of the context clue task a limitation here. Children may do well using context clues when they are presented with them in isolated sentences and the directions of the task (i.e., figure out what a word means using the clues in the sentence) are transparent. However, they may not be apt or able to do this on their own when they encounter words they do not know in what they hear or read. While assessing students' ability to use context clue is important in order to see whether they are able to use these clues when they are prompted to do so, it is also important to evaluate whether students use context clues in more authentic tasks such as the strategy use task we discuss next.

Strategy Use Task

In order to investigate how children tackle tough words on their own, teachers can present children with text that has tricky words (i.e., words teachers know will be hard for their students) and ask them at specific points in the text what they are thinking. If children respond that they heard or read a word they don't know, teachers can ask them how they will figure it out. If children do not respond that they heard or read a word they don't know, teachers can ask them pointed questions such as

"Are there any words you just heard or read that you don't know? If yes, what could you do to figure them out?"

"If you didn't know the word in bold on this page, how would you figure it out?"

Teachers can give students points for correct responses or score the quality of their response using a rubric (e.g., 0 = uses no strategies, 1 = uses limited strategies partially, 2 = uses limited strategies fully, 4 = uses multiple strategies fully). Children can get points for saying they would use word parts, context clues, or resources such as the glossary or dictionary. To a certain extent, asking children questions while they listen or read text interferes with what they would naturally do; however, using this procedure to find out about children's vocabulary strategy use provides a more authentic context (i.e., listening to a book or reading a book) within which teachers can understand how children are developing in their acquisition of independent word learning skills.

Observation and Language Sampling

Two final forms of assessment that can complement the more systematic assessments we have described are observation and language sampling. Throughout explicit and extended instruction and in the course of routine activities in a language-rich classroom environment, children should have many opportunities to demonstrate their word knowledge and use words productively on their own. Teachers can capture children's comprehension of words and word use by collecting systematic observation and language sampling data. For example, they can keep a clipboard with a list of names on the left and a list of words on the top (see Figure 6.12) and check off the boxes when children respond correctly to questions that ask about target words or when children use target words in context themselves. Also, in centers, teachers can transcribe what children say and take notes

Name	build		model		construct		estimate		compare	
	R	E	R	E	R	E	R	E	R	E
Adam	✓	✓			✓		✓	✓	✓	✓
Elliott	✓	✓			✓	✓				
Emily	✓	✓	✓	✓	✓		✓		✓	
Max	✓		✓		✓		✓	✓	✓	
Sarah	✓				✓	✓				

R = Receptive knowledge. E = Expressive use. ✓ = Shows word knowledge or use.

FIGURE 6.12. Observation and language sampling checklist.

about what children do as a way to sample their language comprehension and expression of words in context. Teachers can then review these data on a regular basis to track children's receptive and expressive vocabulary in class.

Combining Assessments to Inform Instruction

All of the assessment tasks we have described here have strengths and limitations. And none fully captures what children know about words. Thus, when possible, teachers should use more than one assessment task so that they can understand children's word knowledge from multiple angles and, thereby, get a more complete picture of what children actually know. Specifically, teachers can combine receptive and expressive tasks, tasks that use pictures and tasks that are completely oral, and tasks that involve both oral and written communication. By looking at children's word knowledge from different perspectives, teachers will get a fuller understanding of children's word knowledge and the extent to which they have internalized the word learning strategies they have been taught. At the same time, we caution against overtesting at the expense of teaching. Ideally, assessments should be quick and to the point and take up as little instructional time as possible so that teachers can implement the instruction that the assessments are meant to inform. It is a delicate balance between testing and instruction, and teachers need to weigh how much information they need to plan instruction and differentiate appropriately as they decide how many and which assessments to use.

Summary

Assessment is essential in prekindergarten through second-grade classrooms to identify children who may need extra support, decide what kind of support they need, and determine how well children are responding to the vocabulary curriculum in place. Although vocabulary is complex and vocabulary assessment is complicated, there are numerous published assessments you can use to evaluate children's vocabulary strengths and needs, as well as a range of assessments you can develop on your own to assess vocabulary learning in your classroom. In this chapter, we have described a variety of these assessments and discussed their strengths and limitations. The value of these assessments lies in their power to inform what you teach and how you teach it and, equally important, how you differentiate instruction for students with different strengths and needs. In the next chapter we discuss how to differentiate classroom instruction for all students and, in particular, for students who may need extra support to acquire the vocabulary they need to succeed in school.

CHAPTER 7

Differentiating
Vocabulary Instruction

- How can teachers differentiate instruction to meet the needs of diverse learners?
- How can teachers use response to intervention to support students' vocabulary?

Like many classrooms across the United States and the world, Ms. Marshall's kindergarten class is incredibly heterogeneous. It is a model of diversity. Her class includes children from diverse cultural and linguistic backgrounds and different socioeconomic levels. Her class also includes children with language-related disabilities. Ms. Marshall is thrilled to have such a diverse class, but sometimes she feels overwhelmed because she isn't sure if her vocabulary instruction truly meets the needs of all her students. How can she possibly plan vocabulary lessons that both scaffold and challenge all of the students in her class? Fortunately, there are a number of strategies Ms. Marshall can use that will allow her to optimize her vocabulary instruction for her students with varying strengths and needs.

More and more children come to school with vastly different backgrounds, experiences, and abilities. Such diversity presents opportunities for children to learn from each other about the world and about different perspectives. But it also poses challenges for teachers in designing instruction to meet the needs of all children in school. Thus, the one-size-fits-all model of instruction is anachronistic, and differentiated instruction is required in all 21st-century classrooms. While, in general, principles of effective vocabulary instruction apply for diverse students (Graves & Silverman, 2010; Jitendra, Edwards, Sacks, & Jacobson, 2004), teachers can chart multiple pathways within the curriculum to reach children from varied backgrounds and with diverse strengths and needs. And by using assessment to guide instruction, teachers can provide accommodations and intensify intervention for children most in need of support. In this chapter, we discuss ways you can differentiate instruction targeting vocabulary breadth and depth to meet the needs of the diverse students in your classroom. We first turn to the notion of Universal Design for Learning (UDL) as a framework for thinking about how to differentiate vocabulary instruction and thereby meet the word learning needs of all children. Then we discuss accommodations for different types of learners. Finally, we review recent research on applying the response-to-intervention (RTI) model, through which children who are struggling receive support as needed, to vocabulary instruction.

Universal Design for Learning

As discussed in Chapter 2, UDL is a framework for instruction meant to "guide the design and development of curriculum that is effective and inclusive for all learners" (Rose & Gravel, 2010, as cited in Hall, Meyer, & Rose, 2012, p. 1). Using the UDL framework to plan curriculum allows teachers to be optimally responsive to the "vast linguistic, cultural, and cognitive variability" (Hall et al., 2012, p. 4) present in 21st-century classrooms. A bit of theory is necessary here. The UDL framework is based on the conceptualization that there are three neural networks in the brain that specialize processing certain kinds of information and performing different types of tasks. Rose and Meyer (2002) note:

> We identify these networks by terms that reflect their functions: the *recognition, strategic*, and *affective* networks. The activities of these networks parallel the three prerequisites for learning described by the Russian psychologist Lev Vygotsky (1962): recognition of the information to be learned; application of strategies to process that information; and engagement with the learning task. (*www.cast.org/teachingeverystudent/ideas/tes/chapter2_2.cfm*)

Children differ in their strengths, weaknesses, and preferences in each of the neural networks. Thus, to optimally support student learning, teachers should design instruction to address students' needs and take advantage of students' strengths and preferences in these networks.

Thus, UDL is organized around the following three principles of instruction (Rose & Meyer, 2002, as cited in Hall et al., 2012, p. 2):

(I) To support recognition learning, provide multiple means of representation—that is, offer flexible ways to present *what* we teach and learn.

(II) To support strategic learning, provide multiple means of action and expression—that is, flexible options for *how* we learn and express what we know.

(III) To support affective learning, provide multiple means of engagement—that is, flexible options for generating and sustaining motivation, the *why* of learning.

In reference to vocabulary development, recognition learning involves the ability to understand words and concepts. Optimal learning and transfer of learning occurs when children are offered multiple means of representing words and concepts. For example, teachers could use verbal explanations, pictures, gestures, and video to support children in understanding words and concepts. Teachers are also encouraged to support children linguistically by clarifying what words mean and how they are used across contexts (e.g., in oral vs. written language, in different grammatical structures, and in different languages). Finally, teachers are urged to support comprehension of words and concepts through activating or supplying background knowledge, highlighting relationships among words and concepts, and fostering "processing, visualization, and manipulation" of information as well as "transfer and generalization" of word and concept knowledge (Hall et al., 2012, p. 14).

Strategic learning involves the ability to "plan, execute, and monitor actions and skills" (Hall et al., p. 3). In the area of vocabulary development, using words and concepts appropriately in different contexts and activating independent word learning strategies require strategic processes. Providing different ways to use words expressively can facilitate word learning. For example, teachers could guide children to use words in sentences, act out words, or draw representations of words to show their understanding of words and concepts. Additionally, nurturing children's word awareness and scaffolding their use of independent word learning strategies can support strategic word learning. Finally, cultivating children's goal-setting and self-monitoring skills such that children plan to use words and concepts in speech and writing and monitor how their word and concept use is received by others will support children in developing their productive language skills and refining their vocabulary knowledge over time.

Affective learning refers to the emotional value we assign to various learning tasks. The more emotionally significant we deem a task, the more likely we are to engage in that task wholeheartedly. To stimulate children's affective learning in the area of vocabulary, teachers can try various options for encouraging their interest in word learning. For example, teachers can identify topics of special interest for children in their class and start by highlighting words and concepts related to those topics before expanding out to other topics in the curriculum. By "hooking" children's interest, teachers may be able to establish a foundation of excitement for word learning on which they can build in future instruction. Giving children some choice in which words are taught and emphasizing the relevance of word learning in all aspects of life can help children recognize the value of learning words and concepts. By fostering collaboration and word learning communities, teachers can establish a culture of vocabulary learning in their classrooms in which all children can participate and contribute. And, by setting high expectations for vocabulary learning and conveying the belief that all children can meet those expectations in one way or another, teachers can help students internalize the sense that they can and should become active learners and users of sophisticated words and concepts.

The principles of UDL can be used to provide different ways for all children to access the same content and meet the same instructional standards. These principles are akin to accommodations for children with identified special needs. Although accommodations are usually considered after lesson development as a means of providing access to the curriculum for students with special needs, UDL principles are intended to guide the entire process of lesson development from start to finish so that instruction meets the needs of all children from the beginning. Accommodations are different from modifications because they provide support for children without lowering expectations. They are adaptations that allow students to interact with content and demonstrate their understanding without changing what children are expected to know or be able to do. Modifications, on the other hand, reduce the expectations in a particular way. For example, making content less complex or limiting the amount of information children are expected to learn are common modifications used in educational settings. Teachers should strive to accommodate all students' individual needs while maintaining high expectations so that all children have the opportunity to learn what they need to know and be able to do to succeed. For vocabulary instruction, this means providing multiple ways for children to access word meanings and demonstrate word knowledge, but it does not mean limiting the complexity or number of words children are taught and expected to learn.

It is important to note that UDL contains principles for instructional design that support children from diverse backgrounds and with different strengths and needs within the same classroom in meeting the same standards. And UDL is a framework from which children below, on, or above grade level can benefit. In the same way UDL principles necessitate extra supports for children who may be struggling to access grade-level context, UDL principles also call for differentiating instruction for students who need greater challenge. Although teachers are most often concerned about children who are struggling to access content, children who require greater challenge may become frustrated and disengaged if their needs are not met as well. UDL principles serve as a model for differentiated instruction that is appropriate for and inclusive of all students. In an era when all students are expected to meet common standards, namely the CCSS, using UDL to help children with varying needs and abilities to meet these standards is crucial. In the following section we discuss specific accommodations for vocabulary instruction within the UDL framework. Then we discuss how these accommodations could be used to support children with diverse strengths and needs.

Accommodations within the UDL Framework

We have classified each of these accommodations under one of the three principles of UDL discussed above to help situate the accommodations within the principles of the framework, but often they could be classified under more than one principle. This list of accommodations is in no way exhaustive, but it should provide an initial framework to consider when designing and developing vocabulary curriculum. Many of these accommodations would be very simple additions to existing classroom practices.

Multiple Means of Representation

Connect to Prior Knowledge

Children learn words more readily when they are able to build on prior knowledge. It is much easier to learn a new word for a known concept than a new word and a new concept simultaneously. When possible, connecting word and concept instruction to what children already know about the world can facilitate their word and concept learning. For example, if teaching the word *elevate*, meaning to lift up, students may be able to draw on their knowledge of using an *elevator*, which is a machine that moves people up and down in a building. Connecting to typical household routines and activities can be helpful as well. For instance, teachers could ask children to think about whether they use a stepstool to *elevate* themselves when they brush their teeth at night. Referencing known constructs is beneficial because it gives students mental "Velcro" upon which to "stick" new vocabulary words that they are acquiring.

Offer Linguistic Support

Some children need more linguistic support than other children do to be able to understand words and concepts that are new to them. Instead of "dumbing down" the curriculum and teaching only easier concepts or words, teachers should help children with less linguistic awareness understand underlying words and concepts so they are capable of learning more advanced words. This support can come in the form of providing definitions and explanations of simpler words and concepts needed to understand more advanced ones, delivering verbal and nonverbal information simultaneously, and, for ELLs, making connections to children's native language. Additionally, adjusting the pace and time for linguistic processing can support children who need extra help.

Consider the linguistic scaffolding the teacher employs during this science lesson to make sure the new vocabulary is comprehensible for all her students, including those with limited English-language skills.

TEACHER: We are going to learn the word *camouflage* today. Say *camouflage*.

STUDENTS: *Camouflage.*

TEACHER: *Camouflage* means to look like to your surroundings. Let's explore the word *camouflage* in this text about animals. (*Reads an excerpt from* Animal Hide and Seek [Smith, *2012*]).

TEACHER: What did the author tell us about animal camouflage?

JACOB: It's got lots of colors.

TEACHER: I think you're on the right track. Colors are something we can see and camouflage has to do with how something looks.

TEACHER: Let's look at the pictures to help us understand more about animal camouflage. What do you see in this picture? (*Picture shows a green tree frog on a leaf*).

MIKEL: A frog holding on to a leaf.

CLAUDIA: It's a little frog with black eyes.

TEACHER: I see that, too. Before Jacob said camouflage had to do with colors. Let's think about the colors in this picture. What color is the frog?

STUDENT: Green.

TEACHER: You're right! I see a green frog. And what color is the leaf?

STUDENT: Green.

TEACHER: So, what's the same between these two? They're both . . . (*pause*)

STUDENTS: Green!

TEACHER: That's correct. The green tree frog is the same color as the leaves it's sitting on. So, I think the green tree frog uses its green color as a camouflage, so it looks like its surroundings.

In this example, the teacher provides the definition of the target word in child-friendly language before reading to alert her students about a key topic from the passage. This linguistic scaffolding, in the form of a brief preteaching moment, is especially helpful for the ELLs in her classroom, who likely do not know the word *camouflage*. Their minds have been primed to listen for the word and think about its meaning. Then, at the conclusion of the passage, the teacher checks to see what the students learned about *camouflage*. Jacob shares his understanding of camouflage, which involves something about color. The teacher acknowledges that his answer is related to the concept and then uses linguistic scaffolding to extend his thinking using picture support. By explicitly making the connection between the green frog and the green leaf, Jacob and his peers learn that camouflage is related to having the same color as something in the environment. On subsequent pages in the book, the teacher will introduce other dimensions of camouflage, such as pattern and texture, to further advance the students' understanding of the concept.

Use Multiple Representations to Present Words and Concepts

Some children may easily understand verbal information about words and concepts such as definitions or explanations. However for children who may have difficulty processing verbal information, the use of nonverbal tools for learning verbal information can help make complex information more accessible. Thus, presenting words and concepts through visual aids, dramatic play, or real objects may help learners access word and concept meaning more readily. This principle expands on the dual coding theory (Paivio, 1986), discussed in Chapter 2, which holds that information encoded both verbally and nonverbally takes cognitive precedence over information encoded only verbally or nonverbally, leading to improved understanding and memory of dually perceived stimuli. Providing both verbal and nonverbal support can be rather simple. For example, after reading *From Head to Toe*, by Eric Carle (1997), a teacher could teach new words related to animal movement by having children act out words such as *bend, raise, wave, arch,* and *stomp.* The teacher can have children pretend to be the animals in the book and do the movements the animals do themselves. She can have children act out the movements during other times of the day as well. She might say, "*Raise* your shoulders like a buffalo if you are ready for lunch." Finally, a teacher can instruct children to apply the words to new contexts. She could say, "What do we usually *raise* when we have something to say? What could we raise instead?" In this way, children are supported in connecting the actions with the words they are learning and the contexts in which they apply.

Use Graphic Organizers to Highlight Critical Features of Words and Relations among Words

Some children may internalize and integrate important information about words on their own, whereas other children may need more help in doing so. And, while some children may automatically recognize connections among words and concepts, others will not appreciate these relations until they are made explicit and transparent. Graphic organizers can be used to help children identify the important information about words and concepts they are learning and detect relations among words, which aids comprehension and flexible language use. For example, graphic organizers can be arranged specifically to compare and contrast vocabulary words. As shown in Figure 7.1, the standard analogy formula (*a* is to *b* as *x* is to *y*) can be adapted for a simple graphic organizer. Teachers can thus use graphic organizers as a visual representation of concepts they are teaching. In Figure 7.2,

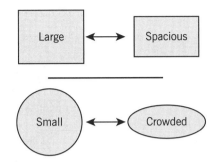

FIGURE 7.1. Analogy graphic organizer.

we show how teachers can use graphic organizers to highlight how words are related morphologically. Seeing the same word part in many different words can make morphological relationships more salient for learners who may not hear the similarities in words.

Use Paraphrasing, Role-Play, Visualization, and Mnemonics to Support Memory for Representations

Children often have difficulty processing and remembering words and concepts they are learning. Teachers can further children's processing of word meanings by having them (1) explain the word or concept in their own words, (2) act out the meaning of words or concepts in ways that make sense to them, and (3) use mental imagery to think of how to represent words and concepts in ways they can understand and remember. For example, a teacher might say, "Oh! My bag is so full I have to *lug* it down to the library. Show me what it looks like to *lug* a big bag of books. Say 'I have to *lug* this heavy bag all the way to the library!' " Or, while preparing her students to use digital texts, a first-grade teacher might say, "Touch the green *icon* to open our story for today. An *icon* is a little picture for something on a computer or tablet that you can touch (*demonstrates touching*). Try it in the

Prefix		Root		Meaning
un	+	safe	=	not safe
un	+	finished	=	not finished
un	+	able	=	not able
un	+	kind	=	not kind
un	+	lucky	=	not lucky

FIGURE 7.2. Graphic organizer showing words with the prefix *-un*.

air with me and say, 'I am touching the icon (*teacher and students gesture to show they are touching the icon*).' Now when I hear the word *icon*, I will think of a little picture and the act of touching it (*gestures again*)."

Memory aids for remembering words or word learning strategies can also be helpful. For example, a teacher could support children in thinking of a mnemonic device for remembering a word or an acronym to remember a word learning strategy. In our own work, discussed in Chapter 4, kindergarteners in our reading buddies program readily learned and effectively used the PET vocabulary strategy we developed. The simple three-step process helped kindergarteners, including kindergartners who were ELLs or otherwise at risk for reading difficulty, remember the vocabulary strategy we had taught them. Memory aids, such as the PET strategy, will help children who need extra attention in remembering words they are learning and strategies for learning new words.

Multiple Means of Action and Expression

Offer Alternative Response Modes

Children may be able to comprehend words but have difficulty demonstrating their comprehension or using words and concepts effectively across contexts. To encourage children to show what they know, teachers can offer them different ways of communicating. The response modes can range from more to less supportive, and supports can be gradually faded out over time as children become more independent and capable of demonstrating their word knowledge and using words on their own. Teachers can ask students forced-choice questions with two response possibilities, fill-in-the-blank questions in which students are expected to supply the missing word, or open-ended questions in which children must think of the answer without provided options. The response modes can also differ in the facet of language tapped. Teachers could encourage students to use words or concepts in drawing, speaking, or writing, depending on their facility with each form of communication.

As an example, during a unit on civic duty and participation in the community, a teacher could ask questions about the target words *responsibility*, *fairness*, and *respect* in several ways. Rather than asking, "What does *responsibility* mean?" the teacher could ask, "Which decision is more responsible: (1) walking next to your little brother or (2) running home ahead of your little brother on the way home from school?" Here the teacher uses a real-life application of *responsibility* in context instead of asking the students to provide a definition without any support. Or the teacher could choose a sentence with a blank for the target word and include several options in a word bank. For older students, a teacher could choose a scenario followed by a fill-in-the-blank sentence, such as: "The referee made sure everyone followed the rules. He made sure the game was _____ [*easy, fair, done*]." Finally, a teacher could ask an open-ended question to probe how a student can connect a target word to his or her own life. For example, she could ask: "How can you show that you *respect* the rules at school?" She can then rate the answer as either correct or incorrect, while taking note of the quality and detail of the response.

Provide Added Support and Opportunities for Practice

Extra support and practice are what many children need to be able to effectively learn words and concepts. Although some children need only 8 to 10 exposures to a word before they can use it on their own productively, others need two or three times that amount to achieve the same level of word learning. It is not that they cannot learn words at the same level as their peers, just that they need extra support and opportunities for practice to perform at that level through small-group instruction, partner activities, or one-on-one tutoring as needed. If they are given previews of words before instruction and reviews of words after instruction, children who need extra support and opportunities for practice are more likely to keep pace with their peers and avoid falling behind in word learning.

For example, a teacher can use a word wall to provide systematic review of the target words from previous units, while connecting those words to current topics. Students can be prompted to copy and illustrate each word in a journal. The teacher can explain to students how their drawings show the target words and write their explanations on their papers. The teacher can provide individualized support and review of the target words as she visits with students individually and listens to their explanations. The teacher can clarify misconceptions about the words and provide additional examples so the students are given multiple opportunities to hear the words used correctly in speech.

Support Strategy Use through Goal Setting, Step-by-Step Instruction, Think-Alouds, and Self-Monitoring

Children generally need extra support in developing independent word learning strategies in particular. They need to learn when and how to use these strategies since eventually the teacher will not be there to support them. Teachers can model think-alouds and guide children to use think-alouds to talk through how to regulate the strategies they are learning. They can also encourage children to set vocabulary learning goals and monitor their progress. For example, teachers can model how to use independent word learning strategies with digital text as follows: (1) before reading set a goal of touching or clicking on three definitions in the digital text, (2) during reading tally the number of times they look up a word, and (3) after reading check whether they met their goal. Even in prekindergarten through grade 2, when this process is highly scaffolded, children can begin to develop independent word learning strategies through think-alouds, goal setting, and self-monitoring.

Consider this example of a teacher modeling how to self-monitor for understanding of complex vocabulary while reading with her kindergarten class. The teacher is reading aloud *Click, Clack, Moo*, by Doreen Cronin (2000).

TEACHER: (*reading aloud*) "So the cows went on strike. They left a note on the barn door. 'Sorry. We're closed. No milk today.' "

TEACHER: Hmm, the cows went *on strike*. I wonder what *strike* means. First, I can think whether I have heard the word somewhere before. Thumbs up if you have heard the word strike.

STUDENTS: (*Some thumbs up, some thumbs down.*)

TEACHER: I'm thinking about baseball. A *strike* in baseball is when a pitcher throws a pitch right down the middle of the plate. The umpire calls it a *strike*. But wait, are the cows playing baseball?

STUDENTS: No.

TEACHER: No, that's right. They're not playing baseball. So, I have to keep thinking. What are they doing here? (*Points to picture.*)

STUDENTS: They are typing.

TEACHER: Right, we see in the picture that they are typing a note to Farmer Brown. And what did the note say?

STUDENTS: No milk!

TEACHER: OK, so the cows aren't going to give their milk to the farmer. They are "closed for business." So, I think going on *strike* means not working because when the cows went on strike they were closed and they didn't give Farmer Brown any milk. Thumbs up if you think that explanation makes sense.

STUDENTS: (*Thumbs up.*)

TEACHER: We just figured out what a new word meant by using what we know, the pictures, and the clues in the story. Next time I want to hear you think out loud to find out a new word.

In this example, the teacher does most of the cognitive work, walking the students through her think-aloud to determine the meaning of the unknown word. By explicitly stating each step aloud in the context of the story, the teacher has modeled appropriate self-monitoring and clarifying skills that the students can begin to internalize for independent reading in the future.

Multiple Means of Engagement

Promote Self-Selection and Facilitate Individualization of Word Learning

To foster engagement in word learning, teachers can encourage children to self-select words to learn from read-aloud books or books they are reading on their own. Or children can choose which words they want to investigate themselves from a list of words chosen by their teachers. This promotes a sense of ownership in the learning process needed by children who may be less motivated to learn words. For prekindergarten and kindergarten students, teachers ask children to listen for new words they hear during read-alouds and raise their hands to have the words written on the board. After reading, teachers can help children learn about the words they chose by reading definitions from a children's dictionary or returning to the story itself to look for clues. For first- and second-grade learners especially, teachers will want to teach students to read independently and identify words that are unknown in texts. Older students can highlight unknown words and write them down in a vocabulary journal to look up after they read. Choosing words to learn more about can empower children to ownership over their word learning.

Foster Peer Collaboration for Word and Concept Learning

Using small groups, same-age peer tutoring, or cross-age peer tutoring can be great ways to encourage children who may be struggling to learn words and to use them in different contexts. Talking about words with peers establishes an authentic context for word learning and sets the stage for developing depth of word knowledge as peers talk about various facets or uses of words together. Peers can also provide timely corrective feedback, if taught to do so, so that children can refine their word knowledge through conversations with their peers. Figure 7.3 is an example of an application activity we used to foster conversation among peers in our reading buddies program with younger and older students working in pairs. This activity could be used with same-age buddies as well.

Encourage Self-Assessment and Reflection

As children learn words and develop word awareness, teachers can promote self-assessment and reflection as ways for children to celebrate what they have learned and recognize what they need to review and practice. The more children can appreciate their own progress and diagnose where they need to continue improve, the more likely they are to invest in the process of word learning and strategy use, and thus become independent word learners over time. For example, at the beginning and end of a learning unit, teachers can provide students with a rubric to evaluate their own knowledge of the target concepts and vocabulary. This helps both the teacher and student in setting goals before instruction and then evaluating progress at the conclusion of an instructional unit. Figure 7.4 shows a self-rating rubric for younger students, and Figure 7.5 shows a self-rating rubric that can be used with older students.

Summary

Multiple means of representation, action and expression, and engagement are strategies that help all children build breadth and depth of vocabulary. Teaching

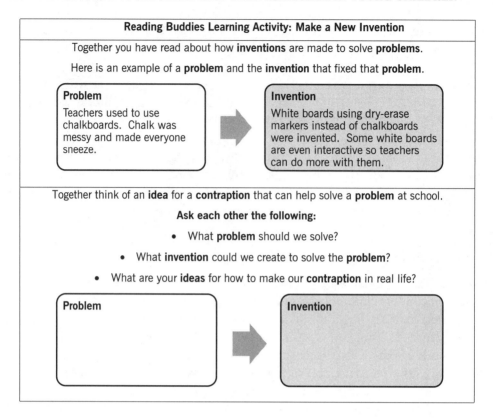

FIGURE 7.3. Sample peer collaboration learning activity about inventions.

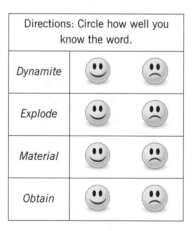

FIGURE 7.4. Sample self-rating vocabulary rubric for emergent readers.

Directions: Rate how well you know each word according to the scale below.				
	I've never heard it.	I've heard it, but I don't know what it means.	I've heard it and I have some idea what it means.	I know what it means and I can explain it well.
Dynamite				
Explode				
Material				

FIGURE 7.5. Sample self-rating vocabulary rubric for beginning and fluent readers based on the word knowledge scales of Dale (1965) and Wesche and Paribakht (1996).

words through verbal and nonverbal methods helps children understand the multiple facets of words and gain a deeper knowledge of words. Asking children to use words in a variety of ways encourages them to see how words can be applied across many contexts. And encouraging personalization of word learning can help children become more active and independent word learners. In Figure 7.6, we provide a checklist of UDL accommodations teachers can use to plan instruction that meets the needs of all learners in prekindergarten through second-grade classrooms.

Meeting the Needs of Diverse Children

As we have already noted, children arrive at school from very different cultural, linguistic, and socioeconomic backgrounds, and with various strengths and needs. In this section, we discuss how the accommodations we have just described can be applied to supporting diverse learners in today's classrooms.

Culturally and Linguistically Diverse Learners

Culturally and linguistically diverse learners live in environments in which the norms and traditions are very different from those that pervade mainstream school culture and in which the home language does not match the language of schooling. The gap between the language of school (i.e., academic language) and the language of home (i.e., conversational language) is wider in some homes, even in English-speaking homes (e.g., homes where African American Vernacular English is spoken), than in others. Often the gap is widest in homes where a language other than English is spoken, though the size of the gap often depends on socioeconomic status. In this section, we will first discuss culturally responsive teaching and accommodations that can be used to support children from diverse cultural backgrounds. Then we focus on vocabulary learning support for ELLs.

Multiple Means of Representation
☐ Connect to prior knowledge.
☐ Offer linguistic support (e.g., clear definitions for unknown words, connections to students' native language when applicable).
☐ Provide multiple representations to present words and concepts (e.g., present verbal and nonverbal information about words simultaneously).
☐ Use graphic organizers to highlight critical features of words and relations among words.
☐ Use paraphrasing, role play, visualization, and mnemonics.
Multiple Means of Action and Expression
☐ Offer alternative response modes (e.g., multiple choice, fill in the blank, open-ended questions, drawing, speaking, or writing).
☐ Provide added support and opportunities for practice (e.g., small-group instruction, partner activities, one-on-one tutoring).
☐ Support strategy use through goal setting, step-by-step instruction, think-alouds, and self-monitoring.
Multiple Means of Engagement
☐ Promote self-selection and facilitate individualization of word learning.
☐ Foster peer collaboration for word and concept learning.
☐ Encourage self-assessment and reflection about word learning.

FIGURE 7.6. Checklist for applying UDL accommodations to vocabulary instruction. Adapted from CAST (2011). Copyright 2011 by CAST. Adapted by permission.

Culturally Responsive Vocabulary Instruction

Culturally responsive teaching involves respect for children's home culture and language, recognition of the funds of knowledge children bring with them to the classroom, and support for children in accessing and negotiating the culture and language of school. Vocabulary instruction can be culturally responsive if it connects to and builds on children's home language and culture and supports children's knowledge of academic language in general and academic vocabulary in particular. When teachers value children's culture and language as a resource and work to bridge the divides between home and school language and cultures, children feel welcome and engaged and learn to navigate home and school cultures fluidly. As part of culturally responsive vocabulary instruction, teachers can provide multiple means of representation through books about different cultures and communities, such as *We're Different, We're the Same*, by Bobbie Kates (1992), *The Name Jar*, by Yangsook Choi (2013), *I Love My Hair!*, by Natasha Anastasia Tarpley (2001), and *Abuela*, by Arthur Dorros (1997). Teachers can focus on words from these books that describe people and activities in different cultures in positive and empowering ways. And, when explaining words, they can use examples that are relevant in different cultures. Figure 7.7 is an example of one way to integrate culturally responsive teaching and vocabulary instruction.

Along with recognizing children's home language and culture, teachers should include activities that foster a sense of the classroom and the school culture, such as a list of classroom rules that encourage respect for differing ideas and the sharing

---

The Calendar Project

At the beginning of the school year, Ms. Parks posted a calendar to her kindergarten classroom wall. The calendar included holidays that Ms. Parks celebrated with her family and friends, such as Christmas, New Year's, and Valentine's Day. The calendar also included holidays that Ms. Parks did not necessarily celebrate herself, such as Kwanzaa, Chanukah, and Eid al-Fitr. She explained to her students that these were holidays that her friends and coworkers celebrated. She wanted to remember when the holidays happened so she could learn more about what made the day special to people she knew and respected. Ms. Parks also sent home a calendar to each student asking the parents, guardians, and older siblings to indicate what holidays were important to them. Ms. Parks then added those holidays to the classroom calendar.

Throughout the year, Ms. Parks recognized the holidays on the calendar. During read-alouds, Ms. Parks introduced books about the holidays and the cultures that celebrate those holidays. During writer's workshop, she encouraged students to draw or write about what made the holiday special. Ms. Parks helped students label their drawings using all the languages the students knew. Throughout these activities, Ms. Parks encouraged the students to think of values that are shared across the holidays and cultures, such as *respect, courage, community, sharing, celebrations, kindness,* and *cooperation*. These words were continually added to the classroom word wall to represent the shared values of the classroom. Ms. Parks's calendar and monthly activities helped ensure that her class was a safe space where students could feel comfortable sharing what makes their family and community special—and they built vocabulary as well.

FIGURE 7.7. An example of culturally responsive vocabulary instruction.

of resources. Furthermore, teachers can foster communication with classrooms from other communities, in the same city or state, or even in another country. Developing relationships that celebrate children's diversity creates a forum for new ideas that capitalize on unique strengths. Each of these practices within culturally responsive teaching provides multiple means of action, self-expression, and engagement for culturally diverse learners.

Vocabulary Instruction for ELLs

ELLs are children whose home language is not English and who have limited English-language proficiency. ELLs are at risk for experiencing difficulty in schools where English is the language of instruction because they have less knowledge of English than their non-ELL peers. Without accommodations, ELLs may have difficulty accessing curriculum that has been developed with only native English speakers in mind (August & Shanahan, 2006).

ELLs have varying levels of English-language proficiency. Some children have little to no exposure to English, whereas others have at least some conversational English-language proficiency. However, even ELLs with conversational English-language skills may struggle with academic language and vocabulary if they have had less exposure to the English language of school with its particular vocabulary and syntax. For example, if a child has three pieces of candy and gives one to a friend on the playground, he may be able to respond correctly when asked, "How many do you have left?" The vocabulary is fairly simple, and the situation provides plenty of contextual support for the child to figure out the question and the answer. However, this same child may have a lot of difficulty if a teacher asks, "If you have a pie divided into three slices and you give one slice to your friend, what number of slices would you have left?" The context of the question is more abstract, and the vocabulary and syntax are more complex.

In addition to having different levels of English-language proficiency, ELLs also have varying levels of native language proficiency, ranging from substantial to limited. Thus, being able to provide native language supports that allow children to access English vocabulary instruction depends on the level of native language vocabulary children already have. Figure 7.8 shows the range of abilities in ELL children found in a single second-grade classroom. Teachers need to be prepared to use instructional supports to meet the needs of ELL children at various levels of English-language proficiency alongside their non-ELL peers. Often, teachers can have all children in the class working on a similar assignment (e.g., "use the words we learned today in your writing journal") as long as there is sufficient instructional support for children who need it.

August et al. (2005) offer guidance on supporting the vocabulary development of ELLs. These researchers suggest that teachers (1) take advantage of students' first language, (2) ensure ELLs know the meaning of basic words, and (3) provide review and reinforcement (pp. 54–55).

Student	Home Language	Observations about the Student	Instructional Supports
Waris	Urdu	Waris can use drawings to share her thoughts with a teacher or peer.	The teacher can provide Waris with a drawing journal to express her ideas and scaffold her language as she uses the drawings to explain her thoughts in words.
Alondra	Spanish	Alondra can complete a sentence with support from her teacher.	The teacher can provide sentence frames in order to help Alondra express her thoughts.
Nien	Vietnamese	Nien can form his own simple sentences with support from his teacher.	The teacher can provide Nien with a word and phrase bank to help him express his ideas.
Enrique	Spanish	Enrique can form his own complex sentences with prompting from his teacher.	The teacher can provide Enrique with prompts to express his ideas in class.

FIGURE 7.8. Example of varying ELL student abilities.

Specifically, if children have sufficient knowledge of their native language and their native language shares cognates with English (e.g., Spanish, which is spoken by nearly 75% of ELLs in the United States, shares many cognates with English), teachers can guide students to use cognate knowledge to infer word meanings. Cognates are words that share similar pronunciation and meaning across two languages. For example, English and Spanish share the following cognates: *family/familia, curious/curioso, perfect/perfecto.* (See *www.colorincolorado.org/educators/background/cognates* for additional information.) Even if children's first language does not share cognates with English, teachers can refer children to translations or to resources to help them access translations on their own so they can comprehend text more readily. Additionally, teachers may need to focus on basic words to ensure that ELLs with limited English vocabulary have the foundation of word knowledge they need to learn new words. Some basic words (e.g., *apple, book, tree*) will be fairly easy to teach because they are concrete and can be portrayed visually. Other words that we often consider basic (e.g., *find, make, time*) are much more abstract and require lots of repeated exposure across contexts for learning. Finally, review and reinforcement are important for all learners, but particularly for ELLs, who are navigating two (or more) languages and trying to remember vocabulary in each.

Other accommodations that we mentioned earlier in this chapter in the sections on multiple means of representation and multiple means of action and expression (e.g., multiple response options) are also important for ELLs, who may need extra nonverbal support to comprehend verbal instruction and extra scaffolding to use language expressively. A model that is useful for thinking about how to support language development in general and vocabulary acquisition in particular for

FIGURE 7.9. Input–interaction–output model. Based on Gass, Behney, and Plonsky (2013).

ELLs is the input–interaction–output model (e.g., Gass, Behney, & Plonsky, 2013). This model, shown in Figure 7.9, suggests that, for learning a second language, students need comprehensible input, meaningful interaction, and purposeful output. Providing explanation and nonverbal support makes advanced vocabulary more comprehensible. In Chapter 3, we discussed making vocabulary comprehensible to young children by providing examples across contexts and using visuals, props, and actions to demonstrate what words mean. These instructional practices can be particularly helpful to ELLs. In the next chapter, we discuss how multimedia can be used as another way to help ELLs understand word meaning. Additionally, as we discussed in Chapter 4, creating opportunities for students to use words in conversation, whether with the whole class (e.g., dialogic reading or Text Talk), small groups (e.g., collaborative reading groups), or partners (e.g., buddy reading or reading buddies), allows children to practice using the words they are learning with feedback from teachers or peers. And encouraging children to use the words they are learning beyond the immediate instructional context (e.g., in presentations or in writing) helps them internalize words and remember them long-term.

Children from Low Socioeconomic Backgrounds

Many children come from homes where resources that promote word learning are not easily available. For example, parents and caregivers with smaller incomes may not be able to purchase books, pay for field trips, or buy educational games that can be used to facilitate vocabulary and concept development. Compared to children who have these resources, children from lower socioeconomic backgrounds may be at a disadvantage. Teachers can help to level the playing field, so to speak, by helping these children access resources to build background and vocabulary knowledge and by scaffolding their language learning so they can catch up with their peers who may have had more exposure to such resources at home. In other words, teachers can offer multiple means of representation, action and expression, and engagement to children from low socioeconomic backgrounds so they can obtain content and material that is not available to them outside of school. Figure 7.10 is an example of how a teacher can provide digital resources in the classroom to engage students in the learning and application of new vocabulary. The effective use of multimedia in the classroom to support vocabulary development is discussed in more detail in Chapter 8.

During their reading rotations, Ms. Sharp allows students to work on digital games in pairs. Children are assigned to a specific category of digital game according to their vocabulary-related needs. Children from low socioeconomic status homes are thus provided ample opportunity to work on their vocabulary-related skills using technology they may not be able to access at home.

Story Games	Meaning Games	Matching Games	Relations Games
Miguel's Sketchpad (*Maya & Miguel*) *Choose words to create a comic strip.*	**Skits' Tricks** (*Martha Speaks*) *Move Skits to demonstrate the vocabulary word.*	**Word Race** (*Oh Noah!*) *Match orally presented vocabulary to pictures (Spanish).*	**Synonym Sam's Lab** (*Between the Lions*) *Find two words that mean the same as a given word.*
Storybook Creator (*Super Why!*) *Choose the correct vocabulary words in an interactive story.*	**Scrap Yard Slice** (*Electric Company*) Break apart compound words.	**Cooking with Caillou** (*Caillou*) *Match orally presented vocabulary to pictures.*	**Face Off** (*Word Girl*) *Defeat the villain using antonyms.*
True Stories (*Martha Speaks*) *Read stories with target vocabulary words and then take a vocabulary quiz.*	**Power Words** (*Word Girl*) *Choose the vocabulary word that that fits the scenario.*	**Match It** (*Oh Noah!*) *Match the correct word to the corresponding picture (Spanish).*	**Reading Power Bingo** (*Super Why!*) *Help Super Why! find the opposites.*

FIGURE 7.10. Digital activities for differentiating vocabulary instruction.

Children with or at Risk for Language-Related Disabilities

Besides having cultural and linguistic and socioeconomic differences, many children are at risk for disabilities that affect how they learn. A variety of disabilities affect language development (e.g., attention deficit disorders, autism spectrum disorders, developmental disabilities, visual or hearing difficulties). As ever more children with disabilities are included in general education classrooms, teachers can seek guidance from school specialists (e.g., special educators, reading specialists, speech–language pathologists, and school psychologists) to support these children in acquiring vocabulary. Since roughly 8% of preschool or kindergarten children have specific language impairment (SLI) and nearly 10% of all school-age children have specific learning disability (SLD), most teachers in general education classrooms will work with children with language-related disabilities (American Speech–Language–Hearing Association, n.d.). Even if teachers do not have children with identified disabilities in their classrooms, they may have children who are at risk for disabilities. In other words, some children may not be identified as having a disability, but they may have language difficulties that, if not addressed, may lead to a disability later in life. In the following section, we discuss SLI and SLD and describe how they may affect vocabulary development. We also suggest accommodations that may be used for children with or at risk for language-related disabilities in developing breadth and depth of vocabulary knowledge.

Children with or at risk for SLI often have trouble articulating words or stringing words together fluently. Being able to pronounce words correctly helps children form a clear phonological representation, which strengthens children's memory for words. Thus, children with SLI may have trouble remembering words they learn. Children who have SLI may have trouble understanding or producing language, and they may struggle with learning new words and participating in conversations with others. Children with SLI may drop word endings (e.g., *-s, -ed, -ing*), use incorrect verb tense (e.g., past instead of present), and have difficulty following directions and answering questions. Since children with SLI may have trouble communicating their thoughts and ideas to others, they may not get the interaction and feedback needed to learn new words and refine word knowledge. Thus, children with SLI may need extra guidance in learning, remembering, and using words accurately across contexts.

Children with or at risk for SLD typically struggle with processing, organizing, and recalling information, which leads to problems in reading, writing, and other language-based activities. SLD can be associated with phonological, auditory, or language processing deficits, all of which affect vocabulary learning. Thus, children with SLD may have limited early vocabulary knowledge, which is exacerbated over time. In order to prevent the snowball effect of SLD on vocabulary development, early intervention in prekindergarten through second grade should provide support for word learning and strategy use with specific supports for processing, organizing, and recalling information related to word learning.

In the vignette in Figure 7.11, we show how regular classroom teachers can work with specialists to embed supports for children with or at risk for SLI or SLD into regular classroom instruction. As can be seen in this example, multiple means of representation, action and expression, and engagement allow children with or at risk for language-related disabilities to participate fully in vocabulary learning in the classroom. Given that children with or at risk for language-related disabilities are required to meet the same high expectations on the CCSS as all other students, using UDL accommodations to provide access and promote learning in the area of vocabulary is crucial. And, by incorporating UDL accommodations into vocabulary instruction, teachers can better meet the needs of all students, including those who have (identified or unidentified) disabilities.

Response to Intervention

Response to intervention (RTI) provides a flexible framework for thinking about how instruction can be differentiated and how to intensify instruction for children who need more support. RTI has not been applied widely to vocabulary yet, but emerging studies suggest that RTI holds promise for serving as a framework for

Mr. Klipstein, a first-grade teacher, collaborates with the speech–language pathologist, Ms. Watts, and the special educator, Ms. Bradley, to include three students with language-based disabilities into his class. At the biweekly planning meeting, Ms. Watts, Ms. Bradley, and Mr. Klipstein review the students' individualized educational objectives. These objectives include "understanding and producing grade-level language." The teachers discuss the accommodations children need to be able to access, participate in, and benefit from all instruction, including vocabulary instruction.

In each vocabulary lesson, Mr. Klipstein clearly articulates his expectations to the children. He breaks down instructions step by step and uses picture and nonverbal cues to remind children what to do at each step. When possible, he provides his students with language-based disabilities with a checklist of steps to help them self-regulate. For example, if children are supposed to complete a graphic organizer with a word, a definition, an example, and a picture, Mr. Klipstein will write out each of these steps on a checklist for students to complete. Additionally, Mr. Klipstein provides these students with extra opportunities to hear and use words they are learning with peers and/or teachers present to provide immediate feedback.

When Mr. Klipstein or one of the specialists is working with any of these children, they provide positive reinforcement for correct language use and clear and manageable suggestions for improvement for incorrect language use. When possible, Mr. Klipstein gives them additional time to complete activities and emphasizes accuracy over fluency. Finally, he provides additional resources besides teacher support that the students can access throughout the day independently. For example, he partners these students with competent and encouraging peers to work together during vocabulary activities. And he provides them with unlimited access to reference materials, such as picture dictionaries, content summaries, and digital libraries, which they can use to fill in gaps in their understanding or memory of the target words and concepts. These measures, along with regular communication with the specialists and with families of his students with language-based disabilities, ensure that all students in Mr. Klipstein's classroom are included to the fullest extent possible in the rich vocabulary instruction in the classroom.

FIGURE 7.11. Example of including children with or at risk for language-related disabilities in vocabulary instruction.

differentiated vocabulary instruction (Loftus & Coyne, 2013), just as it has served as a framework for differentiated phonemic awareness and phonics instruction (Gilbert et al., 2013). A widely adopted model of RTI is one that includes three tiers of instruction. These tiers are not the same as the tiers of words to teach proposed by Beck et al. (2002, 2013). Tier 1 instruction is core instruction. It is the common curriculum provided to all children at a given grade level. Tier 1 instruction should be differentiated to meet the needs of diverse learners with lower and higher levels of vocabulary. Tier 2 instruction is meant for children who are not showing progress in Tier 1. Tier 2 provides an additional dose of instruction for small groups of students. Tier 3 instruction is more intensive, sometimes one-on-one, instruction for children who struggle despite differentiated and research-based Tier 1 core instruction and Tier 2 supplemental instruction. Below we describe features of vocabulary instruction at the various tiers of RTI implementation. Then we discuss the connection between assessment and RTI. Finally, we review a few studies that have investigated the efficacy of using RTI for promoting the vocabulary development of young children.

Differentiated Core Curriculum Instruction (Tier 1)

As part of the core curriculum, or the curriculum that serves as the foundation for instruction for all students, teachers should provide high-quality whole-class instruction aimed at meeting the broad needs of students in their classrooms. Additionally, teachers should offer differentiated opportunities for all children to build on their strengths and have their needs met. The words that teachers teach in the core curriculum should be related to an overarching unit or theme and to each other so that children can develop rich semantic networks of word knowledge. The explicit instructional practices that we outlined earlier in the book should pervade the core curriculum. Teachers should provide comprehensible definitions, examples across contexts, opportunities for children to analyze and use words, repeated exposure and review of words, and direct instruction on word learning strategies. Explicit instruction should be implemented within a language-rich environment that fosters word awareness and excitement about word learning. For children who need more support in learning and using words within core instruction, ways to differentiate for vocabulary instruction include (1) providing additional repetitions of words in various contexts and additional instruction in word learning strategies, (2) providing added prompting to use words and word learning strategies, and (3) offering added scaffolding and wait time when asking students to use words or word learning strategies. For students who need to be more challenged in the area of vocabulary, teachers can introduce them to "bonus" words on the same theme as the other words introduced in class, ask students to use multiple words simultaneously in speaking or writing, and encourage students to use word learning strategies independently in reading advanced text. Teachers are typically given a core curriculum program to implement in their classrooms. If the core curriculum program does not adhere to the principles outlined above, teachers should modify it to ensure there is optimal support for children's development of vocabulary breadth and depth in school.

Supplemental Instruction for Vocabulary (Tier 2)

Children who do not respond to the core curriculum and differentiated instruction alone require additional instruction to improve their vocabulary development. The keyword is *additional*. Rather than replace core instruction with other instructional support, children who are not developing in vocabulary at the same rate as their peers should be given small-group instruction that adds to and builds on differentiated core instruction. Such supplemental instruction can function as an extra "dose" of instruction that is aligned with the core instruction they have already received. Grouping children with similar levels of vocabulary knowledge and similar instructional needs may allow for more targeted supplemental instruction in vocabulary. There are few published programs to support vocabulary at Tier 2, so teachers may need to create their own lessons, based on the core curriculum, that contain this extra "dose" for those in need of more exposure and support.

Intensive Interventions for Vocabulary (Tier 3)

Little research has been conducted on intensive interventions for vocabulary for children who have not made progress in supplemental intervention. For children who are not progressing in vocabulary, despite whole-class and differentiated core instruction and supplemental small-group instruction, one-on-one additional and intensive support may be required. This instruction may be aligned with core instruction, but it may also be qualitatively different. To further the vocabulary learning of children who have not responded to research-based instruction that is proven to be effective for a wide variety of learners, instruction may need to be more tailored and specific to the individual needs of the child. For example, although mental imagery is not a primary instructional practice in explicit instruction recommended for the core curriculum, it may be a cornerstone of Tier 3 instruction for a student who has strong visualization skills but poor language skills. However, since Tier 3 instruction has not been well researched, it is premature to recommend a set of specific instructional practices for children with different strengths and needs.

The Role of Assessment in RTI

At the heart of RTI is the assessment process, discussed in the Chapter 6. As we noted there, assessment plays a critical role in determining whether students are responding to instruction. In RTI, all children are screened on vocabulary knowledge at the beginning of the school year and monitored throughout the year to determine their response to core instruction. Based on what teachers see in these assessments, they may differentiate instruction within the core curriculum to meet children's needs. Children who do not show adequate response to instruction in Tier 1 are provided with Tier 2 instruction and evaluated more frequently so teachers can monitor their progress more closely. If, despite Tier 2 instruction, children show limited progress in vocabulary, teachers may call for administration of diagnostic measures, perhaps by a reading specialist or special educator, to identify the specific difficulties children are experiencing in learning vocabulary words and concepts. This diagnostic information is used to design more individualized and intensive interventions to address the specific needs of children who are unresponsive to both Tier 1 and Tier 2 instruction. Thus, screening, progress monitoring, and diagnostic assessments are essential in the RTI framework.

Research on RTI and Vocabulary Development

In a recent article entitled "Vocabulary Instruction within a Multi-Tier Approach," Loftus and Coyne (2013) summarized a series of studies they conducted that provide initial evidence of the efficacy of RTI for supporting vocabulary breadth and depth. In the first study, the researchers evaluated a Tier 1 read-aloud intervention that included research-based vocabulary instruction practices and extension activities. Before reading, teachers introduced target words and asked students to raise their hands if they heard the words during the read-aloud. During reading, teachers defined the target words, referred to pictures related to the target words, and asked students to say the target words out loud. After reading, the teachers reintroduced the target words by reviewing the definitions, reading the sentences from the book that contained the words, and again referring to the illustrations of the words in the book. Next teachers provided additional examples of the words across contexts. Finally, teachers led a series of activities for children to engage in identifying examples and non-examples of words. This same instructional approach was used with the same books and words twice over the course of a week. Results showed that students who participated in this Tier 1 intervention, which essentially captured all the features of explicit instruction outlined earlier in this book, outperformed children who did not receive the intervention in word learning. However, the effects of the intervention were stronger for children with higher rather than lower initial vocabulary knowledge. Thus, the researchers conducted another study to determine whether supplemental instruction (i.e., Tier 2) given to children with lower vocabulary knowledge would help close this gap.

In their second study Loftus and Coyne (2013) provided all students with Tier 1 instruction modeled on the instruction just described. Students who scored low on a standardized vocabulary measure (the PPVT) were determined to be at risk for experiencing difficulty in vocabulary and provided with Tier 2 instruction. Tier 2 instruction focused on only half of the words covered in Tier 1 so the researchers could evaluate whether children learned words to a greater extent if they appeared in Tier 1 instruction only or in Tier 1 *and* Tier 2 instruction. Tier 2 instruction included three components: (1) a review of word meanings, (2) a repeat of vocabulary activities done in Tier 1, and (3) two additional vocabulary activities not done in Tier 1. These activities involved looking at pictures and creating sentences about them using target words and distinguishing between picture examples of two different target words. Results showed that at-risk students learned the words taught in Tier 1 *and* Tier 2 better than they learned the words just taught in Tier 1, and that at-risk students provided with Tier 2 instruction made gains comparable to their peers who were not at risk. These findings suggest the promise of RTI for supporting word learning in children at risk for experiencing difficulty in school due to limited vocabulary knowledge. We hope that researchers and teachers will continue to explore this important issue.

Summary

Diverse learners can benefit from vocabulary instruction when instruction is tailored to their individual needs. Structuring lessons around the principles of UDL allows teachers to differentiate instruction and provide access and support to children with a variety of backgrounds and abilities. We hope you are able to use the UDL-aligned accommodations described in this chapter in your vocabulary instruction so that all students in your class, including children from culturally, linguistically, and socioeconomically diverse backgrounds and children with different strengths and abilities, gain the vocabulary they need to access texts in school. We also hope you consider using an RTI approach to achieving increasingly intensive vocabulary instruction for students who need extra support in your class. In the next chapter, we focus on how multimedia can be an effective tool for promoting differentiated instruction for word learning in prekindergarten through second-grade classrooms.

CHAPTER 8

Using Multimedia to Support Word Learning in the Digital Age

GUIDING QUESTIONS

- What is the state of research on the effects of multimedia on vocabulary learning?
- How can teachers use multimedia to support vocabulary learning in the classroom?
- How can teachers evaluate multimedia for use in supporting vocabulary learning?
- How can teachers integrate technology into their regular vocabulary instruction?

Mrs. Hagel begins her lesson by dimming the lights and turning on her interactive white board. Her students immediately focus on the screen, where she has displayed a vocabulary word wall. As Mrs. Hagel touches each word, a short video that shows the meaning of the word pops up on screen. After Mrs. Hagel has finished reviewing each word for the day, she displays a digital text on screen. As she reads the text, she highlights the target words and touches them for a quick definition. Once Mrs. Hagel has finished reading the digital text aloud to her students, she engages them in a game in which they come to the interactive white board to move pictures and words to match contexts in the story. Mrs. Hagel uses multimedia to maximum advantage in her second-grade vocabulary instruction.

Some of the information presented in this chapter previously appeared in Silverman and Hines (2012). Copyright by The Guilford Press. Adapted by permission.

In the previous chapter, we focused on ways to differentiate instruction for diverse learners. We discussed the UDL framework, which suggests that curricula should include multiple means of representation, action and expression, and engagement to meet the needs of diverse learners. And we mentioned

> **Multimedia** integrates more than one medium of communication. For example, digital texts are a form of multimedia that includes text, graphics, and sound and video is a form of multimedia that includes visuals, sound, and action.

that the use of multimedia aligned with UDL principles is one way to differentiate curricula for children with different needs. With the explosion of digital learning opportunities in the past decade alone, and the feverous pitch at which new products are becoming available to teachers, we have chosen to dedicate an entire chapter to discussing how you can use multimedia to support vocabulary development in your classroom, and we propose examples of how multimedia can be used effectively in vocabulary instruction. We hope that our extended discussion of multimedia, delivered within the context of UDL and all the principles of vocabulary instruction we listed in the previous chapters, enables you to become a discerning consumer of existing and future media.

How Multimedia Supports Vocabulary Development

Educators often receive conflicting messages about the role of multimedia in education. On the one hand, we are cautioned that too much "screen time" is detrimental to children's health and well-being (e.g., *www.nlm.nih.gov*; *www.mayoclinic.com*). On the other hand, we are encouraged to use multimedia to enhance educational opportunities for students (e.g., *www.pbs.org*; *www.macfound.org*). The debate about whether or not to use multimedia in education presents a false dichotomy. Teachers wouldn't get rid of all of the books in the classroom just because some books are not appropriate for children. Similarly, some multimedia may belong in the classroom and some may not belong there.

By choosing multimedia content that supports educational objectives and using multimedia as an instructional support rather than a non-instructional babysitter, we can harness its power to foster vocabulary learning in particular. Many words represent dynamic concepts that are hard to explain or to depict with simple drawings or still pictures. Multimedia allows the possibility of exhibiting the multidimensionality of words. It also offers the possibility of supporting children in interacting with words in multidimensional ways, which in turn can increase word learning.

> The CCSS call for students to engage with digital sources on a range of topics. (See Standard 10 on Range, Quality, and Complexity.) Thus, using multimedia for vocabulary instruction can also support children in meeting the CCSS.

The use of multimedia is grounded in the dual coding theory proposed by Paivio (1986). According to this theory, depicted in Figure 8.1, the human brain processes information through two separate paths. One path processes verbal information (e.g., the words a teacher says as she reads aloud). The other path processes nonverbal information (e.g., the gestures a teacher uses as she reads and the pictures she shows from the book she is reading).

The dual coding theory proposes that information that is encoded both verbally and nonverbally is represented more fully in memory than information that has been encoded through one channel alone. Multimedia, which typically complements verbal information with robust nonverbal information, including live action and animation, could have an advantage in vocabulary instruction over other means of presentation that are not as multifaceted. As Neuman (1997) suggests, children may learn slightly different and complementary types of information from different sources of verbal and nonverbal representation, which, when taken together, support children's depth of understanding of content and concepts. For example, when learning about *shadows*, children can gain information from a verbal explanation that tells them that shadows occur when something blocks light and from a nonverbal video clip of children performing a shadow puppet show. Experiencing the explanation along with the video clip may enhance learning about *shadows* more than being exposed to either medium alone.

Multimedia has other potential benefits as well. For example, it can be used to focus on salient features of content, to engage students as active participants in knowledge acquisition, to scaffold student learning, and to muster attention and motivation. Close-up video shots can call children's attention to a particular object

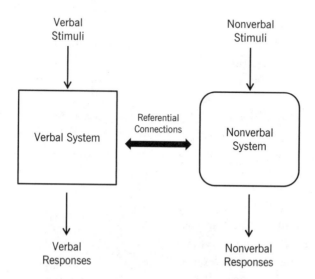

FIGURE 8.1. The conceptualization of information processing according to the dual coding theory. Based on Paivio (1986).

or even a particular aspect of an object being discussed (Salomon, 1981). Computer games, interactive electronic books, and even video in which characters ask the audience to respond all invite children to become actively involved participants (Segers, 2009). Features embedded in electronic storybooks and computer games such as text-to-speech narration, computer assistants (i.e., avatar characters that provide help), and "hotspots" (i.e., areas where users get additional information) can help children acquire content they might not be able to access on their own (McKenna & Zucker, 2009; Shamir & Korat, 2009). The use of multimedia can also serve to motivate children, particularly children who are at risk for difficulties in reading, to engage with content and text that may otherwise be inaccessible or difficult for them (Kamil, Intrator, & Kim, 2000; McKenna & Zucker, 2009). We review several types of multimedia that can be used to support breadth and depth of vocabulary learning and discuss how these technologies might be used in everyday classroom settings. Later in the chapter, we suggest guidelines teachers can use to review new multimedia as it becomes available for classroom use.

Types of Multimedia to Support Word Learning

There are many different types of multimedia available for classroom use, ranging from videos to electronic books to computer programs, games, and applications. While research on the use of multimedia for vocabulary learning is still in the early stages, there are some indications that these different types of multimedia are effective in supporting word learning.

Using Video to Support Vocabulary Learning

One useful form of multimedia is video. Video is an electronic medium that shows moving images with accompanying audio. Much of the research on the effects of video on children's learning has been in the context of at-home or in-school viewing of television programs. Research on the effects of educational television viewing on literacy and numeracy outcomes has been accumulating since the 1970s. In the late 1980s and early 1990s, Rice and colleagues (1988) conducted a series of studies showing positive effects of viewing educational television programs such as *Sesame Street* on children's vocabulary development. In 2001, a study by Wright and colleagues showed the positive effects of viewing *educational* children's television programming on children's vocabulary but the negative effects of viewing *non-educational* children's or general audience television programming on children's vocabulary, suggesting that the content of the television programming matters. Similarly, in 2005, Linebarger and Walker (2005) demonstrated that different television programs had different effects on young children's language and literacy, but that many programs, such as *Dora the Explorer*, *Blue's Clues*, *Arthur*, *Clifford*, and *Dragon Tales*, had positive effects on children's receptive vocabulary and expressive language skills. These studies, taken together, show that educational children's television programs can serve as a fertile ground for supporting vocabulary development in young children.

While growing research suggests that educational television can have a positive effect on children's vocabulary development, an open question is whether this effect is as robust as the effect of reading books. A recent study investigated this issue by analyzing children's vocabulary learning through read-alouds, video, or read-alouds plus video (Silverman, 2013). Two educational programs based on children's literature were chosen for the study: *Arthur* and *Martha Speaks*. *Arthur* is based on a book series by Marc Brown, and *Martha Speaks* is based on a book series by Susan Meddaugh. The educational objective of *Martha Speaks* is to bolster vocabulary development, and, accordingly, target words are explicitly defined and repeated throughout episodes. Note that the first author of this book is the curriculum director for the *Martha Speaks* program.

The study's author chose videos that were based on the program and created books derived from the video scripts so that the videos and books had exactly the same content. Children experienced stories from *Arthur* and *Martha Speaks* in either video only, read-aloud only, or video plus read-aloud . No additional teaching was included in any of these contexts so that the effect of the medium rather than the effect of instruction could be evaluated. Children were tested before and after the instructional period on their knowledge of words from the stories and their general vocabulary knowledge. There was no difference in vocabulary learning in the three contexts, but children learned more vocabulary from experiencing *Martha Speaks* than from experiencing *Arthur*. A second study on *Martha Speaks* (Silverman, 2013) compared one viewing versus three viewings of the television program. This study found that, as with repeated readings of books, repeated viewings of videos led to more positive results than a single viewing. These studies show that the video medium may be as powerful as the book medium for supporting children's vocabulary learning.

However, additional research shows that video may be particularly helpful for certain children. For example, Silverman and Hines (2009) compared read-alouds only to read-alouds plus video with both ELL and non-ELL children in prekindergarten through second-grade classrooms. The intervention was developed around the topic of habitats and included both fiction and nonfiction books. In both the read-alouds only and the read-alouds plus video contexts, teachers provided explicit instruction of target words. Teachers spent 9 days on each of four habitats. For every habitat studied, teachers in the read-aloud only context read three books for 3 days each. Meanwhile, teachers in the read-aloud plus video context read three books for 2 days each and showed video clips over the course of 3 days for each habitat. For non-ELL children, results showed no difference in vocabulary learning by context (i.e., read-aloud only or read-aloud plus video). However, for ELL children, results showed greater vocabulary learning in the read-aloud plus video rather than the read-aloud only context. Many ELL children have limited English vocabulary knowledge compared to their English-only peers; therefore, learning new words and content in English may be a challenge. Nonverbal support in the form of multimedia may provide a scaffold for ELLs so that they can more readily access new information presented in class. Thus, using video to complement read-alouds may be particularly beneficial for ELLs and other students who need nonverbal support for learning from verbal instruction in school.

Figure 8.2 is an example of a 3-day sequence that could be used to support vocabulary learning through read-alouds plus video. In a unit on the ocean habitat, teachers could read any of three National Geographic Kids books—on dolphins (Stewart, 2010), whales (Marsh, 2010), or sharks (Schreiber, 2008)—on days 1 and 2 and then show brief (i.e., roughly 5-minute) segments from the National Geographic Kids *Really Wild Animals: Deep Sea Dive* DVD on dolphins, whales, or sharks on day 3 (Youngdahl & Grupper, 2004). Or teachers could read the National Geographic Kids book *Weird Sea Creatures* (Marsh, 2012) on days 1 and 2 and then show segments from the National Geographic *Amazing Planet: Creatures of the Deep* DVD on day 3. In any of these scenarios, teachers could focus on words such as *shallow, surface, deep, dive, depth, migrate, route, speed, distance, predator,* and *prey.* Although each of these words can be discussed verbally, they are illustrated more fully through the context and action afforded by video.

Other peer-reviewed studies have included video as part of the total instructional curriculum but have not explicitly tested the effects of including the video component. For example, video clips were embedded in daily lessons in the World of Words (WOW) program, a preschool program aimed at improving the vocabulary and conceptual knowledge of low-income preschoolers (Neuman, Newman, & Dwyer, 2011). In this program, teachers focused on teaching taxonomically related content words (e.g., words related to *insects* included *ladybug, grasshopper,* and *butterfly*) and other words related to the content area (e.g., *segment, antennae,* and *creature*). Video clips were taken from *Sesame Street* and were 40 to 90 seconds in length. The clips presented information about the topic of the lesson,

Day 1: Read-Aloud (30 min)	Day 2: Read-Aloud (30 min)	Day 3: Video (30 min)
• Introduce new words. • Read book straight through. • Review words. • Play word game.	• Review new words. • Read book and stop to discuss words and content. • Review words. • Play word game.	• Review new words. • Show video clip (5 min) straight through. • Show video clip (5 min) again and stop and to discuss words and content. • Review words. • Play word game.

FIGURE 8.2. An example of a 3-day read-aloud plus video sequence.

and teachers reinforced learning of this information through follow-up questioning and read-alouds of books aligned with the video clips. In a randomized control trial, children who participated in the WOW curriculum scored higher than peers who did not participate in the program on vocabulary, concept development, knowledge of categories and properties, and inductive reasoning skills. Figure 8.3 outlines activities that are embedded in the WOW program. Incorporating video into lessons to engage children in academic topics and illustrate key concepts may provide the extra motivation and support they need to develop breadth and depth of vocabulary on new content they learn in school.

Given that research shows the potential of video for promoting vocabulary and content learning and using curricula such as WOW as an example, educators should consider including educational television and video in classroom instruction to build and reinforce vocabulary knowledge and conceptual understanding. It is likely that providing information in multiple formats (e.g., read-alouds, direct instruction, and educational television and video) can be beneficial. The nonverbal information in educational television and video (e.g., the darkness of a *blackout*, the *misty* precipitation in the rainforest habitat, and the wiggling *antennae* of a katydid) may be conveyed more clearly and comprehensibly through animation, live action, and other multimedia enhancements than through traditional methods of classroom instruction alone. Therefore, educational television and video should be a part of every educator's toolkit.

Activity	Description
Tuning Video	Teachers showed a short rhyme or song or word-play video to tune children in to the topic (e.g., living things) and category (e.g., insects).
Content Video	Teachers showed a slightly longer content video that presented a particularly salient example of the topic and category through live action.
Teacher–Student Dialogue	Teachers asked *wh-* questions to guide children to think about words and concepts.
Book Reading	Teachers read an information book to children that provided the same content from the video through a different medium (i.e., text and pictures).
Picture Cards	Teachers showed children pictures cards with examples and non-examples of the topic and category at hand.
Time for a Challenge	Children were asked to think analytically about words and make decisions about examples and non-examples of words.
Extension Activity	Children were asked to show their learning of words and content through writing and drawing in journals.

FIGURE 8.3. Instructional content of the WOW program. Adapted from Neuman, Newman, and Dwyer (2011). Copyright 2011 by the University of Michigan. Used with permission.

Using Digital Texts to Support Vocabulary Learning

Digital texts are another form of media that presents opportunities for vocabulary instruction. Digital texts can range from the simple (e.g., words and static pictures on an electronic reader) to the complex (e.g., dynamic texts with text-to-speech narration, hyperlinks from words to definitions, music and animation, and interactive games). Free digital texts are available through local public libraries and through websites such as the International Children's Digital Library (*http:// en.childrenslibrary.org*). Commercial digital texts are available from online bookstores (e.g., Storia, Kindle, and Nook) and educational technology websites. Digital texts can support vocabulary development through the presentation of both verbal and nonverbal information about words and independent word learning through hyperlinks to definitions and online glossaries as well as supportive interactives (i.e., games that are related to the content). (We provide a list of digital resources in the Appendix.)

Research has identified a promising role for digital texts in promoting vocabulary. For example, Korat and Shamir (2012), working with prekindergarten and kindergarten children, and Korat (2010), working with kindergarten and first-grade children, found that children learned vocabulary through the use of a digital text that included dictionary definitions, dynamic visuals, and accompanying music that dramatized the story. Shamir, Korat, and Fellah (2012) conducted a related study with preschool children with developmental delays. The researchers found the digital text format to be particularly beneficial for supporting the vocabulary learning of these children. In another study by members of this research team, Shamir, Korat, and Shlafer (2011) examined vocabulary learning through digital texts with kindergarten children who were typically developing or at risk for developing learning disabilities. The researchers found that children in both the typically developing and at-risk groups who used the digital texts showed significant improvement in vocabulary, suggesting that the digital text format may be useful for promoting the vocabulary learning of children with diverse strengths and needs.

Of course, as with regular books, different kinds of digital texts may support vocabulary differentially. Verhallen and Bus (2010) investigated the effects of two types of digital texts on children's receptive and expressive vocabularies. These researchers were working with 5-year-old children in the Netherlands from immigrant and low socioeconomic backgrounds. Children were randomly assigned to one of two conditions, either digital texts with static (i.e., still) images or digital texts with video images, which

> **Digital texts,** also called electronic books or e-books, are texts that can be read on electronic devices. They can function like traditional books, with static pictures and printed words, or they can include digital features such as hypertext (i.e., links to more information), animation, and narration.

showed action related to the narrative. In both conditions, children listened to the story four times with minimal adult interaction. Before and after viewing the respective text types, all children were assessed on their receptive and expressive knowledge of words that appeared at a low frequency in the story. While children learned words receptively and expressively through using digital texts with static or video images, they acquired more expressive vocabulary through using digital texts with video images. This finding suggests that using digital texts with video may provide extra nonverbal support that is helpful for developing depth of vocabulary knowledge, particularly for children from low-income and immigrant backgrounds who may need extra support to acquire school language.

In addition to examining digital texts with static versus video images, researchers have investigated different modes of engagement with digital texts. For example, Shamir (2009) assigned kindergarten students to experience one of three modes of engagement: "(1) read story only, (2) read story with dictionary, and (3) read story and play" (p. 85). In the read-only mode, children were given an oral reading of the text, which included automatically activated dynamic visuals dramatizing the story. The story reading plus dictionary support mode added explanations associated with pictures of difficult words. Children could activate the dictionary support (i.e., the pictures and explanations) by clicking on specific words, which appeared in clouds. The read-and-play mode included activities (i.e., hotspots) designed to enhance story understanding. After listening to the story, children could click on hotspots to interact with characters, objects, and specific words from the story. These activities were designed to enrich story comprehension.

Children participated in the intervention in pairs, and the researchers recorded and then analyzed their collaborative talk during the intervention sessions. Shamir (2009) found that children discussed word meanings, pictures, and plot in all conditions. Furthermore, activating the hotspots helped trigger collaborative knowledge construction. However, additional analysis of each condition showed mixed associations with vocabulary learning. Results showed that improvement in vocabulary was significantly, positively associated with greater usage of the dictionary option but significantly, negatively correlated with activation of picture hotspots, suggesting that certain digital texts features can detract from vocabulary learning. Thus, while teachers should seek out digital texts that include dictionary options, they should avoid digital texts with an inordinate number of amusement features that can distract from word and content learning.

Beyond choosing high-quality digital texts, teachers have to consider the best contexts for using digital texts with children. Teachers can weigh the benefits of having children use digital texts in partners versus independently. Working with kindergarten students from families with low socioeconomic backgrounds, Shamir, Korat, and Barbi (2008) examined the effects using digital texts in pairs or individually. They specifically selected a digital text that they defined as "high-quality" in that most of hotspots were congruent with and integrated into the story's content. Children in the sample were randomly assigned to one of four groups: tutor, tutee, individual learner, and control group. Tutors and tutees were then randomly paired. Tutors did not necessarily have advanced literacy skills since they were chosen at random, but they were provided some initial instruction on using the digital text before they worked with their partner. In this way, the tutor was supposed to show the tutee how to use the digital text. Meanwhile, the individual learner read the digital text without a peer and children in the control group were not exposed to the digital text.

The intervention consisted of two half-hour digital text sessions in two modes: read the book or read and play with the book. Findings indicated that children who worked in pairs showed more story comprehension than children who worked individually, and, to a certain extent, tutors showed greater story comprehension than tutees. The authors concluded that working in pairs with educational digital texts might be a practical solution as well as an educationally beneficial one. For teachers who have the resources for digital texts in their classrooms, they recommend using highly rated digital texts and carefully planning peer collaboration activities to improve outcomes for preschool- and kindergarten-age children from families of low socioeconomic status.

In the reading buddies project that we have discussed previously, we have also used digital texts with pairs of children, but the pairs in our project consist of fourth-grade big buddies and kindergarten little buddies. In our project, we have used digital texts related to the show *Martha Speaks* called True Stories. The True Stories collection (*http://pbskids.org/martha/stories/truestories*) covers science, technology, engineering, and math (STEM) content through exploration of the environment, transportation, communication and computer technology, inventions, and measurement. In each unit, there is one video and three digital texts. The texts can be accessed through a computer or tablet device and offer text-to-speech capability. We chose to use tablet devices in our program so children could navigate the text with a touch screen and work together in their regular classroom setting (i.e., not in a school computer lab). The True Stories suite includes a variety of built-in components aimed at strengthening students' understanding of the key vocabulary. For example, in the True Stories texts, target words are highlighted and pronounced and students can click on or touch words to access definitions. Additionally, the texts offer interactive features, such as being able to move binoculars across the page to *observe* the animals and plants in their *habitat*. Finally, a quiz-show-style word game is featured at the end of the text to review target words. Feedback is provided in the quiz to support children's review of the words.

In the reading buddies program, teachers previewed the videos and texts with big and little buddies before buddies met together to make sure both buddies had enough prior knowledge to engage with the texts on their own. In the teacher-led lessons, teachers pretaught vocabulary words and comprehension strategies so children would be successful when working together. Also, teacher led lessons for the big buddies focused on using the digital text and following the big buddy guide for what to do when working with little buddies. During the buddies sessions, student pairs watched the video or read or listened to the text together. Then they talked about the text and completed activities related to the text together. Sometimes big buddies read the text to little buddies; at other times big buddies and little buddies listened to the text being read aloud through the text-to-speech feature. When buddies listened to the digital text, they shared a set of ear buds. Each buddy put one ear bud in his or her ear to listen to the story with one ear and to listen to his or her partner with the other ear. We used alcohol wipes to clean the ear buds between sessions. (The devil is in the details.)

We found that children were very engaged with the digital texts and learned the words and content embedded in the texts. The texts provided more support for the buddies as they learned words and content together. And the interactive features made the words come alive. The text-to-speech feature was particularly helpful for big buddies with lower reading skills because they were able to focus their attention on sustaining the oral conversation with their little buddy rather than dividing their attention between decoding and conversing interchangeably. Having had preparation and practice before the reading buddies sessions, the big buddies were positioned as experts and were able to effectively guide the little buddies in learning words and content. In this case, the digital text was a tool that enabled buddies at different levels to work together productively.

When used independently or in pairs, digital texts are a promising important medium to support vocabulary learning. As these projects have demonstrated, digital texts have many affordances, including text-to-speech, hypertext, and interactive capabilities that can bring words and content alive for young children. Digital texts are more likely to accommodate a wide range of learners. Their multimodal representations of words and content help children develop greater understanding of word and concept meaning. Thus, we strongly encourage teachers in prekindergarten through second-grade classrooms to consider using digital texts as a resource for vocabulary instruction in schools.

Using Computer Programs, Games, and Applications to Support Vocabulary Learning

Besides using videos and digital texts as media through which to teach vocabulary, there is a wide world of computer programs, games, and applications that can be used as well, many of which have not been evaluated, however, in formal research studies. Therefore, as we discuss later, teachers must use these assets with caution. But, some studies show that particular programs, games, and applications may be useful resources for supporting children's vocabulary learning.

In one study, Huffstetter, King, Onwuegbuzie, Schneider, and Powell-Smith (2010) evaluated the effects of a computer-based reading program on children's print knowledge and oral language skills. The program under consideration was the Headsprout Early Reading program, now called MimioSprout Early Reading (*www.mimio.com/en-NA/Products/MimioSprout-Early-Reading.aspx*). The program addresses all aspects of reading, including vocabulary, and is designed for children in prekindergarten through second grade. As part of the comprehensive program, children engage in the following vocabulary-related activities: (1) children choose pictures to match words in texts they are hearing or reading, (2) children answer questions about words in texts they are hearing or reading, and (3) children complete sentences with words from texts they are hearing or reading. The program is adaptive to students' levels of language and literacy, and teachers can obtain data on how students are progressing through the program. Huffstetter and colleagues evaluated the program with prekindergarten children in Head Start classrooms. Children were randomly assigned to an intervention or a comparison group. Children in the intervention group used the program for 30 minutes a day over the course of 8 weeks. Children in the comparison group used a math software program for the same amount of time. Results showed that children in the intervention group outperformed children in the comparison group in print knowledge and oral language. The oral language measure used in the study included vocabulary assessment. This study suggests that even very young children can learn vocabulary through computer-assisted learning. Other comprehensive computer-based reading programs that may show similar results include Waterford Early Reading, World Book Early World of Learning, and ABC Mouse.com Early Learning Academy.

In another study, Silverman (2009) evaluated the effect of playing vocabulary-focused computer games on kindergarten children's word learning. The study was conducted in a school in which most children were from low-income and non-English-speaking homes. Included in the evaluation were three vocabulary-focused games on the *Martha Speaks* website (*http://pbskids.org/martha/games/index.html*). The three games were (1) Catch, a quiz-show-like game in which children are asked a question using a target word and given two choices to answer the question; (2) Scrub-a-Pup, an interactive game in which children "do" target words (e.g., *spray* the water) as they wash dogs; and (3) Funny Photos, a "what's wrong with this picture" game in which children hear a voice-over of Martha using target words as they play. In Catch, words are used explicitly; in Scrub-a-Pup, words are used interactively; and, in Funny Photos, words are used ambiently. Children in the intervention group played each game in pairs for roughly 8 minutes per day for 3 days. Children in the comparison group did not play the games. We pretested and posttested all children on their knowledge of target words (i.e., words targeted in the games). We also monitored the engagement of children in the intervention group as they were playing each game. Results indicated that, compared to children in the comparison group, children in the intervention group made significant gains on words targeted in Catch, but not in the other two games. Results also showed that children were more engaged playing the Scrub-a-Pup game. These findings suggest that different kinds of games have different effects on children's word learning. Games in which words are explicitly taught and assessed may be more supportive of children's word learning, but games in which children are able to engage interactively may be more motivating. Games that combine explicit teaching and engagement may be optimal.

In a final study, Fehr et al. (2012) evaluated an early version of a vocabulary-building program called The First 4000 Words (*www.sewardreadingresources.com/fourkw.html*). In this program for children in first through fourth grades, children listen to a story read aloud on the computer. Then they are introduced to target words from the story through definitions, examples, and pictures. They are also able to listen to the pronunciations of words and record their own pronunciations for practice. Next, children listen to the story read aloud again. During this reading of the text, children can click on words for definitions, examples, and pictures throughout the read-aloud. Finally, they play interactive games that reinforce learning of the words targeted in the read-aloud text. One game children play is a puzzle game in which they are given a definition and are expected to click on the word that goes with the definition to reveal pieces of the puzzle. In another game, children are given pictures and asked to identify as quickly as possible which of three words best describes the picture. Children get points for speed and accuracy. All aspects of the program are adaptive to students' vocabulary level so that those need more support receive that support and those who need more challenging vocabulary are accommodated as well. In the study Fehr and colleagues conducted with struggling readers in grades 2–4, children were assigned to an intervention or control group. Children in the intervention group participated in 10 lessons from the First 4000 Words program on the computer. Children in the control group did not participate in the program. All children were pre- and posttested on knowledge of words in the intervention. While there was no difference in children's target word knowledge at the start of the program, children in the intervention group outperformed children in the control group at the end of the program. Thus, this study shows that computer-assisted vocabulary programs, particularly ones that provide context and definitions, promote interaction with words, and adapt to students' vocabulary level, may be beneficial for promoting children's vocabulary learning.

Evaluating Multimedia
to Support Vocabulary Development

While evidence upholds the use of certain multimedia resources for teaching vocabulary, there is a plethora of resources that have not been formally evaluated. As the world of multimedia has expanded in recent years, new tools for instruction come on the market every day. The problem for educators is determining which tools are likely to promote vocabulary development and which are a waste of time and money. Given that time and resources are precious in the school context, teachers need to be critical consumers of multimedia products. Some products include a lot of bells and whistles that make them appealing to children but actually detract from their learning (e.g., Parish-Morris et al., 2013). Other products seem to adequately address the learning objectives but are not engaging or adaptive. Teachers need to weigh the pros and cons of each type of multimedia they adopt to support vocabulary instruction. In this section, we outline criteria teachers can use to evaluate multimedia resources so they can adopt those most likely to further student vocabulary learning.

In selecting videos, teachers will want to evaluate the extent to which the content is artful (for fiction) or accurate (for nonfiction) and engaging. Teachers will want to be sure that target words are well supported in the video. Specifically, teachers can ask the following questions:

- Are target words used repeatedly?
- Are definitions provided in the video?
- Do target words appear on the screen?
- Is the context supportive of word learning?
- Do visuals and animation support rather than detract from word learning?
- Is the pace appropriate (not too fast or too slow) to support word learning?

Finally, teachers should choose videos that are well aligned with their objectives and with how they are teaching content and words in class.

For choosing high-quality digital texts to use in instruction, we turn to criteria recently suggested by Cahill and McGill-Franzen (2013). These authors suggest choosing digital texts with:

- Engaging and artful writing
- Pictures and/or animation that support comprehension
- Expressive and fluent narration
- Meaningful and extensive interaction

Additionally, for vocabulary instruction, teachers should consider the following:

- Are target words printed and pronounced?
- Are definitions for target words easily accessible?
- Does the context provide support for word learning?
- Do pictures and animation support word learning?
- Do interactives foster vocabulary learning in a meaningful way?
- Is there review and repetition of words?

In general, teachers should make sure that digital texts have few distractions so that children can focus on the text and the words in the text. And teachers should make sure treatment of vocabulary in the digital text is consistent with treatment of vocabulary in regular classroom instruction.

To evaluate computer programs, games, and applications on the market, we refer to evaluation criteria suggested by Bishop and Santoro (2006) and Wood (2001). Bishop and Santoro (2006) provide a comprehensive approach to evaluating software that focuses on the interface design, the instructional design, and the content as three separate but related aspects to consider. Criteria related to the interface design, which refers to how the user interacts with the software, assess the extent to which the software is aesthetically pleasing, operationally supportive (i.e., instructions are clear and help is easily accessible), and interactive. Figure 8.4 lists some questions teachers can use to evaluate the interface design of software programs.

Criteria related to the instructional design, which refers to how the software is set up to support learning, evaluate the extent to which the software is systematic (e.g., builds on prerequisite knowledge and uses assessment data to pace instruction and review), is instructionally supportive (e.g., provides scaffolds and feedback), and is motivating. In Figure 8.5, we list some questions teachers can use to evaluate the instructional design of software programs.

Content-related criteria are particular to the components of reading targeted by the software program. Bishop and Santoro (2006) focused on phonological awareness and alphabetic skills in their review, so these content criteria are not appropriate for evaluating software targeting vocabulary learning. For guidance, we turn to research by Wood (2001), who developed five theoretically driven and research-based guidelines for evaluating the extent to which software programs support vocabulary learning. Figure 8.6 shows criteria for content that we adapted from Woods (2001).

Wood (2001) also developed a taxonomy for teaching vocabulary, adapted from Watts (1995), that captured research-based instructional practices for supporting vocabulary development. Based on our own work in classrooms (Silverman

Interface Design Criteria	Yes	No
1. Is the program's interface appealing to young children?		
2. Is the program's interface well organized and easy to navigate?		
3. Does the program's interface support rather than detract from student learning?		
4. Does the program's interface promote interaction with content?		
5. Is the interface modifiable for individual learners?		

FIGURE 8.4. Interface design criteria for digital vocabulary media. Adapted from Bishop and Santoro (2006). Copyright 2006 by Wiley Periodicals, Inc. Used with permission.

Instructional Design Criteria	Yes	No
1. Is the program set up to progress from easier to more difficult content?		
2. Is progression through the program based on students' performance?		
3. Does the program offer ample opportunity for practicing new skills?		
4. Does the program include support (e.g., prompts) and feedback when needed?		
5. Does the program incorporate review and recycling of previously learned skills?		
6. Does the program (a) save student work, (b) summarize student performance for teachers, and (c) use student assessment data to adjust pace and difficulty?		
7. Is the program fun and does it promote sustained engagement with content?		

FIGURE 8.5. Instructional design criteria for digital vocabulary media. Adapted from Bishop and Santoro (2006). Copyright 2006 by Wiley Periodicals, Inc. Used with permission.

& Crandell, 2010), we have modified this taxonomy somewhat to provide a checklist of types of research-based vocabulary instruction that could be included in educational software targeting vocabulary learning. (See Figure 8.7.) Of course, no one program could or should include all of these types of instruction at once, but teachers can use this list to determine how specific programs address vocabulary.

Since many software products become commercially available each day from relatively unknown publishers who claim that their program will drastically

Content Criteria	Yes	No
Does the software relate the new to the known?		
Does the software promote active, in-depth processing?		
Does the software provide multiple exposures of new words?		
Does the software teach students to be strategic readers?		
Does the software promote additional reading and exposure to words?		

FIGURE 8.6. Content criteria for digital vocabulary media. Adapted from Wood (2001). Copyright 2001 by Julie M. Wood. Used with permission.

Specific Content Criteria *Does the software program include the following?*	Not Included	Partially Included	Extensively Included
Well-chosen target words.			
Student-friendly definitions.			
Examples across contexts.			
Illustrations and animations of words.			
Attention to how words are related.			
Opportunities for word analysis and interaction with words.			
Attention to the sound and spelling of words.			
Attention to using word parts to figure out words.			
Attention to using context clues to figure out words.			
Attention to using resources to figure out words.			
Native language supports for ELLs.			

FIGURE 8.7. Specific content criteria for digital vocabulary media based on the criteria of Silverman and Crandell (2010) and Wood (2001).

From *Developing Vocabulary and Oral Language in Young Children*, by Rebecca D. Silverman and Anna M. Hartranft. Copyright 2015 by The Guilford Press. Permission to photocopy this figure is granted to purchasers of this book for personal use only (see copyright page for details). Purchasers can download a larger version of this figure from *www.guilford.com/silverman-forms*.

improve vocabulary, we feel we should discuss how to evaluate software. There-fore, we evaluate several products, from the many available software applications, using the criteria we discussed. We hope that these reviews can serve as models for teachers to use when reviewing programs they come across on their own.

In looking for applications to review, we referred to the Reading Rockets list of Top 13 Vocabulary Apps (*www.readingrockets.org/teaching/reading101/vocabu-lary/literacyapps_vocabulary*). Unfortunately, many of the apps (e.g., Bookworm, Chicktionary, Wurdle, Spelling Bee) used crossword, word search, or spelling bee formats, which confound spelling and vocabulary; some of the apps were outdated in terms of their look and feel (e.g., Opposite Ocean, Same Meaning Magic, Same Sound Spellbound); and some of the apps focused more on grammar than vocabulary (e.g., MadLibs, Word Sort, Preposition Builder). Thus, we deemed only two apps to be worth reviewing here. In the first app, the Opposites, children try to quickly match antonyms. The game is fast and fun; words are read orally to provide support for decoding; and the focus on word relations is valuable educationally. However, children already need to know the meaning of the words to succeed in the game, and there is little feedback for incorrect answers. Therefore, this app, like many other apps we have encountered, functions more like an assessment than a teaching tool.

In the second app, Word SLapPs, children are shown a set of pictures (e.g., of animals) and are asked to touch the picture that goes with the word they hear. Children might be asked to "find the ape" when shown a set of four pictures that include an ape, a cow, a zebra, and a lion. Teachers and parents can customize the app with their own pictures and words. The interface is simple and attractive for children, and the ability to touch pictures to play the game makes it easy to navigate. Content-wise, there are no definitions or examples across contexts included in the app, and children are not able to interact with words in meaningful ways beyond choosing the pictures that go with the words. Thus, children are unlikely to learn anything about the word beyond a specific association with a picture. Instructionally, the game begins by presenting one picture to go with one word and then increases in difficulty so that children are expected to choose one picture that matches the word out of a field of two, three, or more choices. If teachers or parents enter their own thematically related pictures and sequence them in a particular order, then words can be encountered in a systematic way. However, there appears to be little meaningful feedback in the program. If children touch the wrong answer, an X appears without any explanation or feedback on why the answer was incorrect. In general, this app could be useful for reviewing words already taught in class and building basic receptive vocabulary breadth of fairly imageable concepts. But its usefulness is narrow; and teachers and parents should employ the app only if they recognize its limitations. Hundreds of new apps come on the market every day, very few of which are vetted. Developers can make grand claims about the educational value of particular apps with little oversight. Therefore, teachers muct critically evaluate each app they consider for instruction.

Beyond apps, we identified specific websites that focus on vocabulary learning. On the PBS Kids website, there are a variety of games that focus on different reading and math skills. Teachers and parents can search for specific games related to specific skill sets. For example, games in the Curious George suite focus on math-related vocabulary such as *more* and *less*. Games that are part of the Dinosaur Train suite, which teaches science content, focus on words used to compare plants and animals such as *fastest* and *largest*. Another set of games, which are part of the Sid the Science Kid suite, target words having to do with our senses, the weather, and measurement. The interface for each of these games is kid-friendly and easy to use. The connection to familiar characters that children watch on TV is powerful for promoting motivation and engagement. The interface of these games promotes interaction with the content. The content within the games is related thematically, and there are multiple opportunities to engage with the words and content within the games. However, there are few definitions and examples of words across contexts. The games are interactive, but children are expected to know the words before they play the games, and there is little support for word learning embedded in the program. There is little feedback, and there is no way to differentiate the levels of the games or individualize them for students with particular needs. Thus, teachers could use these games for reinforcement of words, concepts, and content already taught in class, but children are unlikely to learn much vocabulary through these games without classroom-based instruction.

Aside from discrete web-based games, children can also explore virtual worlds that promote self-guided learning on various topics. The example we reviewed for this chapter was the National Geographic Kids Animal Jam website (*www.animal-jam.com/home*), which enables children to explore a fictional world called Jamaa and learn about real animals on Earth. For example, in an area of Jamaa called Brady's Expeditions, children can learn about constrictor snakes through video and text. Content words such as *constrictor* are highlighted through on-screen text. The video and text include a lot of sophisticated words such as *powerful, modify,* and *device.* The interface is interesting and easy to use and allows children to explore different areas within the fictional world of Jamaa. In terms of content, words are used in context and are related thematically to the content, but words are not explicitly taught through definitions and examples across contexts. Words are used multiple times as children explore the content, but they are not expected to interact with words in any meaningful way. And, despite the fact that words are used in context, there is no support for children to figure out word meaning using context clues, morphological word parts, or glossary resources. Instructionally, there is very little opportunity to practice using words or feedback on word use, and there is no leveling of children's experience based on assessment data. Overall, the National Geographic Kids Animal Jam program, like other programs in this genre (e.g., Discovery Kids Scuba Adventures, *http://kids.discovery.com/games/apps/discovery-kids-scuba-adventures*), offers exposure to lots of content-area and general academic words, but the instruction is not explicit and systematic. Thus, the program could, perhaps, be used as a supplement to regular classroom instruction on animal characteristics and habitats, for example, but it could not be used as a more comprehensive vocabulary program.

Besides websites that immerse children in virtual worlds, other websites aid children in exploring various topics of interest to them. One such website is Wonderopolis (*http://wonderopolis.org*), which was developed by the National Center for Families Learning and can be used at home and school to help parents and teachers "find learning moments in everyday life." The website explores everyday wonders through videos, text, and activities. For example, in one "wonder," children can explore how fairy tales may change if the ending is changed. The website provides "wonder words" that children can click on to look up a definition and a matching game to practice connecting words to their meaning. For example, on the fairy tales page, children can learn about the words *character, classic,* and *imagination.* It also includes story-, picture-, and video-sharing capability for students to upload their own work related to the topic. Because the interface is text heavy and the navigation is not kid-friendly, this website could be most effectively used by parents and teachers working with children to navigate the content. Parents and teachers could easily guide children to explore certain "wonders" related to the theme of focus in class. And the file-sharing features make the website interactive, so children can use words expressively and creatively in their own way. Thus, this kind of exploration website could be a great tool to use to enrich children's vocabulary learning in and out of school.

In addition to websites children can explore and Internet games children can play, there are software programs that can be purchased. Some software focuses specifically on vocabulary. Lakeshore Learning publishes several options. One is Vocabulary Tic-Tac-Toe for children in first through third grade. In this multiplayer game, children answer vocabulary-related questions in order to place an X or O in a square. As in traditional tic-tac-toe, children try to get three Xs or Os in a row to win. This game requires reading as the words and contexts are not read aloud to children. As with most software programs we have seen, there is little instruction and the game operates with an assessment-like format. There is little feedback. The program says, "Nice Try! Better luck next time!" when children get answers incorrect. But the questions in the game are meaning related (e.g., "What does the suffix *-est* in smartest mean? (a) more (b) most (c) less"). Questions focus on definitions, contexts, multiple meanings, and meaningful word parts, and many of the questions have picture support. If the skills included in the program align with skills taught in class, teachers could use this program to reinforce instruction.

Finally, some software programs that focus on reading in general include an emphasis on vocabulary. The two we review here are Reading Blaster and Reader Rabbit. Both programs cover a wide range of reading skills, but the attention to vocabulary is somewhat limited. In Reading Blaster, one of the games requires children to identify objects that fit within a semantic category (e.g., vegetables, clothing, things in the city) to reveal a hidden picture. The interface is child-friendly, the design is somewhat engaging, and the focus on word relations is aligned with research-based content. The game gets harder as children use it, and the game stores some, albeit minimal, data for teachers or parents to review after the children are done playing. However, the attention to vocabulary in the program does not appear systematic. There is no explicit instruction, and the game operates more like an assessment than an instructional support. In Reader Rabbit, students are exposed to vocabulary through an electronic text that functions like a book. Words such as *prize, trick, critter, prepare,* and *trade* are embedded in the text. Objects are labeled throughout the text, and children can click on them to hear them, but no definitions are provided when children click on objects or words and the target words are fairly basic (e.g., *swing, cloud, spaceship*). After reading, children are quizzed on vocabulary and comprehension and teachers and parents are given a brief report. As with Reading Blaster, the interface is child-friendly. However, the design is less engaging and interactive. Content-wise, exposure to vocabulary in the context of reading supports vocabulary learning, but explicit instruction with definitions, examples, and word analysis support children's word learning more than incidental exposure alone. In both of these programs, the focus is on decoding and sight word recognition more than vocabulary and comprehension, although the programs purport to address these areas as well. To truly support vocabulary learning, the programs would need to be much more systematic and explicit and give children more opportunities to interact with and use words across contexts.

In summary, although there are many different types of computer programs, Internet games, and software applications that address vocabulary to some extent, many of these assets do not fully align with research-based practice for effective vocabulary instruction. However, vocabulary programs that are more aligned with research-based practice may be on the horizon. As these programs, games, and applications become available for use in schools, teachers may wish to evaluate them using the criteria we have suggested to ensure that they are providing children with high-quality multimedia to promote their vocabulary development.

Enhancing Vocabulary Instruction through the Use of Multimedia

In addition to using specific software programs to support vocabulary development, teachers can use multimedia throughout instruction. Teachers can enhance vocabulary instruction with multimedia in several ways. One way to include multimedia in vocabulary instruction is through the use of PowerPoint or other presentation software programs such as Prezi and Keynote. In our research, we have created PowerPoint presentations that introduce new vocabulary, show how vocabulary can be used across contexts, and support student engagement in vocabulary learning. For example, on the slide in Figure 8.8, we wrote the word *habitat* so children could see it in print. We also provided the definition and two examples of the word. Finally, we included a Spanish translation for the Spanish-speaking ELLs in class. On the next slide we displayed two habitats and asked children to say which animals lived in each habitat using the target word. Thus, children were supported in using the word in new contexts.

Another way teachers can incorporate technology into their vocabulary lessons is through multimedia word investigations. Teachers can sequence websites for children to explore with the whole class, in small groups, in pairs, or individually through programs like QuestGarden and TrackStar. Then teachers can guide

habitat

A **habitat**
means a place where people or
animals live.

Español: habitat

PET

☐ Pronounce

☐ Explore

☐ Try it out

Camels live in a desert **habitat**.
Penguins live in an icy **habitat**.

FIGURE 8.8. Multimedia slide for vocabulary instruction. Desert image Copyright 2006 by Steve D. Brown. Arctic image Copyright 2011 by Liam Quinn. Reprinted by permission.

children through a web-based experience in which they hear or read definitions, synonyms, and examples involving target words (*http://visual.merriam-webster.com/index.php*). Children can learn about the etymology of target words (*http://public.oed.com/aspects-of-english/word-stories*) and examine a visual thesaurus (*www.visualthesaurus.com*) showing how words are related to the target words. They can hear the word translated (*http://translate.google.com*) and can see visual maps of texts using the word through Wordle (*www.wordle.net*) or WordSift (*www.wordsift.com*).

Finally, teachers can use multimedia to engage children in expressing their knowledge of words through such programs as Kidspiration (*www.inspiration.com/kidspiration*), in which children can create concept maps that show important features of words or word webs that show how words are related. Teachers can also support children in using words they are learning in their own multimedia stories or blogs through websites like Glogster (*www.glogster.com*), Kerpoof (*www.kerpoof.com*), Storybird (*storybird.com*), Smories (*www.smories.com*), and Voice Thread (*voicethread.com*). Using any of these sites, teachers can help children create personal stories, reports, or word walls that include the new words they are learning. Thus multimedia can be an effective tool throughout vocabulary instruction for introducing words to children, helping them engage with words, and supporting them as they use words in multiple contexts.

Summary

In this chapter, we reviewed a host of ways that you can incorporate multimedia into vocabulary instruction to promote children's breadth and depth of word knowledge. The value of multimedia is that it inherently provides verbal and nonverbal information and multiple means of representation, action and expression, and engagement. Thus, multimedia offers access to words and support for word learning to a wide range of children. Teachers need to be critical consumers of multimedia programs and evaluate them carefully to ensure they are optimally designed to support student learning. But, if wisely integrated into a comprehensive, research-based vocabulary program, multimedia can enhance instruction and optimize vocabulary learning for children with diverse strengths and needs in prekindergarten through second-grade classrooms. In the next chapter, we turn to how home–school connections, which can include multimedia, may be used to foster vocabulary development in and out of school.

CHAPTER 9

· · · · · · · · · · ·

Home–School Connections to Support Word Learning

GUIDING QUESTIONS

· ·

- How can home–school communication support vocabulary learning in school?
- How can parent involvement support vocabulary learning in school?
- What are the characteristics of home–school connection programs that have been shown to promote vocabulary?

Back to School Night at Hillside Elementary is a festive event. The school is packed with parents and children. Excitement is in the air. Mr. Frazier introduces himself to the parents of the first graders in his class. He explains the curriculum and tells the parents that vocabulary will be a major instructional focus in his first-grade class this year. The parents nod their heads and smile broadly. At the end of the night, as he cleans up his classroom, Mr. Frazier is somewhat somber. Last year after Back to School Night, he didn't see many of the parents again until the end-of-school-year celebration. He wishes he could build on parents' excitement from Back to School Night and somehow develop a more productive and collaborative home–school partnership this year. He knows that he needs to do more to draw parents in and get them involved in supporting their children's vocabulary learning in school.

There are too many words to learn and not enough time in the school day for teachers to provide all of the support students need for development of vocabulary breadth and depth. Fortunately, teachers can work with parents to provide support word learning beyond the classroom. Parents are children's first vocabulary teachers, and they encourage children's word learning whenever they read to or talk with their children. However, teachers and parents are often not on the same page, so to speak, on how they read to children or how they support children's word learning. When teachers and parents are aligned in this endeavor, children are likely to learn more words, more quickly, and in more depth. For children who have limited academic English vocabulary, greater alignment of vocabulary instruction between home and school could be crucial. Thus, teachers should work with parents to foster home–school connections to support children's vocabulary breadth and depth.

Teachers must understand, value, and respect what parents are already doing on a regular basis to immerse their children in language. Among other things, parents read to their children, sing to their children, and share stories with their children. They also ask children to tell them about their day and use words effectively to communicate, politely, their wants and needs. Teachers should build home–school connections that are bidirectional so that parents can learn from what teachers are doing in school and teachers can learn from what parents are doing at home to provide optimal support for vocabulary development. In fact, recent research shows that educator outreach and family involvement are both important predictors of children's vocabulary and early literacy skills (Hindman & Morrison, 2011).

In this chapter, we discuss various ways you can work with parents to support your students' vocabulary learning in and out of school. In the first half of the chapter, we review ways you can communicate with and involve parents in their children's vocabulary learning. The research on communicating with and involving parents is thin, so we offer suggestions based on lessons learned from studies that have looked at relationships between parent involvement and home literacy practices and students' academic success (e.g., Bracken & Fischel, 2008; Fischel & Ramirez, 2005), studies of multicomponent programs that have included home–school connection activities (Meier & Sullivan, 2004), and studies of larger home–school connections programs (e.g., Jordan et al., 2000). In the second half of the chapter, we take a close look at a few of these programs that have had positive effects on children's vocabulary development. Whether you implement small-scale or large-scale initiatives to connect with parents, your efforts will pay dividends in both immediate and long-term effects on children's vocabulary development.

Home–School Communication

Bridging home and school through consistent communication with parents is a promising way to support vocabulary learning beyond the classroom. Teachers can send home traditional newsletters, post information on their websites or blogs, or send information to parents through e-mail, text, or Twitter. Regardless of the medium, the content of the communication is critically important. The content should be focused on (1) specific themes and words that are being studied in the classroom and (2) general strategies and activities parents can use to support children's word learning. We discuss how to involve parents in both of these tasks.

Communication about the Classroom Curriculum

In order to reinforce words taught in school at home, parents need to know what themes and words teachers are teaching and what activities parents can do to support children's learning of the words and content. Since parents may not have time or access to look up words and research content, teachers should provide enough information so that parents can figure out what to do fairly easily. Projects that require a lot of extra materials and time will be hard for parents to implement. And, since vocabulary learning should be fun, teachers should avoid adding any stress to the situation. Even assignments that seem so simple, such as "Send in a picture of your child and his or her *relatives* to share with the class," can be stressful for parents who do not have pictures already printed out at home. Completing this assignment could require going to a store after work with hungry and tired kids in tow to print out pictures. Ugh! If a child does not bring in a home-based project, a teacher should not assume that the parents are lazy or uninterested. Rather, teachers should recognize that parents are often overwhelmed with all that they must do to care and provide for their families. So, teachers should be thoughtful about how to engage parents in simple and stress-free ways. Figure 9.1 shows the kinds of information and resources parents need in order to reinforce word learning. Figure 9.2 is a sample newsletter for parents that has information on the theme and the words that are being taught in school, definitions for parents to use when they talk with children, and a fairly easy activity that reinforces word learning. Other activities that can motivate parents to support children's word learning at home are described in Figure 9.3.

Information	Resources
• What theme are you working on? • What words are you teaching? • What are the definitions you are teaching? • What are some examples you have used in class? • How should I talk with my children about these words?	• What books should I read with my child on this theme? Can I check them out of the classroom or school library? • What games or activities should I do with my child to reinforce themes and words?

FIGURE 9.1. What parents want to know about teaching vocabulary.

Wonder Words to Review at Home Monthly Theme: *Habitats*	
Weekly Word List	**Activity for the Week**
• *Identify*: When you identify something, you say what it is. • *Habitat*: A habitat is a place where an animal lives. • *Observe*: When you observe something, you look at it closely. • *Depend*: When you depend on something, you need it.	• Observe the habitat in your backyard. • Identify the plants and animals (e.g., bugs) that live there. • Talk about what the plants and animals depend on. • Write in your home-school connections journal about what you saw and discussed.
Parents, please ask children about their wonder words and do the activity with them. Ask them questions about what they observe and identify in the backyard!	

FIGURE 9.2. Weekly parent newsletter example.

The most important characteristics of these activities are that (1) they encourage use of the target words, (2) they are interactive and support parent–child conversation about words, and (3) they are easy to implement in the everyday lives of busy families. Teachers can use these activities or devise their own ways of engaging parents in using words taught in school with their children. In fact, teachers may enlist parents in coming up with new ways to support word learning at home!

REINFORCING VOCABULARY AT HOME

The Miller family, which includes second grader Kelly and kindergartener Miles and their parents, Mike and Sam, has a Wonder Words dry-erase board in their kitchen. When the children get off the bus on Mondays, Mike looks through Kelly's bag to find her homework folder for the week. In her folder, he finds a newsletter with the weekly theme and vocabulary words along with suggestions of books to read and websites to explore. When they get inside, Mike writes the weekly words on a chart on the dry-erase board. This week, the words are related to transportation (i.e., *speeding, accelerate, decelerate, travel, vehicle, depart, arrive, delay*). Mike proceeds to fix dinner while the children watch television. When Sam gets home, the family sits down to eat. Mike asks Kelly to read the Wonder Words for the week. Throughout dinner, each family member, even Miles, tries to weave the Wonder Words into conversation about the day. Sam talks about the delay on the commute home on the metro; Mike talks about their plans for traveling over winter break; Kelly talks about all the different kinds of vehicles she saw on the way home from school; and Miles talks about how his toy cars can speed really fast. As they eat and talk, Kelly puts a tally by each word that is used. After dinner, she tallies up the number of times they used the words and records that number on a progress chart in her homework folder. Using Wonder Words at dinner is a fairly easy way to integrate reinforcement of school vocabulary into regular Miller family activities.

Activity	Description
Favorite word activity	Parents and children vote on their favorite word and talk about why it is their favorite. Families send in votes and they are tallied in class. The winning word is announced each week.
Word-use game	Parents and children try to use a target word appropriately in context as many times as they can at dinner. Parents keep a tally and send it in the next day so teachers can celebrate classwide word use.
"Guess my word" game	Parents can choose one of the words they have learned in school over the past month and ask children to guess their word. They can give children clues about the word, or children can ask questions about the word as they try to guess.
Word puzzles	Teachers can send home word puzzles for parents and children to do together. Teachers can provide clues for the parent to read that lead children to figuring out the mystery word.
Word art	Teachers can ask parents to help their children make artwork through drawing, painting, or collage making to illustrate certain words. Parents and children can work together to decide what to make. Then children can bring their creation to school to share with their classmates.
Word journals	Teachers can ask parents to keep a word journal with their children about when they have heard or used words taught in school on a particular theme. Parents can send in the journal periodically so the teacher can use examples from different families when she reviews words in class.
Reading books related to taught words	Teachers can send home lists of books that include either target words or content related to target words. These books could have been read in class or they could be new. Teachers can create a lending library in class for parents to check these books out or have them on reserve in the school library for parents to check out. They can even include bookmarks in the book for questions parents can ask about content and words in the books while they are reading. Reading additional books with words and content connected to class is a great way to reinforce children's word learning.

FIGURE 9.3. Parent and child activities that support word learning at home.

Communication about Strategies and Activities beyond the Classroom Curriculum

Beyond enlisting parents in supporting vocabulary instruction introduced in class, teachers can help parents create a language-rich environment at home that builds children's vocabulary breadth and depth. Specific routines and activities can be used at home on a regular basis to support children's word learning. As with the suggestions for supporting parents in reinforcing words taught in school, implementing these routines and activities on a regular basis should be easy to do and lots of fun too. They should also fit well into parents' regular routines so parents can incorporate them seamlessly into their lives and use them consistently over time. Teachers should encourage parents of ELLs to use their native language when using these activities. Research shows long-term academic benefits for ELLs who have a solid foundation in their native language (August & Shanahan, 2006). Figure 9.4 features some primarily oral language and book-based suggestions for general vocabulary-related activities that parents can use.

Besides these suggested activities, parents can also foster vocabulary learning through multimedia. Specifically, parents can co-view educational television programs with their children and ask questions or call attention to words in the programs while they are watching. Recently, Strouse, O'Doherty, and Troseth (2013) studied parents' use of the dialogic reading approach during co-viewing of educational television programs and found positive effects on preschoolers' story comprehension and story vocabulary. Similarly, parents can foster children's language and literacy learning in the context of digital texts. Korat, Shamir, and Heibal (2013) conducted a study with kindergarten children and their mothers from families of low socioeconomic status. Children and their mothers were assigned to one of three conditions: (1) digital text reading, (2) regular book reading, and (3) a

---

PROMOTING VOCABULARY LEARNING IN EVERYDAY ROUTINES

Ms. Desai drives her three boys, including a second grader, a first grader, and a preschooler, to school and day care each morning. To avoid the inevitable scuffles that ensue when there is no structured activity in place, Ms. Desai tells the children it is time to play 20 Questions. She says she will start and think of something. (She tries to think of a subject at least one of the boys is studying in school.) Each boy gets a turn to ask a question about what she is thinking and make a guess. Whichever boy guesses correctly first gets to think of something and have the other boys and their mother guess. If the boys get to 20 questions before they guess, Ms. Desai gets to pick again. The boys play this game with their mother for a half hour in the car, and before they know it they have arrived at school without bickering. Ms. Desai has implemented a routine to get her sons to use language in an engaging (and practical) way.

Routine	Description
Read and talk about books every day	Parents can establish a time for daily book reading and encourage children to talk about books and words every day.
Establish a family theater time to act out stories together	Parents can support children in acting out a story or putting on a puppet show portraying a story for other family members. Parents can encourage children to use words they heard in the original story.
Write books about family adventures and children's interests	Parents can help children write books at home. These books can be about family activities or anything of interest to the child. Parents can even help children research information children would like to include in their books. Parents can encourage children to use interesting words in their writing.
Keep a family journal or create a family scrapbook	Parents and children can capture memories of family activities in a family journal that they can add to over time. Or parents and children can annotate pictures in a family photo album that is kept over time. Parents can encourage children to use interesting words to describe what they did or what they see in the picture. Parents and children can revisit these again and again once they are made.
Engage in family storytelling	Parents and children can hold a weekly storytelling time in which they tell a story about something that happened to them that week or something that they made up. All family members can gather around and listen and ask questions throughout the story. In this activity, parents can model use of sophisticated words during storytelling, and children can engage in use of sophisticated words as well.
Encourage oral language use in art and building activities	Parents can encourage children to express themselves through a variety of different forms of art including drawing, painting, and collage making. They can also encourage children to express themselves through building structures with a variety of different materials. While children are working on their projects, parents can ask children to name and describe what they are making and ask children questions about what they are making that encourage active language use.
Play Categories, I Spy, and 20 Questions	Whether in the grocery store or on a long car ride, parents often need to keep children entertained during regular daily activities so they don't get out of control. Playing word games is a great way to support vocabulary and keep children occupied at the same time. In Categories, parents give children the name of a category, such as *occupations*, and children have to name as many things in that category as they can. This game helps build semantic awareness. In I Spy, parents can describe something they see (e.g., "I spy with my little eye something *enormous*") and children have to try to guess what it is. This game supports awareness of descriptive words. Finally, in 20 Questions, parents think of something (e.g., a skyscraper), and children can ask up to 20 questions to help them guess what it is (e.g., "Is it a person, place, or thing? Is it big or small? Is it colorful or black and white?"). Like I Spy, this game encourages use of descriptive language skills.

FIGURE 9.4. Parent and child routines that support word learning at home.

regular classroom program with no additional intervention. Mothers were given guidance on effective ways to read to their children. They practiced reading with their children in the context of the study over the course of 5 weeks. Children in both the digital text and regular book-reading conditions showed significant progress in phonological awareness and vocabulary, suggesting that digital texts are at least as useful as regular books for supporting students' language and literacy skills. However, Parish-Morris et al. (2013) caution that digital texts with too many bells and whistles (e.g., gimmicky hotspots and non-content-related interactive features) may deter rich parent–child communication during storybook reading, so parents should be provided with information on how to choose digital texts that will promote rather than deter dialogic conversation. Finally, there are many apps and software programs that parents can access to encourage word learning. Not all apps and programs are created equal, as we discussed in the previous chapter, but parents can be steered toward choosing the apps and programs that best adhere to research-based practice. (Note that teachers can adapt some of our recommendations in Chapter 8 for parents' use.)

Involving Parents
in Vocabulary Instruction in School

In addition to helping parents reinforce children's use of words learned in school at home, teachers can invite parents to actively participate in vocabulary instruction in school. This kind of parent involvement serves several purposes:

1. Parents become engaged in their children's school learning.
2. Parents learn how teachers are talking about books and words in school.
3. Parents can share experiences and words important in their cultural context.
4. Teachers can have help managing a roomful of busy students.
5. Children can have more opportunities to learn from and talk with others about content and words they are learning in school.

Here are some ways teachers can invite parents into their classrooms to support word learning.

- Teachers can invite parents to come tell a story or read a book to the class that is related to the theme and the words children are learning in school.
- Teachers can ask parents to come to school to read with individual children or with pairs of children working together who may need extra support.
- Teachers can invite parents to introduce a weekly mystery word in class. Parents can describe the word before revealing it. Then they can tell a story or read a book using the mystery word.

- Teachers can encourage parents to come to school to help with class projects related to themes and words taught in school. For example, parents can help make class books, murals, or dioramas on particular themes using target words.
- Teachers can ask parents to attend field trips that broaden the experiences related to the theme and words introduced in class.
- Teachers can also invite parents to lead their own virtual field trip in school related to the theme or words taught in class.

Getting parents involved with supporting children's word learning in school can be a great way to engage parents in the classroom community and capitalize on their knowledge, expertise, and creativity.

Programs to Promote Home–School Connections

A wide range of programs supports parents in helping their children in reading and writing. Recently, van Steensel, McElvany, Kurvers, and Herppich (2011) reviewed family literacy programs to determine the effects of these programs on comprehension-related and code-related skills. These researchers borrowed Hannon

INVOLVING PARENTS IN VOCABULARY LEARNING AT SCHOOL

Mrs. Gonzales, whose daughter, Maria, is in kindergarten, volunteers in her daughter's classroom on Tuesday and Thursday mornings. Mrs. Gonzales does not go in to work at a local grocery store until noon on those days. When she is at school, she works with children during centers time. In particular, she reads with children in the library area and helps children make books in the writing area. When she gets to school, Maria's teacher, Ms. Gregory, communicates with Mrs. Gonzales about the theme and words that were introduced that week and points toward the vocabulary word wall so Mrs. Gonzales can use it as a reference when she works with children. In the library center, Mrs. Gonzales reads books on the weekly theme with children as they take turns in the center. She refers to the word wall to remember which words are targeted that week. After a while, Mrs. Gonzales moves to the writing center. She prompts children to write about the theme and use the words in their writing. She provides encouragement for children to use invented spellings and draw about what they are writing. (Mrs. Gonzales has been in the classroom for a couple of months now, and she has learned a lot of the language that Ms. Gregory uses when she is working with children.) Mrs. Gonzales also helps children publish their work by laminating and binding pages for the children. Besides being a great help to Ms. Gregory, Mrs. Gonzales is able to see what her daughter is working on in school and what kind of vocabulary she can use to support her. In fact, she now regularly reviews words and concepts at home with her daughter and brings home books on the class theme to read with her daughter at home.

and Bird's (2004) definition of family literacy programs: "programmes to teach literacy that acknowledge and make use of learners' family relationships and engagement in family literacy practices" (p. 24). After reviewing 30 studies conducted across two decades, these researchers found that, although content, implementation, and effects varied across studies, family literacy programs, on average, show positive effects on children's literacy skills. Within the set of studies that focused on comprehension-related skills, many specifically included attention to and effects on vocabulary. In the following section, we review studies that include attention to vocabulary and evaluate the strengths and limitations of each approach.

Dialogic Reading Family Literacy Programs

One approach to supporting parents in promoting their children's early language and literacy skills is the dialogic reading approach that we discussed in Chapter 4. Several studies have been conducted over the years in which parents of children ages 3–5 were trained to use the dialogic reading approach at home while reading books with their children (e.g., Lonigan & Whitehurst, 1998; Whitehurst et al., 1994). Research comparing the effect of dialogic reading at school, at home, and at school and home together show that school-plus-home intervention had the strongest effects on children's vocabulary development. As we discussed in Chapter 4, the dialogic reading approach includes questioning and prompting children during reading to foster extended conversations about text. In the dialogic reading approach, parents are taught to: (1) ask their child open-ended questions, (2) follow their child's answers with questions, (3) repeat their child's answers, (4) assist their child as needed, (5) praise and encourage their child, and (6) follow their child's interests. Specifically, parents are taught to follow the sequence in Figure 9.5 during book reading. Using this approach, parents support children in learning both contextualized (i.e., in the book) and decontextualized (i.e., outside of the book) language to talk about text and the world outside of the text.

In 2004, Pearson published a program called Read Together, Talk Together (Whitehurst & National Center for Learning Disabilities, 2004) that guides parents

---

- Introduce the book by reading the title and author and asking children to predict what the book might be about.

- Read the book using:
  o CROWD Questions (Completion, Recall, Open-Ended, *Wh-*, and Distancing)
  o The PEER Sequence (Prompt, Evaluate, Expand, and Repeat)

- Close the book and ask questions that help children connect the book to their everyday lives.

FIGURE 9.5. Parent procedures in the dialogic reading approach. Based on Zevenbergen and Whitehurst (2003).

of children from ages 2–5 on how to use dialogic reading with young children. The Read Together, Talk Together kit includes a program handbook, a video for teachers and a video for parents, and materials for program implementation (i.e., books and notes for teachers and parents to use while reading books with children). The videos describe dialogic reading and include demonstrations of teachers and parents reading with children using the approach. Typically, training occurs over two sessions. In these sessions, parents watch the video on dialogic reading and then participate in one-on-one role play with a parent educator. Role play includes having parents practice responding to different types of child behaviors and providing feedback on parents' response. The program can be modified according to the needs of the school and community, but having been implemented worldwide, it can easily be applied in most contexts.

There are several advantages in teaching parents to use the dialogic reading approach in reading books with their children to promote vocabulary development. The program requires few materials and minimal parent training. Therefore, it is cost effective and logistically easy to implement. Parents can use a wide variety of books as they implement the program, which allows for flexibility and differentiation depending on the student's interests and the available books in the home. Most important, effects across studies are robust, particularly on children's expressive vocabulary (e.g., Lonigan & Whitehurst, 1998; Whitehurst et al., 1994). This means that the resources invested in the dialogic reading program, both from the school's and the parent's perspective, are highly likely to yield substantial and positive results. However, the limitations of the program should be noted as well. Dialogic reading lacks an explicit vocabulary instruction component, meaning that parents are not taught how to provide child-friendly definitions of words and examples across contexts. Furthermore, the program does not discuss how parent-to-child language can be extended beyond storybook reading time. Finally, the approach does not tap into what parents may already be doing naturally in the home to support children's language development. Despite these limitations and because of the ease of implementation and the positive effects of the program, holding workshops to teach parents to use the dialogic reading approach at home is a good option for teachers who want to build home–school connections. Teachers of children ages 6–8 could easily adapt the dialogic reading prompts to be appropriate for slightly older learners and teach parents to use these prompts when reading with their children, thus leveraging dialogic reading to help parents in their efforts to support the vocabulary development of older children as well.

A Family Literacy Program Focused on Oral Language

Although less well known than the dialogic reading approach, Project EASE (Easy Access to Success in Education) is another family literacy program that has demonstrated positive effects on young children's vocabulary growth. Jordan et al. (2000) found that kindergarten children whose parents participated in the program advanced more in vocabulary, as well as in comprehension and storytelling, than children whose parents did not participate in the program. The Project EASE program consisted of monthly meetings at children's schools and weekly follow-up activities to be conducted at home. The program ran for 5 months, and each month focused on a different aspect of early language and literacy. The topics addressed in the program are (1) storybook reading, (2) working with words, (3) letter recognition and sound awareness, (4) retelling family narratives, and (5) talking about the world through the use of nonfiction text. Language was addressed throughout each program topic, but, obviously, vocabulary was the primary focus of the second topic.

Each month, parents met with a parent educator who presented information on the topic at hand. Then, immediately following the presentation, parents engaged in activities related to the topic of that session with their children. Finally, parents were provided with activities to implement at home with their children on a regular basis. During the month focused on vocabulary, the parent educator discussed the main points listed in Figure 9.6. Parents were given examples of activities to foster word learning and encouraged to help their children to label, define, describe, and relate words and their attributes across activities. Then parents participated in the activities outlined in Figure 9.7, which had been introduced in the parent session, with their children in school.

Following the session on vocabulary, parents were given a guide reviewing what the parent educator had presented. They also received tools and materials each week in the month after the vocabulary session to support trying out what had been presented in the session. For example, parents were given books, suggestions for discussing the books with their children, and activities to do with their children to support vocabulary learning. The activities that were sent home were designed to promote defining, categorizing, and relating words and using words to describe and discuss concepts and topics that are important to children and their families.

---

1. Parents are the first source of vocabulary development for their children and they continue to be a critical source for verbal interactions.

2. Parents can influence and broaden their child's vocabulary by the kinds of interactions they have at home.

3. Activities that help broaden a child's vocabulary include book reading, extended conversations (e.g., at mealtimes), and discussions about events and/or concepts that go beyond the "here and now."

4. Vocabulary will greatly impact their child's literacy development throughout the school years; in particular it will impact reading comprehension and written language performance.

FIGURE 9.6. Vocabulary information presented to parents in Project EASE. Adapted from Jordan, Snow, and Porche (2000). Copyright 2000 by the International Reading Association. Used with permission.

1. Making pictorial word webs about a single topic (e.g., things to do outside, things about school, favorite things to do on vacation).

2. Guessing the names of items from verbal clues. Children describe items to parents and have them guess, and parents read riddles to children to have them name the items.

3. Reading books together that have an array of words centered on a single topic.

4. Reading books that require the child to guess items hidden under a flap.

5. Making associations between words as to how they are alike and different.

FIGURE 9.7. Parent and child vocabulary activities in Project EASE. Adapted from Jordan, Snow, and Porche (2000). Copyright 2000 by the International Reading Association. Used with permission.

As noted, while vocabulary was the main focus of one of the sessions in Project EASE, the other topics addressed in the project also encouraged parents to introduce words and support word learning. For example, in the session on reading narratives, parents learned that "children are introduced to rare words, longer and more complex sentences, and distant concepts" through fiction texts. And in the session on reading nonfiction books with young children, parents were taught that "text centered on a single topic introduces rare and specific words which help develop their vocabulary." Thus, parents were encouraged to read with children and discuss words with children throughout the entire program.

The strength of the Project EASE program lies in the ongoing guidance and support it gives parents in encouraging their children's language and literacy development beyond school. The program focused on integrating language and literacy into regular routines such as book reading and mealtime, car trips, and bedtime conversation. The program supplied parents with (1) information on how to support their children's language and literacy, (2) practice implementing strategies to support their children's language and literacy, and (3) activities to carry out with their children at home to reinforce language and literacy learning. Given the sustained support parents received in the program, it is likely that they continued using many of the practices they learned in Project EASE well after the program had ended.

Project EASE was initially implemented in a suburban school district with a limited number of students from minority or ELL backgrounds. Thus, the gap between the language and culture of the school and the language and culture of the home was likely not as wide as it would be in a district with a greater number of students from minority or ELL backgrounds. If Project EASE were to be implemented in a school with high numbers of children from minority and ELL backgrounds, teachers would want to modify the program to reflect the cultural and linguistic diversity of parents and students in the population. For example, San Francisco, Mo, Carlo, August, and Snow (2006) developed a Spanish-language version of the program for use with low-income families in Costa Rica. Research on the Costa Rican adaptation of the project did not show robust effects on vocabulary, but the authors suggested that the intervention may have needed to be more intensive to show meaningful differences in the vocabulary development of children from low-income backgrounds in the Costa Rican context. Thus, teachers who want to implement a program like Project EASE to support the vocabulary learning of children at risk for experiencing difficulty in school should consider developing maximally intensive programs to foster strong and stable home–school connections over time.

A Family Literacy Program Focused on Reading *and* Writing

Saint-Laurent and Giasson (2005) studied a family literacy program targeting parents of first graders with a special emphasis on writing in addition to reading. The program focused on book reading that adapts to children's growing skills and interactive writing for a variety of purposes. The program included nine bimonthly workshops, each of which lasted for 90 minutes. The content for each workshop is outlined in Figure 9.8. During each workshop, the facilitator guided discussion on previous workshop topics, led discussion on the new workshop topic, demonstrated key strategies parents could use within each topic, supported parent practice with other parents or children, reviewed key points about the topic, and presented activities related to the topic that parents could do at home. Parents were provided with a guide, materials to use throughout the program, and a refrigerator magnet with key points from the program to help them remember what they learned over time.

Saint-Laurent and Giasson (2005) then compared the outcomes of students whose families had participated in the program with the outcomes of students whose families did not participate in the program. Parents who participated in the program reported that they were very satisfied with the program and had applied what they learned in the program with their children. Overall, children whose parents participated performed better on reading and writing measures. Significantly, they produced longer narratives that included better vocabulary, sentence structure, and spelling.

The strength of this program was threefold: (1) it focused on reading and writing and attention to vocabulary within each domain, (2) it focused on how children develop over time and how parents can support them at different stages of development, and (3) it focused on the role of parents in modeling and guiding children to become proficient readers and writers. The program also provided parents with strategies and materials as well as time to practice, discuss, and ask questions about what they were learning in the workshops. The program's limitations included its potential lack of generalizability to contexts with high numbers of minority and ELL students. As with Project EASE, this program was conducted subsequently with children of nonminority status. The study, conducted in Quebec, Canada, included mostly Caucasian, French-speaking children. However,

Workshop	Description
Book reading and school success	This session included an introduction to the program and information about the importance of book reading at home.
Importance of book reading in grade 1	This session focused on asking children questions to support vocabulary and comprehension before, during, and after reading.
Library visits	This session included a guided tour of the library to support book borrowing.
Playing with letters	This session focused on writing and invented spelling.
Everyday literacy	This session focused on literacy activities to do regularly at home.
Listening to a beginning reader	This session focused on the reading strategies of beginning readers and the power of parental scaffolding through dialogue.
Writing plays	This session focused on using writing to communicate messages and the role of parents in supporting writing development.
Listening to a developing reader	This session focused on guiding developing readers who are beginning to read on their own using prompting to support decoding and questioning to support vocabulary and comprehension.
Synthesis and party	This session provided a review of all of the content in the program and a celebration of parent and student success in the program.

FIGURE 9.8. Components of family literacy workshops. Adapted from Saint-Laurent and Giasson (2005). Copyright 2005 by Saint-Laurent and Giasson. Used with permission.

children in the study were from middle *and* lower socioeconomic backgrounds. Interestingly, results did not differ for children from different backgrounds. For teachers looking for comprehensive family literacy program that engages parents in supporting children's vocabulary through reading *and* writing, a program such as the one described by Saint-Laurent and Giasson (2005) may be of interest. As with all programs reviewed here, though, the program may need to be modified to meet the needs of parents and children in different contexts.

A Family Literacy Program Focused on ELLs

Project FLAME (*www.uic.edu/educ/flame/index.html*), which stands for Family Literacy: Aprendiendo, Mejorando, Educando (Learning, Bettering, Educating), is a family literacy program focused on meeting the needs of Latino parents learning to speak English alongside their children (Shanahan et al., 1995). Targeting parents of children ages 3–9, the program includes English as a second language (ESL) instruction to parents and teaches parents how to support their children's language and literacy development. Parents attend twice-weekly ESL classes and twice-monthly parenting education classes. Parents also participate in less structured field trips and meetings to learn about community resources.

Project FLAME focuses on the importance of family in the Latino culture and strives to provide culturally responsive instruction for parents and their children. Parent input and feedback are critical components of the program. And to empower parents in supporting their children's language and literacy development, the program positions parents as teachers and integrates the experiences of parents and children. It builds on social relationships, using group classes to foster community and support, and adapts to the needs and concerns of parents. Yet, the program is structured and includes ways to support children in strengthening the academic language and literacy needed for school success. The topics covered over the course of 14 parent workshops are featured in Figure 9.9.

Shanahan and colleagues (1995), who studied the program over the course of 5 years, found that participation in the program led to positive results for parents and children. As noted on the Project FLAME website:

> Annual evaluation results show that children of participating families show significant gains. These gains are evident in cognitive development, pre-literacy and literacy skills, and vocabulary development in both Spanish and English. Results further show that parents change their attitudes towards teaching their children and also become more proficient in English as shown by significant gains in English proficiency as measured by the Language Assessment Scales (LAS). (*www. uic.edu/educ/flame/flameobjectives.html*)

Shanahan et al. suggest that the strength of the program rests in its sensitivity to cultural context, its use of collaborative learning among parents, and its responsiveness to the experiences, needs, and abilities of the parent participants. Project FLAME was designed to be situated in Spanish-speaking Latino communities to support the language and literacy of both parents and their children. One of its drawbacks, however, is that while it strongly focuses on book reading and writing in general, it does not include a full session on supporting vocabulary at home. Thus, programs for parents from other cultural and linguistic backgrounds may need to be structured differently to be optimally responsive to students' needs. Given that vocabulary is a major barrier to comprehension for many ELLs (August & Shanahan, 2006), teachers who choose to implement a program similar to this one may want to consider spending a full workshop session on supporting vocabulary development.

A Family Literacy Program
Specifically Targeting Vocabulary

The final family literacy program we review is one we conducted as part of our reading buddies program (Silverman, Martin-Beltran, Peercy, & Meyer, 2014). The reading buddies family literacy program was closely tied to the curriculum

Workshop Title	Workshop Description
Creating home literacy centers	Parents learn how to create a home literacy center with such items as pencils, crayons, paper, scissors, paste, magazines, and pictures and use it to foster children's literacy.
Book sharing	Parents learn how to effectively share books and talk about books with children even if parents have limited literacy.
Book selection	Parents are taught criteria for selecting appropriate books for their children.
Library visit	Parents are taught how to use the library to find books for their children.
Book fairs	Parents are provided with support for purchasing books for their home library in English or Spanish.
Teaching the ABCs	Parents are taught simple ways to teach letters and sounds.
Songs, games, and language*	Parents are taught to use songs, games, and language experience activities to promote language and literacy.
Children's writing	Parents are provided information on how children develop writing and how to support writing development.
Community literacy	Parents are guided to think about how they can share their own language and literacy with children through everyday experiences in the community (e.g., grocery shopping).
Classroom observations	Parents are invited to observe in their children's classrooms so they gain an understanding of how language and literacy are taught in schools.
Parent–teacher get-togethers	Parents are invited to participate in guided discussions with teachers and principals about their children's education in school.
Math at home	Parents are provided with games and activities to do at home to encourage math skills.
Homework help	Parents are taught how to support children in doing their homework even when they can't do it themselves.

FIGURE 9.9. The components of the Project FLAME parent workshops. *Not included in the original session plan but listed on the Project FLAME website. Adapted from Shanahan, Mulhern, and Rodriguez-Brown (1995). Copyright 1995 by the International Reading Association. Used with permission.

and, in fact, taught parents to use the same vocabulary learning strategies teachers and children were using in school. We implemented the family literacy program in the evenings in a school with large numbers of Spanish-speaking ELL students. While the reading buddies family literacy program focused on both fourth grade and kindergarten, we will discuss just the kindergarten family literacy program here. The program was implemented over the course of 4 nights.

On the first night, we introduced the parents to the central vocabulary strategy their children were learning as part of the reading buddies program in school, known as PET (Pronounce, Explore, and Try It Out), and we talked about choosing words to focus on with young children and defining words for young children.

On each subsequent night we reviewed the strategy and took the time to let parents try using the strategy with their children. We explained to parents the value of pronouncing a word in English and Spanish, the many ways to explore words, and the importance of encouraging and supporting children in trying out words. While we focused on the words that were part of the reading buddies program during the family literacy nights, we stressed to parents that they could use the PET strategy to focus on any words children may not know during their regular family activities. Finally, we sent home suggestions for extending word learning beyond the PET strategy. Specifically, we suggested creating family word walls, playing word games such as I Spy on walks to and from places in the community, and identifying a "word of the day" for all family members to try to use.

Since all the parents of children in the reading buddies program were invited to participate in the family literacy nights, we were unable to test its specific effect on children's vocabulary learning. However, qualitative observations of parent–child interaction revealed that parents became more adept at using the PET strategy over the course of the family literacy night sessions. And we found through parent interviews that parents felt more confident in teaching words to their children after the sessions. Finally, parents reported using the strategy at home with their children between the family literacy night sessions, suggesting they found it feasible to implement the strategy on their own at home. The strengths of this program were that it focused specifically on vocabulary over an extended period of time and was clearly connected to the classroom curriculum. The limitations of the program were that it did not focus on vocabulary in writing and it did not include an adult language-learning component. Teachers who plan to introduce family literacy programs in their school have to determine the appropriate scope of such programs for their context and resources.

Common Themes of Family Literacy Programs

A few themes emerge from the family literacy programs we reviewed. We highlight them here as guidelines for effective family literacy programs that aim to support vocabulary development.

1. Family literacy programs should provide sustained support for families.
2. Family literacy programs should focus explicitly on supporting vocabulary in the context of reading and writing.
3. Family literacy programs should be responsive to parents' strengths and needs.
4. Family literacy programs should offer resources or help families identify resources in their community for supporting language and literacy.
5. Family literacy programs should build a bridge between what children are learning in school and at home so that their language and literacy learning can be seamless.

Implementing thcsc programs requires substantial funding and school and community support. Resourceful teachers with leadership and organization skills can write grants for funding and seek support from organizations such as Reading Is Fundamental (*www.rif.org*), the National Center for Families Learning (*http://familieslearning.org*), and the National Education Association's Read Across America Program (*www.nea.org*). But even if teachers cannot implement intensive programs such as these, they can learn from effective practices in these programs and integrate these practices to whatever extent possible to bridge home and school vocabulary learning.

Summary

In this chapter, we discussed various programs and strategies you can use to forge connections between home and school for the purposes of supporting children's vocabulary breadth and depth. Whether teachers involve parents on a large or small scale, including parents as partners in the vocabulary development of children is essential. Children who are immersed in words before, during, and after school in a variety of different contexts will be poised to make the greatest gains in vocabulary knowledge and will be most likely to maintain that knowledge over time. When children see the importance of words in every aspect of their lives, they will be motivated and eager to learn new words and use them. We have now reviewed each of the principles set forth for effective instruction that promotes the vocabulary breadth and depth of children in prekindergarten through second grade. In the next chapter we offer you a series of four vignettes that include all of these instructional principles within the context of real-life prekindergarten through second-grade classrooms.

CHAPTER 10

Implementing Vocabulary Instruction in Prekindergarten through Second-Grade Classrooms

GUIDING QUESTIONS

- How do teachers bring together all of the components of effective instruction to support vocabulary breadth and depth?
- What does instruction to support vocabulary breadth and depth look like at different grade levels?

In Chapter 2, we introduced Mrs. Calhoun, who asked for a road map for effective vocabulary instruction. In this book, we have tried to create a road map for Mrs. Calhoun and you to use as a guide for effective vocabulary instruction in prekindergarten through second grade. In further conversation with Mrs. Calhoun after our professional development session that day, she said that, in addition to a road map, she also needed a model. She said, "I just need to see what it looks like." So, in this chapter, we provide some models to show what effective vocabulary instruction looks like in action.

Throughout this book, we have explained the various aspects of effective vocabulary instruction that we outlined in Chapter 2. In this chapter, we highlight four grade-based vignettes that show how to pull it all together. While we previously devoted a separate chapter to each principle in order to explain it in detail, it is important to note that all of these principles are related. Explicit and extended instruction should be implemented in a language-rich environment, which fosters word awareness and development of word learning strategies. Assessment

212

should drive all instruction and, in particular, be used to differentiate instruction according to children's various strengths and needs. Using multimedia is a great way to reinforce word learning in a language-rich environment and to differentiate instruction through multiple means of representation, action and expression, and engagement. Finally, home–school connections, especially ones that are well matched with in-school instruction and that build bridges between the home and school contexts, provide additional reinforcement for word learning beyond the rather circumscribed school day.

We recognize, however, that when you put into practice all of these facets of effective instruction for vocabulary breadth and depth, it will be within the constraints of the broader context in which you teach. Today, teachers must use the CCSS to guide instruction; they must use the curriculum mandated in their schools; and they must show improvement for student learning on state-, district-, and schoolwide assessments. It is our position that the principles we have outlined will enable you to accomplish all of these goals and more. Supporting children's breadth and depth of word knowledge aligns with the CCSS, fits into any curriculum, and, if done well, will help children improve in areas assessed on state, district, and schoolwide assessments. In addition, instruction for vocabulary breadth and depth will help children comprehend and communicate effectively in school and beyond for years to come. In this chapter, we describe contextual factors that support teachers in implementing effective vocabulary instruction, and we provide our Inventory of Vocabulary Instruction (IVI) that can be used to determine the strengths and needs of your own vocabulary curriculum. Then, we offer you a series of grade-based vignettes to show what effective vocabulary instruction looks like in action. We hope this chapter illustrates the variety of ways you can put it all together to employ effective vocabulary instruction in your classroom.

Putting It All Together

Vocabulary Instruction as a Schoolwide Priority

Creating a strong vocabulary program begins with the full investment of several instructional stakeholders: administrators, classroom teachers, teacher specialists, and parents. Because word learning occurs in all aspects of school and home life, it is not just the responsibility of one teacher to support children's breadth and depth of vocabulary. Vocabulary instruction should be considered a shared responsibility among administrators, teachers, and parents to substantially impact student performance and maintain lasting effects in early childhood and beyond. While implementing the principles we have outlined is possible in any classroom context, we find that schools with certain characteristics provide the most fertile ground for the effective vocabulary instruction we describe in this book. These schools (1) prioritize vocabulary as an important area of focus, (2) allocate time for teachers to co-plan so they work together to figure out how best to integrate vocabulary across the curriculum, and (3) encourage reflective evaluation of instruction so teachers can continuously improve their vocabulary instruction within the larger picture of the reading and writing curriculum.

Administrators can set the tone by making vocabulary learning a schoolwide priority and instituting schoolwide initiatives to promote it. One low-cost, high-impact initiative is the establishment of a set of schoolwide academic vocabulary words that everyone— from the principal to the administrative and maintenance staff to the specialist teachers (e.g., special education, ESL, and reading) and specialty teachers (e.g., art, music, library, and physical education)—uses and that children are encouraged to use as well. Schoolwide words can be announced each week and schoolwide activities could focus on these words. Students' use of these words can be reinforced with schoolwide incentives. Teacher specialists and specialty teachers can incorporate words into their instruction, and administrative and maintenance staff can ask children about the words they are learning each week. Principals can host family literacy nights or use other forms of outreach to include parents in the schoolwide vocabulary program. Employing these schoolwide initiatives creates a culture of word learning and ensures children are immersed in opportunities to develop vocabulary breadth and depth.

Principals can also make vocabulary a priority by ensuring that vocabulary assessments are administered and results from these assessments are part of the school's process of strategic planning and school improvement. Including vocabulary data in schoolwide discussions of curriculum and instruction demonstrates to the school community that vocabulary is of primary importance and creates the space for discussion about adjustments to vocabulary curriculum and instruction when needed. Devoting time to professional development and coaching specifically for vocabulary instruction also sends a message that teachers should concentrate on vocabulary in their classrooms and helps them continuously improve their instruction.

Vocabulary Instruction across Classrooms and Teachers

Once vocabulary instruction is established as a schoolwide priority, grade-level teacher teams can focus on it as part of their regular conversations about classroom instruction and student learning. Teachers can co-plan and learn from each other about how to best implement the principles of vocabulary instruction we have set forth in this book. When teachers focus on the same themes and teach the same words, they can share responsibility for lesson planning and effective vocabulary instruction. Including classroom teachers and teacher specialists, who bring different skill sets to these conversations, can ensure that their ideas for how to differentiate for different learners and how to integrate vocabulary across the curriculum inform instruction. Classroom teachers are knowledgeable about grade-level standards and curriculum, reading specialists have expertise in reading and writing development and instruction, ESL teachers have expertise in English language development and instruction, and special educators have expertise in differentiating and intensifying instruction for those students who need extra support. Together, these experts can collaborate to set goals, develop action plans, and solve problems related to scheduling, grouping, and other logistics so that vocabulary instruction can be implemented optimally in the classroom. Additionally, including teacher specialists in grade-level planning for vocabulary instruction enables them to align their instruction with particular students with the grade-level curriculum. Therefore, when teacher specialists work with students who need extra instruction in or outside of the classroom, their instruction will be synchronized with the grade-level vocabulary curriculum. Co-planning can also include specialty teachers such as the art, music, physical education, and library teachers, who can review and reinforce vocabulary through activities related to the theme and content of instruction. Occasionally, teachers can co-plan with teachers in other grades as well. This allows for productive discussions about the alignment of the vocabulary curriculum across grade levels and about how cross-age learning opportunities might reinforce concepts for both younger and older learners.

When resources allow, co-teaching is a great way for teachers to learn from one another and work together to support student vocabulary learning. Co-teaching may be possible when there are two teachers assigned to one class or when teacher specialists "push in" to the classroom. There are a variety of co-teaching options (Friend & Cook, 1996):

- The One Teaching and One Supporting Model—One teacher provides instruction while the other teacher circulates to keep students on task.
- The Station or Center Teaching Model—Each teacher focuses his or her attention on one or two centers while students rotate through all of the centers in small groups.
- The Parallel Teaching Model—Each teacher works with half the class on the same concepts and then groups share what they learned.
- The Alternative Teaching Model—One teacher guides the class in extension activities while the other teacher provides additional support to students who need it.
- The Team Teaching Model—Both teachers work simultaneously to trade off roles in the lesson. Teachers can model how students can work together in pairs and small groups.

Co-teaching, like any close partnership, takes communication from both partners to be successful. Despite the extra effort it may take to develop a successful co-teaching relationship, having two teachers work together on promoting vocabulary instruction creates optimal conditions in which children can learn and use words with teacher guidance. In schools where vocabulary instruction is a priority, co-planning and co-teaching should be encouraged.

Vocabulary Instruction in Individual Classrooms

At the individual classroom level, teachers can reflect on their own vocabulary instruction to identify areas of strength and areas for improvement. To support teachers in this endeavor, we have developed the IVI based on the principles we have outlined throughout this book. (See Figure 10.1 on pp. 217–220.) First, teachers can record and rate the vocabulary components they are currently implementing in their instruction. Then they can focus on improving aspects of instruction they are already implementing or trying aspects of instruction they do not already incorporate into their curriculum. Using this tool, teachers can work independently or with other teachers and/or literacy coaches to set goals and devise an action plan to continuously improve their vocabulary instruction in certain areas. Teachers who seek to do this will be best poised to help their students succeed in learning vocabulary.

Classroom Examples

Vocabulary instruction changes as students develop. Therefore, in the following section, we provide case studies of four diverse classrooms ranging from prekindergarten through second grade to show how effective vocabulary instruction looks at different grade levels. In each example, we describe: (1) the setting, including the student population; (2) the context, including the unit theme and instructional objective; (3) the lesson, including teachers' instructional moves and students' responses; and (4) the instructional significance, including the vocabulary practices exhibited in the example.

Prekindergarten

The first vignette, presented in Figure 10.2 (pp. 221–222), takes place in an urban school in which the majority of students are from English-only, African American, and low socioeconomic backgrounds. The school employs an RTI model. Thus, children are assessed in the beginning of the year for screening purposes and throughout the year for progress-monitoring purposes. Children who are at risk for experiencing difficulty are given supplemental instruction. While there are no prekindergarten standards in the CCSS, the school uses a curriculum that supports children in developing the skills that are precursors to those highlighted in the CCSS. The school puts a major emphasis on oral language and vocabulary development as it recognizes that children from low socioeconomic backgrounds may need extra instruction in building their nascent academic language skills.

Ms. Williams and Ms. Aberra are the classroom teachers we describe in this vignette. They co-teach seamlessly throughout the day. They follow a thematic curriculum and focus on thematically related vocabulary words throughout the unit. The curriculum includes a dual focus on advanced and basic words within

(text resumes on p. 221)

Check aspects of instruction you already include in your curriculum. Then rate these aspects of instruction in the column to the right. Use the following rating scale: (1) always, (2) sometimes, (3) rarely. Aspects of instruction without a check or with a rating of 2 or 3 are areas you may want to target in your own professional development, if applicable.

Academic Standards, Word Choice, and Materials	
Alignment to Standards	Rating
☐ I align vocabulary instruction to the appropriate CCSS grade-level standards for speaking, listening, reading, and writing.	
Appropriate Word Choice	
☐ I target words that are useful for comprehending academic texts across the content areas.	
☐ I target words that children do not already know and need to know to learn in school.	
☐ I target words that are related thematically, taxonomically, or semantically to support vocabulary breadth and depth.	
Appropriate Texts and Materials	
☐ I choose texts and materials with rich language and vocabulary.	
☐ I choose texts and materials across genres.	
☐ I choose texts and materials with ample pictorial support.	
☐ I choose texts and materials that are optimally challenging.	
☐ I choose texts and materials that reflect diverse cultures and experiences.	
☐ I choose multimedia resources that support active word learning.	
Explicit Instruction	
Multidimensional Vocabulary Instruction	Rating
Through-out the day, I implement multidimensional vocabulary instruction:	
☐ I say words for students and have them say the words back.	
☐ I show printed words on word cards and have students attend to the letters and sounds in the words.	
☐ I use pictures, actions, gestures, and props to illustrate words.	
☐ I provide comprehensible definitions of words.	
☐ I provide examples of words across contexts.	
☐ I guide children to analyze how words are used in context and how they are related to other words.	

(continued)

FIGURE 10.1. Inventory of Vocabulary Instruction (IVI).

Multidimensional Vocabulary Instruction *(continued)* | **Rating**

    ☐ I encourage children to use words in new contexts on their own.

    ☐ I provide repeated exposure and review to reinforce word learning across contexts.

Strategic Use of Read-Alouds

I use the read-aloud process strategically:

    ☐ I introduce target vocabulary before reading.

    ☐ I call attention to target vocabulary during reading.

    ☐ I provide opportunities for students to use target vocabulary after reading.

    ☐ I provide corrective feedback as needed.

    ☐ I provide extended opportunities for students to hear and read target vocabulary beyond the read-aloud context.

Language-Rich Environment

Teacher Practices | **Rating**

I foster a language-rich environment:

    ☐ I establish a positive classroom climate.

    ☐ I provide teacher language modeling.

    ☐ I provide opportunities for extended conversation.

    ☐ I support student expression.

    ☐ I provide feedback, and I am responsive to students' needs.

    ☐ I provide access to a variety of books and materials.

    ☐ I organize and manage my classroom so language learning can take place.

Instructional Routines and Activities

I support vocabulary development throughout the following routines and activities:

    ☐ Morning Meeting

    ☐ Dialogic Reading

    ☐ Text Talk

    ☐ The Language Experience Approach

    ☐ Vocabulary Visits

    ☐ Buddy Reading and/or Reading Buddies

    ☐ Collaborative Reading Groups

    ☐ Talking Time Centers

    ☐ Conversation Stations

    ☐ Storytelling and Storyacting

    ☐ Story Dictation

    ☐ Writing Workshop

(continued)

FIGURE 10.1. *(continued)*

Word Awareness and Independent Word Learning	
Fostering Word Awareness	**Rating**
I foster students' word awareness:	
☐ I attend to word choice in reading.	
☐ I attend to word choice in writing.	
☐ I encourage students to collect words.	
☐ I encourage students to play with words.	
☐ I encourage students to investigate words.	
Fostering Independent Word Learning	
I foster students' independent word learning:	
☐ I teach students to use context clues to figure out unknown words.	
☐ I teach students to use word parts to figure out unknown words.	
☐ I teach students to use reference materials to figure out unknown words.	
Assessment	
Assessment Purposes	**Rating**
I use assessments for their intended purposes:	
☐ I screen all children in my class at the beginning of the year to determine their vocabulary strengths and needs.	
☐ I use progress monitoring measures to track children's vocabulary development over time.	
☐ I use diagnostic assessment to determine students' strengths and needs if they are struggling in vocabulary.	
☐ I use outcome assessment to determine the efficacy of my vocabulary instruction program overall.	
☐ I create my own vocabulary assessments to evaluate children's learning of target vocabulary and strategies.	
I use assessment data strategically:	
☐ I use information from assessments to plan vocabulary instruction.	
☐ I use information from assessments to differentiate vocabulary instruction.	
Differentiation	
Universal Design for Learning	**Rating**
I use the principles of Universal Design for Learning to make my vocabulary instruction accessible for all learners.	
☐ I include multiple means of representation in my vocabulary instruction.	
☐ I include multiple means of action and expression in my vocabulary instruction.	
☐ I include multiple means of engagement in my vocabulary instruction.	

(continued)

FIGURE 10.1. *(continued)*

Diverse Learners	Rating
I provide accommodations and modifications in my vocabulary instruction to meet the needs of diverse children.	
☐ I use culturally responsive instruction to support vocabulary.	
☐ I provide linguistic supports for ELL students.	
☐ I provide access to resources for students from low socioeconomic backgrounds.	
☐ I provide accommodations to meet the vocabulary learning needs of children with disabilities.	
Response to Intervention	
I use Response to Intervention to support students in vocabulary learning:	
☐ I provide differentiated vocabulary instruction in my core curriculum (Tier 1).	
☐ I provide supplemental (Tier 2) vocabulary instruction for those who need it.	
☐ I provide intensive (Tier 3) vocabulary instruction for those who need it.	

Multimedia	

Multimedia	Rating
I use a variety of multimedia to support vocabulary learning:	
☐ I use video in my vocabulary instruction.	
☐ I use digital texts in my vocabulary instruction.	
☐ I use computer games, programs, and applications in my vocabulary instruction.	
I am a critical consumer of multimedia that I use in my classroom:	
☐ I evaluate the instructional design of multimedia for vocabulary instruction.	
☐ I evaluate the interface design of multimedia for vocabulary instruction.	
☐ I evaluate the content included in multimedia for vocabulary instruction.	

Home–School Connections	

Home–School Connections	Rating
I foster home–school connections to support vocabulary learning:	
☐ I communicate with parents about my vocabulary curriculum.	
☐ I encourage parents to support vocabulary outside of the curriculum.	
☐ I involve parents in the vocabulary curriculum during the school day.	
☐ I implement a home–school connections program to involve parents in supporting vocabulary.	

FIGURE 10.1. *(continued)*

each theme so that children can increase their knowledge of words and concepts. Whole-class, small-group, and centers instruction is used. Teachers introduce words in whole-class read-alouds. They use small-group differentiated instruction to support children who are at different levels of learning. And, they structure centers activities to encourage children to use vocabulary words as they play. Despite the fact that their students are young, these teachers hold high expectations for what their students can learn and do independently. In the lesson we describe below, the teachers are midway through a monthlong unit on anatomy and physiology. Children are learning the words *anatomy* and *physiology* as well as words having to do with body parts and the five senses (e.g., *see, hear, taste, touch,* and *smell*). The vignette described in Figure 10.2 includes a read-aloud and discussion about differences in human bodies and the respect that all persons deserve, regardless of how their bodies work and what physical supports they may use (e.g., glasses and hearing aids). Among the standards addressed in this lesson is the following: "With guidance and support from adults, explore word relationships and nuances in word meanings" (CCSS.ELA–Literacy.L.K.5).

Activity	Description	Principles Exhibited
Morning Meeting	Ms. Williams reminds the class that they are studying *anatomy* and *physiology*. She asks for volunteers to come up to the front of the classroom and point out and name a part of their anatomy. On a blank diagram of a human body, Ms. Aberra labels the body parts the children show to their classmates. At the end of the lesson, Ms. Williams says, "You know a lot about the anatomy. Today we are going to read a book about the physiology of the senses. We use our body parts to sense things. You are going to learn about the senses of seeing, hearing, tasting, touching, and smelling."	Explicit instruction including review and reinforcement and use of actions and visuals
Read-Aloud	Ms. Aberra then reads aloud a book called *My Five Senses* (1989) by Aliki. When she gets to the target words in the book, she does the following: • Has children say the word. • Gives a brief definition. • Shows a picture. • Provides an example. • Has children do a gesture to go with the word. For example, when she gets to the word *hear* she says, "Say *hear*. [The children say *hear*.] When you *hear* something, you listen to sounds with your ears. [She shows a picture of ears.] If a drum is being played, you can *hear* the sound it makes with your ears. Cup your ear like this to show *hearing*. [She gestures to indicate cupping her ear and the children cup their ears as well.]"	Explicit instruction using pronunciation, definitions, visuals, examples, and gestures

(continued)

FIGURE 10.2. Prekindergarten classroom vignette.

Activity	Description	Principles Exhibited
Extension Activity	Ms. Williams leads a matching game. She asks children to match a body part with a sense. She calls out a sense and asks children which body part matches that sense. After the game, Ms. Williams tells children that sometimes people have difficulty with their senses. She introduces hearing aids and eyeglasses as devices that help people hear and see. She has children complete the sentence frames, "The boy uses a hearing aid to help him _____." and "The girl uses glasses to help her _____." She shows the children pictures of people with hearing aids and glasses and asks children if they know people in their community who wear them. She ends by telling children that they should respect all people regardless of their differences.	Explicit Instruction including word analysis, word use across contexts, and connections to personal experiences
Centers and Small-Group Instruction	Ms. Aberra then introduces the centers for the day. In the dramatic play center, children can play ophthalmologist and audiologist and help stuffed animals with their eyesight and hearing. (The words *ophthalmologist* and *audiologist* are defined and pictures of people doing these jobs along with various devices children can use to pretend to do these jobs are placed in the center.) In the math center, children can taste different fruits and vegetables and count how many are sweet and how many are sour. At the music center, children can play instruments they can hear. At the science center, children can use binoculars and a magnifying glass to see different objects. And at the art center, children can make an art collage with fabrics of different textures they can touch and feel. Children are encouraged to use their sense words as they play.	Language-rich environment
Small-Group Instruction	During centers time, Ms. Williams meets with small groups to guide them in writing a class book about the senses. Ms. Williams provides different levels of support and reinforcement for different groups of students depending on their vocabulary level. For example, she asks children with higher levels of language to use the vocabulary words on their own, but she provides sentence frames for children with lower levels of language. During centers time, Ms. Aberra calls over individual children to administer progress monitoring assessments.	Differentiation of core instruction Assessment

FIGURE 10.2. *(continued)*

This example illustrates a host of effective vocabulary instruction practices that are appropriate for prekindergarteners. The teachers continuously review concepts and words they had previously introduced. They provide explicit instruction of the words related to the five senses. And they use a variety of research-based practices within explicit instruction such as defining words, providing examples, and using gestures and acting out to illustrate words. They also encourage use of words in a language-rich environment and differentiate instruction based on assessment data. The thematic instruction allows for the teaching of basic words like *eyes* and *ears*, slightly more advanced words like *see* and *hear*, and very advanced words like *ophthalmologist* and *audiologist*. By carefully planning how to implement instruction purposefully throughout the day, these teachers are able to provide children with lots of rich experiences around the words and concepts they are teaching. And they are able to connect their vocabulary instruction to other content areas such as science and social studies as well. Thus, Ms. Williams and Ms. Aberra present an elegant example of how effective vocabulary instruction can be integrated into prekindergarten classrooms.

Kindergarten

The second vignette, presented in Figure 10.3, is situated in a kindergarten classroom in a semi-urban school with a majority of students who are ELLs. Spanish is the native language for most of these students. Recently, the administrators and teachers in the school decided to focus on two big initiatives: (1) implementing UDL to engage all learners and (2) integrating technology across the curriculum. Teachers have received professional development on using multiple means of representation (e.g., using pictures and gestures in their instruction), action and expression (e.g., having children draw, act out, or explain their understandings), and engagement (e.g., using collaborative learning and authentic activities throughout the curriculum). Teachers are also encouraged to use media presentations and various technologies to support instruction. Since the majority of the children in the school are ELLs, teachers regularly include accommodations such as native language support in their instruction. This year, the kindergarten classes are working with the fourth-grade classes in a reading buddies program to support vocabulary and comprehension through collaborative learning. In the reading buddies program, children read digital texts together. In the lesson we describe here, Ms. Martin prepares her kindergarten students to work with their big buddies by preteaching vocabulary and previewing content for their upcoming buddy lesson. The unit theme is *technology* and the target vocabulary words for this lesson include *communicate, innovation, information, signal*, and *message*. The following Common Core standard guides the lesson: "Use words and phrases acquired through conversations, reading and being read to, and responding to texts" (CCSS.ELA–Literacy.L.K.6).

This vignette from Ms. Martin's kindergarten classroom demonstrates multiple practices for effective instruction of vocabulary depth and breadth. First, Ms. Martin briefly prompts the students to recall the target words for the technology unit using the picture word wall as a resource and print reference. Then, Ms. Martin delivers approximately 10 minutes of focused, explicit instruction about the meaning and application of the four target vocabulary words. To accommodate her ELL students, who are still acquiring basic English words, she includes multiple means of representation for the target words besides just stating them

Activity	Description	Principles Exhibited
Vocabulary Review	*Students are seated on the carpet in front of a screen. Ms. Martin turns on her projector and starts her PowerPoint presentation for the lesson.* Ms. Martin says, "This month you have been learning about different technologies with your big buddies. What words have you been learning in this technology unit?" (Ms. Martin points to the vocabulary picture and word wall to provide students with support. Students raise their hands to share words and concepts from the previous weeks.) Then Ms. Martin says, "Tomorrow you are going to read a digitial book about different kinds of technology you can use to communicate with your friends. Let's preview the book so you are ready to read and talk with your buddies about the book tomorrow." Ms. Martin asks children what they see in the book and what they think the book will be about as she does a digital picture walk through the book.	Use of multimedia Explicit instruction including review and reinforcement and attention to the printed form of words
Vocabulary Instruction	Ms. Martin says, "Now let's review some words you will hear with your buddies tomorrow. First, let's talk about the word *communicate*." Ms. Martin shows the target word on her first PowerPoint slide. Each slide has the target word, the Spanish translation, the definition, and a picture with an example. She says, "Say the word *communicate*." (The students pronounce the word in unison.) Ms. Martin says, "The Spanish word for *communicate* is *comunicarse*. Those words sound a lot alike." Ms. Martin gives a definition: "When two people *communicate*, they give each other information, or they say or show what they are thinking or feeling to each other. I *communicate* with my mom over the phone to tell her that I love her. How did I *communicate*?" (Ms. Martin lets students respond.) Then she says, "I *communicated* using my phone." Ms. Martin makes a gesture as if she is talking on the phone and then says, "Everyone pretend you are talking on the phone. Turn to your partner and say, 'I am *communicating* on the phone.' [Students turn to each other and act out talking on the phone while using the sentence provided.] Now pretend you are typing a message on a computer. Turn to your partner and say, 'I am *communicating* on the computer.' [Again, students act out and use the word in the provided sentence.] Now pretend you are writing a message on paper. Turn to your partner and say, 'I am *communicating* with a paper and pencil.'" Ms. Martin then goes on to introduce the other target words in a similar way. After the last target word, Ms. Martin initiates a vocabulary review game. She wants to see how well the students learned the words she introduced. She takes note of who may need additional small-group instruction on the vocabulary later in the day. She says, "Let's check how well we know our new words." Ms. Martin asks questions such as the following: "Which is *communicating*: Talking on the phone or sleeping in your room? Why is 'talking on the phone' *communicating*? What are some other ways we can *communicate*?" Ms. Martin asks such questions about all of the target words.	Use of multimedia Explicit instruction including pronunciation, definition, attention to the printed word form, pictures, examples, gestures, word analysis, review, and reinforcement Differentiation including multiple means of representation, native language supports, and supplemental instruction Assessment
Vocabulary Extension Activity	Ms. Martin says, "Tomorrow you will meet with your big buddies and read a digital book about *innovations* in *communication*. Try to use your new words when you are talking with your big buddy. At the end of your buddy session tomorrow, you and your buddy will devise, or make, your own *innovation* for sending messages to friends. Have fun and be creative!"	Language-rich environment including opportunities for extended conversation and expression

FIGURE 10.3. Kindergarten classroom vignette.

verbally. For example, she uses pictures and gestures to represent words along with the definitions. She also allows for multiple means of expression by having the students talk in partners and use gestures to try out the words. Finally, the purpose of this lesson is to prepare kindergarteners to talk with their big buddies the next day. This authentic purpose for instruction and the collaborative learning that will take place in the buddies session promotes children's engagement and motivation to learn the words and concepts in the curriculum. Ms. Martin's kindergarten lesson illustrates how multiple principles of effective vocabulary instruction can be woven together to create a fun, accessible, and stimulating lesson.

First Grade

Our third vignette, presented in Figure 10.4, takes place in a first-grade classroom in a suburban school with students of middle socioeconomic status. The racial and ethnic makeup of the school is truly diverse: 40% African American, 30% Hispanic, 20% Caucasian, and 10% Asian. Most of the children in the classroom speak English only. An overarching goal in this first-grade classroom, as with other lessons at this grade level, is developing early reading skills, such as decoding and sight word fluency. However, Mr. Edwards also focuses on vocabulary depth and breadth and comprehension during his read-alouds, reading groups, content-area lessons, and home–school connection activities. The language arts block we describe occurs during a unit on nonfiction biographies. In this lesson, Mr. Edwards introduces the text *Mae Jemison*, by Nancy Pollette, which chronicles the accomplishments of the first African American astronaut. When possible, Mr. Edwards chooses texts that parallel the content-area learning objectives. For example, since the students are learning about space and the planets in science, this biographical text about an astronaut provides a great opportunity to expose students to similar vocabulary words across content areas. As an extension to the read-aloud, Mr. Edwards selects vocabulary words from the text that are ripe for deeper investigation. He focuses on the words *star, space, shuttle,* and *train* to get his students thinking about multiple-meaning words and using context clues to figure them out. While some children in the class may already know these words, Mr. Edwards uses this lesson to foster word awareness and teach independent word learning strategies to his students. He aligns his lesson objective to meet the following Common Core standard: "Determine or clarify the meaning of unknown and multiple-meaning words and phrases based on grade 1 reading and content, choosing flexibly from an array of strategies" (CCSS.ELA–Literacy.L.1.4).

Mr. Edwards provides a stellar example of how teachers support independent word learning through explicit instruction. He begins with explicit instruction on the target words for the story and on figuring out multiple-meaning words using context. Then he provides guided practice determining words using context through the reading of a rich and authentic text. Next, Mr. Edwards models using

Activity	Description	Principles Exhibited
Morning Warm-Up	While Mr. Edwards takes attendance, students complete a warm-up activity. As part of the space unit, students have been observing the sky with their parents on the way home from school, before bed, and in the morning to detect similarities and differences in the visible stars and planets at different times during the day. For their warm-up activity, Mr. Edwards asks the students to write their recent observations in their home–school connections journal. He distributes gold star stickers to students who use the science vocabulary words in their journal entry: *sun, moon, stars, planets, galaxy,* and *constellation.* Students who struggle to write the words are encouraged to draw pictures or refer to the word wall.	Home–school connection Explicit instruction including review and reinforcement Differentiation including accommodations
Vocabulary Introduction	Mr. Edwards prefaces the read-aloud with a brief preview of focal vocabulary words in the text (i.e., *star, space, shuttle, train*). He writes each word on the board and asks students to say the words aloud. He tells the children that these words are tricky because each of these words has more than one meaning. He reviews the two meanings of each word with his students. He then explains that when words have more than one meaning it is important to look for clues in the text to help them figure out which meaning is intended. He reads a sentence from the text, "Would you like to be a *star* or travel to the *stars*?" and models figuring out which meaning is intended using context clues. He then asks students to listen for the multiple-meaning words he has written on the board as he reads a text about the first African American astronaut, Mae Jemison, because they will talk about how to figure out these multiple-meaning words using content clues as they read.	Explicit instruction including pronunciation and attention to the printed word Support for word awareness and independent word learning
Read-Aloud	Mr. Edwards reads aloud from *Mae Jemison* (Polette, 2003), while the students follow along in their own texts in partners. When he reads one of the target vocabulary words, the students make a *v* in sign language for *vocabulary*. This is a word awareness cue that he has built into his classroom expectations. When he comes to a target word, he asks students to think about which meaning is intended using context clues. At the end of the reading, Mr. Edwards leads a discussion about the main idea of the book.	Support for word awareness and independent word learning
Word Analysis	After the read-aloud, Mr. Edwards tells students it is time for some word work. He rereads a sentence from the book with the word *space*, models completing a graphic organizer to show the multiple meanings of the word, and reminds children about how they figured out the intended meaning of the word using context.	Support for word awareness and independent word learning

(continued)

FIGURE 10.4. First-grade classroom vignette.

Activity	Description	Principles Exhibited
Word Analysis *(continued)*	Finally, he puts a star next to the meaning of the word intended in the context of the book. He follows this same process to provide students with guided practice using the words *train* and *shuttle*. 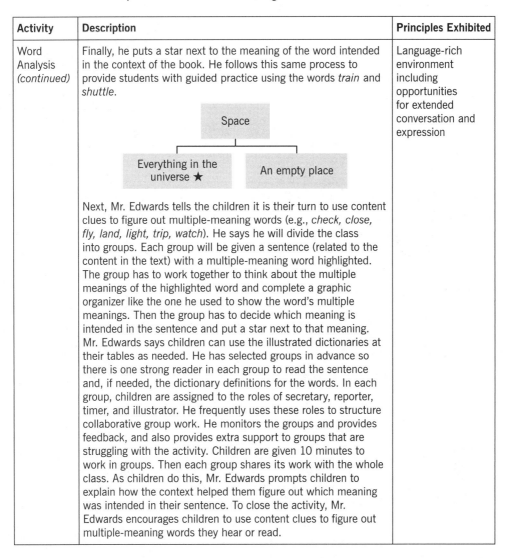 Next, Mr. Edwards tells the children it is their turn to use content clues to figure out multiple-meaning words (e.g., *check, close, fly, land, light, trip, watch*). He says he will divide the class into groups. Each group will be given a sentence (related to the content in the text) with a multiple-meaning word highlighted. The group has to work together to think about the multiple meanings of the highlighted word and complete a graphic organizer like the one he used to show the word's multiple meanings. Then the group has to decide which meaning is intended in the sentence and put a star next to that meaning. Mr. Edwards says children can use the illustrated dictionaries at their tables as needed. He has selected groups in advance so there is one strong reader in each group to read the sentence and, if needed, the dictionary definitions for the words. In each group, children are assigned to the roles of secretary, reporter, timer, and illustrator. He frequently uses these roles to structure collaborative group work. He monitors the groups and provides feedback, and also provides extra support to groups that are struggling with the activity. Children are given 10 minutes to work in groups. Then each group shares its work with the whole class. As children do this, Mr. Edwards prompts children to explain how the context helped them figure out which meaning was intended in their sentence. To close the activity, Mr. Edwards encourages children to use content clues to figure out multiple-meaning words they hear or read.	Language-rich environment including opportunities for extended conversation and expression

FIGURE 10.4. *(continued)*

a graphic organizer and context clues to figure out unknown words and allows for ample practice through small-group collaborative work. He has carefully planned the groups so children can learn from and support each other, and he provides feedback and support as needed. To promote generalization of the strategy, he reminds children they should think about multiple meanings and use context clues in other contexts as well. Teaching children to use independent word learning strategies will take consistent and continued instruction and support. In the lesson we describe here, Mr. Edwards has taken one step toward ensuring that his students eventually become self-sufficient word learners.

Second Grade

Our final vignette, presented in Figure 10.5, is set in a semi-urban school that draws from a linguistically and economically diverse neighborhood that has seen rapid growth in the past few years. The school serves a large population of Hispanic and Asian families who recently moved to the area for new job opportunities. The primary educators have quickly acclimated to principles for supporting ELLs, and the ESL teachers play a large role in the students' instructional day. In this example, we introduce Ms. Cook, the second-grade teacher, and Mr. Guzman, the ESL specialist assigned to second grade. Ms. Cook integrates instruction throughout the content areas and differentiates instruction so that all students have access to the content she is teaching. Since there are so many ELL students in Ms. Cook's classroom, Mr. Guzman co-teaches with Ms. Cook for a portion of the language arts block every day. Mr. Guzman provides ELLs with linguistic scaffolding, nonverbal supports, and explicit English language instruction tied to the second-grade curriculum so that they can fully participate in class activities. While Mr. Guzman supports the ELL students in particular, he works with groups that include both ELLs and non-ELLs so that students can learn from each other and can all benefit from lower student–teacher ratios and differentiated instruction.

Ms. Cook and Mr. Guzman are part of a strong grade-level instructional team that meets weekly to discuss student data and plan lessons. At the beginning of the year, the second-grade team created a list of academically useful words that they planned to introduce across the school year in every second-grade classroom. On the first day of each week throughout the year, homeroom teachers introduce the Weekly Wonder Words. Students are then "on the hunt" for those words throughout the week. Whenever a student uses a word independently, the student earns a token. On Fridays, the students count their tokens and exchange them for classroom privileges such as extra art, computer, or library time. In this way, both the teachers and the students are keenly aware of these sophisticated vocabulary words and make a point of using them in their everyday language. Teachers also introduce content-specific words each week so that children develop strong vocabulary knowledge not only across but also within subject areas.

The language arts block we describe next took place at the beginning of a unit on the plant life cycle. Over the course of the unit, children observe and explore how plants grow. In this lesson, students are learning basic concepts that they build on throughout the unit. The general academic words targeted in this lesson are *change, grow,* and *cycle.* The content-area words targeted in this lesson are *seed, sprout, plant, flower,* and *fruit.* In this lesson, Ms. Cook aligns her teaching with the following Common Core standard: "Use words and phrases acquired through conversations, reading and being read to, and responding to texts, including using adjectives and adverbs to describe" (CCSS.ELA–Literacy.L.2.6).

Activity	Description	Principles Exhibited
Read-Aloud	Ms. Cook gathers the students to the carpet for read-aloud time. She previews the target words with a PowerPoint presentation that includes definitions, examples, and pictures of the target words. Then she reads to the whole class the book *From Seed to Plant* (1991) by Gail Gibbons. As she reads, she calls attention to the target words in context. After reading, she reviews the target words by doing a picture walk through the book she just read. Then she shows children the pictures from the PowerPoint presentation and asks them to identify the different stages of the plant life cycle (i.e., *seed*, *sprout*, *plant*, *flower*, and *fruit*) using the target words.	Explicit instruction including review and reinforcement Use of multimedia Assessment
Transition	After the read-aloud, Mr. Guzman enters the classroom to co-teach with Ms. Cook. Ms. Cook explains the literacy stations for the day and what students are expected to complete during each station. The stations are as follows: 1. Guided reading with Ms. Cook 2. Exploration station with Mr. Guzman 3. Independent reading and writing station 4. Computer station with partners The class breaks up into their four reading groups, which were set by Ms. Cook and Mr. Guzman using the most recent benchmark data.	Differentiation of core instruction
Guided Reading	In the guided reading station, children read leveled texts about plants from the National Geographic Language, Literacy, and Vocabulary (Windows on Literacy) collection. In this series, there are different texts at each level on various topics, including *plants*. In each group, Ms. Cook introduces the text, supports students in reading the text, and leads a discussion of the important details in the text. Ms. Cook also guides word work to aid students' decoding and word recognition skills. Finally, Ms. Cook asks questions about the target vocabulary and provides varying levels of support for students at different levels. For example, she asks higher-level students to use multiple target words together as they explain what they learned while she asks lower-level students to use the target words in single sentences and provides sentence frames for support.	Differentiation of core instruction
Exploration Station	At the exploration station, Mr. Guzman focuses on vocabulary and comprehension skills. He first shows students a short time-lapse video of the plant life cycle (*www.fastplants.org/life_cycle*) and asks them to describe what they see using the target words. Then he models completing a graphic organizer to depict the plant life cycle. Finally, he guides students to use their own graphic organizer (in partners) to depict the plant life cycle using the target words. For high-level groups, he asks them to use complete sentences. For lower-level groups, he supports them in drawing and labeling pictures to express their understanding of the content and to use the target words on their own.	Differentiation of core instruction

(continued)

FIGURE 10.5. Second-grade classroom vignette.

Activity	Description	Principles Exhibited
Exploration Station *(continued)*	Seed → Sprout → Plant → Flower → Fruit → (cycle back to Seed)	
Independent Reading and Writing Station	At the independent reading and writing station, students choose a book from several choices at different levels in the class library (e.g., *Seeds Grow!*, by Angela Shelf Medearis, 1999; *How a Seed Grows,* by Helene Jordan, 1992; *How a Plant Grows*, by Bobbie Kalman, 1997; *The Carrot Seed,* by Ruth Krauss, 2000). As they read, they are expected to write down interesting words in their journal. Children are encouraged to look up these words in the dictionary if they don't know what they mean. Then they are expected to draw and write in their journal about the important ideas in the book using those words. Ms. Cook and Mr. Guzman review the journals every day to monitor children's progress in this center.	Language-rich environment including language-rich texts and opportunities for expression Word awareness and independent word learning
Computer Center	In the computer center rotation, students work in pairs on one of the three classroom computers. Students explore the Brain Pop Jr. *Plants* module. In this module, children can watch a movie, with or without closed captioning, about the plant life cycle, play a game in which they sequence the stages of the plant life cycle, and review word definitions on an electronic word wall. The module prompts students to draw, write, and talk about what they are learning.	Use of multimedia
Wrap-Up	At the conclusion of the literacy stations portion of the language arts block, Ms. Cook and Mr. Guzman call everyone to the carpet to review the words and concepts addressed throughout the day. Children are invited to share what they learned in the independent reading and writing and computer center stations. And teachers preview how children will use the words and concepts they have learned throughout the plant life cycle unit.	Explicit instruction including review and reinforcement
Home–School Connection Activity	At the end of the day, Ms. Cook sends each student home with a bean seed and instructions about how to grow a seed from the book *From Seed to Plant* by Gail Gibbons (1991). Along with the instructions, Ms. Cook provides a list of target vocabulary, including definitions and examples, for parents to use as they help their children care for their bean plant. The students are encouraged keep a home journal to record stages of the bean plant and use target words in their journal. Parents are urged to support students in completing their journal entries. Ms. Cook sets up a class bean sprout so that students who cannot grow a bean sprout at home for whatever reason can monitor and record information about the class bean sprout each morning.	Home–school connection

FIGURE 10.5. *(continued)*

With a wide range of literacy levels represented in her classroom, Ms. Cook begins with a whole-class lesson to introduce the theme and target words. Then she groups children according to their language and literacy level (i.e., emergent, early, fluent, and advanced) to participate in small-group activities that reinforce students' learning and address their needs. Ms. Cook draws on her knowledge of UDL and Mr. Guzman draws on his knowledge of accommodations for ELLs in designing the lesson. Many of the principles described in this book are apparent in the classroom vignette in Figure 10.5.

This second-grade example shows how a diverse group of students at varying levels can participate actively during the language arts block through the use of reading stations. Ms. Cook values differentiation based on assessment data, which is made clear by her strategic grouping of students. In this way, the strongest students are challenged to extend their thinking, while the students who need the most linguistic support are still able to access sophisticated vocabulary and participate in academic discussion. The use of reading stations also emphasizes the importance of independent word learning and self-sufficiency with regard to vocabulary learning. Although Ms. Cook and Mr. Guzman model for the students at their respective stations, they provide ample opportunity for students to practice using the words and concepts they have been learning. When needed, Ms. Cook and Mr. Guzman can redirect or clarify children's misunderstandings. Both teachers provide review and reinforcement of the target vocabulary at each reading station and integrate vocabulary instruction into their lessons on decoding, fluency, and comprehension throughout the language arts block. Multiple means of engagement are also evident in this lesson. The variety of tasks offered at the reading stations foster student engagement. In particular, the use of multimedia to spark discussion at the computer center motivates student participation. Finally, Ms. Cook provides an opportunity for extended learning beyond the classroom by distributing a single bean seed and a copy of the instructions for growing the seed. For students who have the opportunity to work on this project with a parent at home, the bean activity will foster a meaningful connection between the home and school environments.

Summary

In this chapter, we have focused on how school-level, grade-level, and teacher-level support can pave the way for effective vocabulary instruction for students. We have also provided a classroom inventory to help teachers evaluate their curriculum to identify how to teach vocabulary most effectively. Finally, we have presented four vignettes showing how individual teachers with whom we have worked have implemented the principles we describe in the first nine chapters of this book. We hope this chapter has helped you see how to put it all together for effective vocabulary instruction in your classroom.

Concluding Comments

As we discussed in Chapter 1, vocabulary knowledge is essential for comprehending and participating in the academic discourse of school. Children who have limited vocabulary and academic language skills will be at an academic disadvantage. Luckily, effective instruction in the early grades can accelerate children's vocabulary learning and prepare children to understand and use academic language throughout their school careers. Over the course of this book, we have presented six principles to guide vocabulary instruction in prekindergarten through second-grade classrooms. By providing explicit instruction, fostering a language-rich learning environment, supporting word awareness and independent word learning, assessing and differentiating instruction, incorporating multimedia, and establishing home–school connections, you can effectively reinforce children's vocabulary breadth and depth in school and beyond. Provided with instruction that aligns with these principles, children will learn a vast number of individual words and develop deep knowledge of many of the words they are learning. They will be able to determine and clarify their understanding of what words mean, recognize relations among words, and use words effectively in listening, speaking, reading, and writing. Effective vocabulary instruction in the early grades will provide children with the foundation they need to become confident, independent, and successful learners in the years to come.

APPENDIX

• • • • • • • • • •

Resources for Vocabulary Instruction

Selecting Words for Vocabulary Instruction

The optimal vocabulary program begins with careful word choice. As discussed in Chapter 2, we base our recommendations for selecting words on the work of numerous researchers before us. As you endeavor to select words for your own instruction, we recommend you select words that are (1) useful, (2) known, (3) frequent in academic texts, and (4) related to the theme, content, or other words selected for instruction. The resources below may help you get a sense of which words to teach and how to define them.

Resources for Choosing Words

Books

- *Creating Robust Vocabulary* (Beck, McKeown, & Kucan, 2008)
- *Words Worth Teaching* (Biemiller, 2010)
- *A Cluster Approach to Elementary Vocabulary Instruction* (Marzano & Marzano, 1988)

Websites

- *WordZones(tm) for 4,000 Simple Word Families* at *http://textproject.org/library/resources/wordzones-for-4000-simple-word-families* based on research by Hiebert (2005).
- The Academic Word List at *www.victoria.ac.nz/lals/resources/academicwordlist/information* based on research by Coxhead (2000, 2011).
- The Academic Vocabulary List at *www.academicvocabulary.info* based on research by Gardner and Davies (2013).

233

Resources for Defining Words[1]

Wordsmyth

- Collins-COBUILD
- Word Central

Selecting Texts to Support Vocabulary Instruction

Text selection is also central to any successful vocabulary program. Prekindergarten through second-grade libraries should include a majority of "read-aloud" books, as children's listening comprehension is far more advanced than their reading comprehension at this age. Texts to be read aloud should introduce children to a wide variety of contexts and a vast supply of words that are not typically part of children's everyday conversations. In Figure A.1 we present a list of local, national, and international children's literature awards, organized around the principles of text selection for vocabulary instruction that we presented in Chapter 2.

Selecting Multimedia to Support Vocabulary Instruction

A range of multimedia content has been shown to foster vocabulary learning. The varying means of representation, action and expression, and engagement afforded by multimedia allow all students, including struggling readers, ELLs, and learners with disabilities, to access the same academic content. The programs, applications, and websites listed in Figure A.1 reflect the most promising multimedia offerings for vocabulary instruction at this time. Although we recognize that some programs on this list may quickly become outdated and, as discussed in Chapter 8, the effectiveness of each of these media depends on the quality of the interface design, instructional content, and user engagement, we hope this list is a useful starting point in your search for multimedia to support your own students' vocabulary learning.

---

[1]Additional online word resources are listed below in the section on multimedia resources.

Principles of Text Selection	Corresponding Book Awards for Each Principle
Language and complexity *Teachers should choose texts with rich language and vocabulary that are optimally challenging.*	• **(John) Newbery Medal** Named for the bookseller John Newbery and awarded to the author of the most distinguished contribution to American literature for children. • **(Theodor Seuss) Geisel Award** Awarded to the author(s) and illustrator(s) of the most distinguished contribution to the body of American children's literature for beginning readers. • **Charlotte Zolotow Award** Named after the renowned children's book editor Charlotte Zolotow and bestowed annually to the author of the best picture book. • **E. B. White Read-Aloud Award for Picture Books** Awarded to books that embody the quintessential "read-aloud" standards first demonstrated by the celebrated children's author E. B. White.
Genre *Teachers should choose texts across genres.*	• **NCTE Orbis Pictus Nonfiction Award** An award named after Johannes Amos Comenius, who wrote *Orbis Pictus— The World in Pictures* (1657), the first children's book. • **(Robert F.) Sibert Informational Book Medal** Presented annually to the author(s) and illustrator(s) of the most distinguished informational book published in English. • **Scott O'Dell Award for Historical Fiction** Awarded to the author of the best book of historical fiction published in the previous year for children or young adults.
Support and multimedia *Teachers should choose texts with ample pictorial support.*	• **(Randolph) Caldecott Medal** Presented annually to an artist for the most distinguished picture book for children and named after the illustrator Randolph Caldecott. • **(Andrew) Carnegie Medal** Given to the producer of the most outstanding video production for children released during the preceding year. • **Odyssey Award for Excellence in Audiobook Production** Awarded to the producer of the best audiobook produced for children and/or young adults and available in English in the United States. • **The Cybils Awards** Presented annually for the year's best children's and young adult titles by the online blogging community.
Diversity *Teachers should choose texts that reflect diverse cultures and experiences.*	• **(Mildred L.) Batchelder Award** Awarded to an American publisher who translates a celebrated book from another country and language into English for publication in the United States. • **Coretta Scott King Book Awards** Presented to outstanding African American authors and illustrators of books for children and young adults that demonstrate an appreciation of African American culture and universal human values. • **Pura Belpré Medal** Awarded to a Latino/Latina writer and illustrator whose works best portrays, affirms, and celebrates the Latino cultural experience in an outstanding work of literature for children and youth. • **Schneider Family Book Award** Given to an author or illustrator for a book that embodies an artistic expression of the disability experience for children.

(continued)

FIGURE A.1. Selecting texts to support vocabulary instruction.

Principles of Text Selection	Corresponding Book Awards for Each Principle
Diversity (continued)	• **Jane Addams Children's Book Award** Presented to the author(s) of the most outstanding children's books that promote peace and justice. • **Amelia Bloomer Project** Given to authors whose work highlights the power of the individual and the collective voices of women across time and around the world.
Additional lists	• Bank Street College of Education Best Children's Books of the Year • Notable Children's Books listed annually by the New York Times • Boston Globe–Horn Book Awards • Notable Children's Books recognized annually by the ALSC • International Reading Association annual Children's Choices reading lists • Reading Rockets Themed Booklists • PBS Kids Writers Contest • And recommended reading lists at your local public library!

FIGURE A.1. (continued)

Media	Providers/Programs	Websites
Video	BrainPopJR	brainpopjr.com
	Learn360	learn360.com
	National Geographic Kids	video.nationalgeographic.com/video/kids
	NeoK12	neoK12.com
	PBS KIDS Video	pbskids.org/video
	TeacherTube	teachertube.com
	WatchKnowLearn	watchknowlearn.org
Digital and audio texts	Audible, Inc.	audible.com
	The International Children's Digital Library	en.childrenslibrary.org
	iTunes	apple.com/itunes
	Kindle	kindle.amazon.com
	LibriVox	librivox.org
	Nook	barnesandnoble.com/nook
	Project Gutenberg	gutenberg.org
Digital voice recording programs	Glogster	glogster.com
	Kerpoof	kerpoof.com
	Smories	smories.com
	Storybird	storybird.com
	Voice Thread	voicethread.com

(continued)

FIGURE A.2. Selecting multimedia to support vocabulary instruction.

Media	Providers/Programs	Websites
Computer games and applications	MimioSprout Early Reading	www.mimio.com/en-NA.aspx
	Waterford Early Learning	www.waterfordearlylearning.org
	World Book Classroom Early World of Learning	www.worldbookonline.com/training/world_of_learning
	ABC Mouse.Com Early Learning Academy	www.abcmouse.com
	PBS KIDS Games	pbskids.org/games
	The First 4,000 Words	sewardreadingresources.com/fourkw.html
	Reading Rockets Educational Literacy Apps	www.readingrockets.org/teaching/reading101/literacyapps
	PBS KIDS Apps	http://pbskids.org/apps
	National Geographic Kids Animal Jam	www.animaljam.com/home
	Discovery Kids Scuba Adventures	http://kids.discovery.com/games/apps/discovery-kids-scuba-adventures
	Wonderopolis	wonderopolis.org
	Lakeshore Learning	http://products.lakeshorelearning.com/learning/Vocabulary-Games
Website sequencing programs	QuestGarden	questgarden.com
	TrackStar4Teachers	trackstar.4teachers.org
Online dictionaries	Collins COBUILD	collinsdictionary.com/dictionary/english
	Merriam-Webster	visual.merriam-webster.com/index.php
	Online Etymology Dictionary	etymonline.com
	Oxford English Dictionary	public.oed.com/aspects-of-english/word-stories
	Wordsmyth	wordsmyth.net
Visual thesauri and text maps	Graph Words	graphwords.com
	Lexiwords	lexipedia.com
	Snappy Words	snappywords.com
	VisualThesaurus	visualthesaurus.com
	Wordle	wordle.net
	WordSift	wordsift.com
Translation programs	Babylon	translation.babylon.com
	Bing Translator	bing.com/translator
	Collins English for Learners	collinsdictionary.com/dictionary/american-cobuild-learners
	Google Translate	translate.google.com

(continued)

FIGURE A.2. *(continued)*

Media	Providers/Programs	Websites
Graphic organizers and templates	AIM Center	aim.cast.org/learn/historyarchive/backgroundpapers/graphic_organizers
	Education Place	eduplace.com/graphicorganizer
	Kidspiration	www.inspiration.com/kidspiration
	Scholastic Teachers	www.scholastic.com/teachers
	Teacher Vision	www.teachervision.com/graphic-organizers printable/6293.html
	ThinkPort	thinkport.org/technology/template.tp
Presentation programs	Keynote	apple.com/mac/keynote
	PowerPoint	office.microsoft.com/en-us/powerpoint
	Prezi	prezi.com
Clip art	ClipArt ECT	etc.usf.edu/clipart
	Creative Commons	creativecommons.org
	Discovery Education Clip Art	school.discoveryeducation.com/clipart
	Openclipart	openclipart.org
	Tech4Learning	pics.tech4learning.com
	University of Victoria Language Teaching Clipart Library	hcmc.uvic.ca/clipart
	Wikipedia Commons Clip Art	commons.wikimedia.org/wiki/Clipart
Photographic images	Free Digital Photos	freedigitalphotos.net
	Image*After	imageafter.com
	ImageBase	imagebase.net
	Morguefile	morguefile.com
	Public-Domain-Photos	public-domain-photos.com
	Wikipedia Commons Images	commons.wikimedia.org/wiki/Category:Images
Sounds	British Library Sounds	freesound.org
	FindSounds Palette	findsounds.com
	Freesound	sounds.bl.uk
	Free Sound Effects Archive	grsites.com/archive/sounds
	Sounds—The Pronunciation App	soundspronapp.com

FIGURE A.2. *(continued)*

238

References

Al Otaiba, S., Connor, C., Lane, H., Kosanovich, M. L., Schatschneider, C., Dyrlund, A. K., et al. (2008). "Reading First" kindergarten classroom instruction and students' growth in phonological awareness and letter naming-decoding fluency. *Journal of School Psychology*, *46*, 281–314.

American Speech–Language–Hearing Association. (n.d.) Typical speech and language development. Retrieved from *www.asha.org/public/speech/development/chart*.

Apel, K., Brimo, D., Diehm, E., & Apel, L. (2013). Morphological awareness intervention with kindergartners and first- and second-grade students from low socioeconomic status homes: A feasibility study. *Language, Speech, and Hearing Services in Schools*, *44*, 161–173.

Apthorp, H., Randel, B., Cherasaro, T., Clark, T., McKeown, M., & Beck, I. (2012). Effects of a supplemental vocabulary program on word knowledge and passage comprehension. *Journal of Research on Educational Effectiveness*, *5*, 160–188.

August, D., Carlo, M., Dressler, C., & Snow, C. (2005). The critical role of vocabulary development for English language learners. *Learning Disabilities Research and Practice*, *20*, 50–57.

August, D., Kenyon, D., Malabonga, V., Louguit, M., Caglarcan, S., & Carlo, M. (2001). *Extract the Base Test—English*. Washington, DC: Center for Applied Linguistics.

August, D., & Shanahan, T. (2006). *Developing literacy in second-language learners: Report of the National Literacy Panel on Language Minority Children and Youth*. Mahwah, NJ: Erlbaum.

Bates, E., Marchman, V., Tahl, D., Fenson, L., Dale, P., Reznick, J. S., et al. (1994). Developmental and stylistic variation in the composition of early vocabulary. *Journal of Child Language*, *21*, 85–123.

Baumann, J. F., Edwards, E. C., Boland, E. M., & Olejnik, S. (2003). Vocabulary tricks: Effects of instruction in morphology and context on fifth-grade students' ability to derive and infer word meanings. *American Educational Research Journal*, *40*, 447–494.

Baumann, J. F., Ware, D., & Edwards, E. C. (2007). "Bumping into spicy, tasty words that catch your tongue": A formative experiment on vocabulary instruction. *Reading Teacher*, *62*, 108–122.

Beck, I. L., & McKeown, M. G. (2001). Text talk: Capturing the benefits of read-aloud experiences for young children. *Reading Teacher*, *55*, 10–20.

Beck, I. L., & McKeown, M. G. (2007). Increasing young low-income children's oral vocabulary repertoires through rich and focused instruction. *Elementary School Journal*, *107*, 251–271.

Beck, I. L., McKeown, M. G., & Kucan, L. (2002, 2013). *Bringing words to life: Robust vocabulary instruction* (1st and 2nd eds.). New York: Guilford Press

Beck, I. L., McKeown, M. G., & Kucan, L. (2008). *Creating robust vocabulary*. New York: Guilford Press.

Beck, I. L., McKeown, M. G., & Omanson, R. C. (1987). The effects and uses of diverse vocabulary instructional techniques. In M. G. McKeown & M. E. Curtis (Eds.), *The nature of vocabulary acquisition* (pp. 147–163). Hillsdale, NJ: Erlbaum.

Belsky, J., Vandell, D., Burchinal, M., Clarke-Stewart, K. A., McCartney, K., Owen, M., et al. (2007). Are there long-term effects of early child care? *Child Development*, *78*, 681–701.

Berglund, E., Eriksson, M., & Westerlund, M. (2005). Communicative skills in relation to gender, birth order, childcare and socioeconomic status in 18-month-old children. *Scandinavian Journal of Psychology*, *46*, 485–491.

Biemiller, A. (2001). Teaching vocabulary: Early, direct, and sequential. *American Educator*, *25*(1), 24–28.

Biemiller, A. (2005). Size and sequence in vocabulary development: Implications for choosing words for primary grade vocabulary instruction. In E. H. Hiebert & M. L. Kamil (Eds.), *Teaching and learning vocabulary* (pp. 223–242). Mahwah, NJ: Erlbaum.

Biemiller, A. (2010). *Words worth teaching*. Columbus, OH: SRA/McGraw Hill.

Biemiller, A., & Boote, C. (2006). An effective method for building meaning vocabulary in primary grades. *Journal of Educational Psychology*, *98*, 44–62.

Biemiller, A., & Slonim, N. (2001). Estimating root word vocabulary growth in normative and advantaged populations: Evidence for a common sequence of vocabulary acquisition. *Journal of Educational Psychology*, *93*, 498–520.

Bishop, M. J., & Santoro, L. E. (2006). Evaluating beginning reading software for at-risk learners. *Psychology in the Schools*, *43*, 57–70.

Blachowicz, C. L. Z., & Fisher, P. (2000). Vocabulary instruction. In R. Barr, P. Mosenthal, P. S. Pearson, & M. Kamil (Eds.), *Handbook of reading research* (Vol. 3, pp. 505–523). White Plains, NY: Longman.

Blachowicz, C. L. Z., Fisher, P., Ogle, D., & Watts Taffe, S. (2013). *Teaching academic vocabulary K–8: Effective practices across the curriculum*. New York: Guilford Press.

Blachowicz, C. L. Z., & Obrochta, C. (2005). Vocabulary visits: Virtual field trips for content vocabulary development. *Reading Teacher*, *59*, 262–268.

Bond, M., & Wasik, B. (2009). Conversation stations: Promoting language development in young children. *Early Childhood Education Journal*, *36*, 467–473.

Bracken, S. S., & Fischel, J. E. (2008). Family reading behavior and early literacy skills in preschool children from low-income backgrounds. *Early Education and Development*, *19*, 45–67.

Burchinal, M. R., Howes, C., Pianta, R., Bryant, D., Early, D., Clifford, R., et al. (2008). Predicting child outcomes at the end of kindergarten from the quality of pre-kindergarten teacher–child interactions and instruction. *Applied Development Science*, *12*, 140–153.

Burchinal, M. R., Peisner-Feinberg, E., Pianta, R. C., & Howes, C. (2002). Development of academic skills from preschool through second grade: Family and classroom predictors of developmental trajectories. *Journal of School Psychology*, *40*, 415–436.

Cadima, J., Leal, T., & Burchinal, M. (2010). The quality of teacher–student interactions: Associations with first graders' academic and behavioral outcomes. *Journal of School Psychology, 48,* 457–482.

Cahill, M., & McGill-Franzen, A. (2013). Selecting "app"ealing and "app"ropriate book apps for beginning readers. *Reading Teacher, 67*(1), 30–39.

Carey, S. (1978). The child as word learner. In M. Halle, J. Bresnan, & G. A. Miller (Eds.), *Linguistic theory and psychological reality* (pp. 264–293). Cambridge, MA: MIT Press.

Carey, S., & Bartlett, E. (1978). Acquiring a single new word. *Proceedings of the Stanford Child Language Conference, 15,* 17–29.

Carlo, M., August, D., McLaughlin, B., Snow, C., Dressler, C., Lippman, D., et al. (2004). Closing the gap: Addressing the vocabulary needs of English language learners in bilingual and mainstream classrooms. *Reading Research Quarterly, 39,* 188–206.

Carrow-Woolfolk, E. (1999). *Comprehensive assessment of spoken language.* Circle Pines, MN: American Guidance Service.

Carta, J., Greenwood, C., Walker, D., & , Buzhardt, J. (2010). *Using IGDIs: Monitoring progress and improving intervention for infants and young children.* Baltimore, MD: Brookes.

Carver, R. P. (1994). Percentage of unknown vocabulary words in text as a function of the relative difficulty of the text: Implications for instruction. *Journal of Reading Behavior, 26,* 413–447.

CAST. (2011). *Universal Design for Learning Guidelines version 2.0.* Wakefield, MA: Author.

Chapin, L. A., & Altenhofen, S. (2010). Neurocognitive perspectives in language outcomes of Early Head Start: Language and cognitive stimulation and maternal depression. *Infant Mental Health Journal, 31,* 486–498.

Christ, T., & Wang, X. C. (2011). Closing the vocabulary gap?: A review of research on early childhood vocabulary practices. *Reading Psychology, 32,* 426–458.

Christ, T., & Wang, X. (2012). Young children's opportunities to use and learn theme-related vocabulary through buddy "reading." *Literacy Research and Instruction, 51,* 273–291.

Christ, T., Wang, X. C., & Chiu, M. M. (2011). Using story dictation to support young children's vocabulary development: Outcomes and process. *Early Childhood Research Quarterly, 26,* 30–41.

Cohen, J. S., & Mendez, J. L. (2009). Emotion regulation, language ability, and the stability of preschool children's peer play behavior. *Early Education and Development, 20,* 1016–1037.

Collins, M. F. (2010). ELL preschoolers' English vocabulary acquisition from storybook reading. *Early Childhood Research Quarterly, 25,* 84–97.

Coker, D. (2006). The impact of first-grade factors on the growth and outcomes of urban school children's primary-grade writing. *Journal of Educational Psychology, 98,* 471–488.

Connor, C. M., Son, S. H., Hindman, A. H., & Morrison, F. J. (2005). Teacher qualifications, classroom practices, and family characteristics: Complex effects on first graders' language and early reading. *Journal of School Psychology, 43,* 343–375.

Cooper, P. M. (2005). Literacy learning and pedagogical purpose in Vivian Paley's "storytelling curriculum." *Journal of Early Childhood Literacy, 5,* 229–251.

Cooper, P. M., Capo, K., Mathes, B., & Grey , L. (2007). One authentic early literacy practice and three standardized tests: Can a storytelling curriculum measure up? *Journal of Early Childhood Teacher Education, 28,* 251–275.

Correa-Connolly, M. (2004). *99 activities and greetings: Great for morning meeting . . . and other meetings too!* Turners Falls, MA: Northeast Foundation for Children.

Coxhead, A. (2000). A new academic word list. *TESOL Quarterly, 34,* 213–238.

Coxhead, A. (2011). The academic word list ten years on: Research and teaching implications. *TESOL Quarterly, 45,* 355–362.

Coyne, M. D., McCoach, D. B., Loftus, S., Zipoli, R., Jr., & Kapp, S. (2009). Direct vocabulary instruction in kindergarten: Teaching for breadth versus depth. *Elementary School Journal, 110,* 1–18.

Cunningham, A. E., & Stanovich, K. E. (1997). Early reading acquisition and its relation to reading experience and ability 10 years later. *Developmental Psychology, 33,* 934–945.

Dale, E. (1965). Vocabulary measurement: Techniques and major findings. *Elementary English, 42,* 895–901.

Dale, E., & O'Rourke, J. (1979). *The living word vocabulary.* Boston: Houghton Mifflin.

Davis, B. H., Resta, V., Davis, L. L., & Camacho, A. (2001). Novice teachers learn about literature circles through collaborative action research. *Journal of Reading Education, 26*(3), 1–6.

Diamond, L. (2008). *Assessing reading: Multiple measures* (2nd ed.). Consortium on Reading Excellence. Novato, CA: Arena Press.

Dickinson, D. K., & Porche, M. V. (2011). Relationship between language experiences in preschool classrooms and children's kindergarten and fourth-grade language and reading abilities. *Child Development, 82,* 870–886.

Dickinson, D. K., & Smith, M. W. (1994). Long-term effects of preschool teachers' book readings on low-income children's vocabulary and story comprehension. *Reading Research Quarterly, 29,* 104–122.

Dockrell, J. E., Stuart, M., & King, D. (2010). Supporting early oral language skills for English language learners in inner city preschool provision. *British Journal of Educational Psychology, 80,* 497–515.

Duin, A. H., & Graves, M. F. (1986). Effects of vocabulary instruction used as a prewriting technique. *Journal of Research and Development in Education. 20*(1), 7–13.

Duke, N. K., & Pearson, P. D. (2008). Effective practices for developing reading comprehension. *Journal of Education, 189,* 107–122.

Duncan, G. J., Dowsett, C. J., Claessens, A., Magnuson, K., Huston, A. C., Klebanov, P., et al. (2007). School readiness and later achievement. *Developmental Psychology, 43,* 1428–1446.

Dunn, L. M., & Dunn, D. M. (2007). *Peabody Picture Vocabulary Test* (4th ed.). Minneapolis, MN: Pearson.

Dunn, L. M., Lugo, D. E., Padilla, E. R., & Dunn, L. M. (1981). *Test de vocabulario en imagenes Peabody.* Minneapolis, MN: Pearson.

Elleman, A., Lindo, E., Morphy, P., & Compton, D. (2009). The impact of vocabulary instruction on passage-level comprehension of school-age children: A meta-analysis. *Journal of Research on Educational Effectiveness, 2,* 1–44.

Espin, C. A., Busch, T., Shin, J., & Kruschwitz, R. (2001). Curriculum-based measures in the content areas: Validity of vocabulary-matching measures as indicators of performance in social studies. *Learning Disabilities Research and Practice, 16,* 142–151.

Fehr, C. N., Davison, M. L., Graves, M. F., Sales, G. C., Seipel, B., & Sharma, S. S. (2012). The effects of individualized, online vocabulary instruction on picture vocabulary scores: An efficacy study. *Computer Assisted Language Learning, 25,* 87–102.

Fien, H., Santoro, L., Baker, S. K., Park, Y., Chard, D. J., Williams, S., et al. (2011). Enhancing teacher read alouds with small-group vocabulary instruction for students with low vocabulary in first-grade classrooms. *School Psychology Review, 40,* 307–318.

Fischel, M., & Ramirez, L. (2005). Evidence-based parent involvement interventions with school-aged children. *School Psychology Quarterly, 20,* 371–402.

Fisher, R., Henry, E., & Porter, D. (2006). *Morning meeting messages, K–6: 180 sample charts from three classrooms.* Turners Falls, MA: Northeast Foundation for Children.

Friend, M., & Cook, L. (1996). *Interactions: Collaboration skills for school professionals* (2nd ed.). White Plains, NY: Longman.

Gardner, D., & Davies, M. (2013). A new academic vocabulary list. *Applied Linguistics, 35*, 1–24.

Gass, S. M., Behney, J., & Plonsky, L. (2013). *Second language acquisition: An introductory course.* New York: Routledge.

Gilbert, J. K., Compton, D. L., Fuchs, D., Fuchs, L. S., Bouton, B., Barquero, L. A., et al. (2013). Efficacy of a first-grade responsiveness-to-intervention prevention model for struggling readers. *Reading Research Quarterly, 48*, 135–154.

Good, R. H., & Kaminski, R. A. (Eds.). (2002). *Dynamic indicators of basic early literacy skill* (6th ed.). Eugene, OR: Institute for the Development of Educational Achievement.

Gough, P. B., & Tunmer, W. E. (1986). Decoding, reading and reading disability. *Remedial and Special Education, 7*, 6–10.

Graves, M. F. (2006). *The vocabulary book: Learning and instruction.* New York: Teachers College Press.

Graves, M. F., August, D., & Mancillia-Martinez, J. (2012). *Teaching vocabulary to English language learners.* New York: Teachers College Press.

Graves, M. F., & Silverman, R. D. (2010). Innovations to enhance vocabulary development. In R. Allington & A. McGill-Franzen (Eds.), *Handbook of reading disability research* (pp. 315–328). Danvers, MA: Routledge.

Graves, M. F., & Watts-Taffe, S. (2008). For the love of words: Fostering word consciousness in young readers. *Reading Teacher, 62*, 185–193.

Hall, T. E., Meyer, A., & Rose, D. H. (Eds.). (2012). *Universal design for learning in the classroom.* New York: Guilford Press.

Hannon, P., & Bird, V. (2004). Family literacy in English: Theory, practice, research, and policy. In B. H. Wasik (Ed.), *Handbook of family literacy* (pp. 23–39). Mahwah, NJ: Erlbaum.

Heath, S. B. (1983). *Ways with words: Language, life, and work in communities and classrooms.* Cambridge, UK: Cambridge University Press.

Hiebert, E. H. (2005). In pursuit of an effective, efficient vocabulary curriculum for elementary students. In E. H. Hiebert & M. L. Kamil (Eds.), *Teaching and learning vocabulary* (pp. 243–263). Mahwah, NJ: Erlbaum.

Hindman, A. H., & Morrison, F. J. (2011). Family involvement and educator outreach in Head Start: Nature, extent, and contributions to early literacy skills. *Elementary School Journal, 111*, 359–386.

Hindman, A. H., & Wasik, B. A. (2012). Morning message time: An exploratory study in Head Start. *Early Childhood Education Journal, 40*, 275–283.

Hoffman, J. V., & Roser, N. (2012). Reading and writing the world using Beautiful Books: Language experience re-envisioned. *Language Arts, 89*, 293–304.

Hooper, S. R., Roberts, J. E., Zeisel, S. A., & Poe, M. (2003). Core language predictors of behavioral functioning in early elementary school children: Concurrent and longitudinal findings. *Behavior Disorders, 29*, 10–24.

Hoover, W. A., & Gough, P. B. (1990). The simple view of reading. *Reading and Writing: An Interdisciplinary Journal, 2*, 127–160.

Hu, M., & Nation, I. S. P. (2000). Vocabulary density and reading comprehension. *Reading in a Foreign Language, 13*, 403–430.

Huffstetter, M., King, J. R., Onwuegbuzie, A. J., Schneider, J. J., & Powell-Smith, K. A. (2010). Effects of a computer-based early reading program on the early reading and oral language skills of at-risk preschool children. *Journal of Education for Students Placed at Risk, 15*, 279–298.

Huttenlocher, J., Waterfall, H., Vasilyeva, M., Vevea, J., & Hedges, L. V. (2010). Sources of variability in children's language growth. *Cognitive Psychology, 61*, 343–365.

Jitendra, A. K., Edwards, L. L., Sacks, G., & Jacobson, L. A. (2004). What research says about vocabulary instruction for students with learning disabilities. *Exceptional Children, 70*, 299.

Johnson, C. J., Beitchman, J. H., & Brownlie, E. B. (2010). Twenty-year follow-up of children with and without speech–language impairments: Family, educational, occupational, and quality of life outcomes. *American Journal of Speech–Language Pathology, 19*, 51–65.

Jordan, G. E., Snow, C. E., & Porche, M. V. (2000). Project EASE: The effect of a family literacy project on kindergarten students' early literacy skills. *Reading Research Quarterly, 35*, 524–546.

Juel, C. (1988). Learning to read and write: A longitudinal study of 54 children from first through fourth grades. *Journal of Educational Psychology, 80*, 443–447.

Juel, C., Griffith, P. L., & Gough, P. B. (1986). Acquisition of literacy: A longitudinal study of children in first and second grade. *Journal of Educational Psychology, 78*, 243–255.

Justice, L. M., Meier, J., & Walpole, S. (2005). Learning new words from storybooks: An efficacy study with at-risk kindergartners. *Language, Speech, and Hearing Services in Schools, 36*, 17–32.

Kame'ennui, E. J., & Baumann, J. F. (2012). *Vocabulary instruction: Research to practice* (2nd ed.). New York: Guilford Press.

Kamil, M. L., Intrator, S. M., & Kim, H. S. (2000). The effects of other technologies on literacy and literacy learning. In M. L. Kamil, P. B. Mosenthal, P. D. Pearson, & R. Barr (Eds.), *Handbook of reading research* (Vol. 3, pp. 771–790). Mahwah, NJ: Erlbaum.

Kearns, G., & Biemiller, A. (2010/2011). Two-questions vocabulary assessment: Developing a new method for group testing in kindergarten through second grade. *Journal of Education, 190*(1/2), 31–42.

Kim, Y. S., Petscher, Y., Schatschneider, C., & Foorman, B. (2011). Does growth rate in oral reading fluency matter in predicting reading comprehension achievement? *Journal of Educational Psychology, 102*, 652–667.

Kong, A., & Fitch, E. (2002/2003). Using book clubs to engage culturally and linguistically diverse in reading, writing, and talking about books. *Reading Teacher, 56*, 352–362.

Korat, O. (2010). Reading electronic books as a support for vocabulary, story comprehension and word reading in kindergarten and first grade. *Computers & Education, 55*(1), 24–31.

Korat, O., & Shamir, A. (2012). Direct and indirect teaching: Using e-books for supporting vocabulary, word reading, and story comprehension for young children. *Journal of Educational Computing Research, 46*, 135–152.

Korat, O., Shamir, A., & Heibal, S. (2013). Expanding the boundaries of shared book reading: E-books and printed books in parent–child reading as support for children's language. *First Language, 33*, 504–523.

Kriete, R. (2002). *The morning meeting book*. Turners Falls, MA: Northeast Foundation for Children.

Lane, H. B., & Allen, S. A. (2010). The vocabulary-rich classroom: Modeling sophisticated word use to promote word consciousness and vocabulary growth. *Reading Teacher, 63*, 362–370.

Lattanzi Roser, S. (2012). *80 morning meeting ideas for grades K–2*. Turners Falls, MA: Northeast Foundation for Children.

Leung, C. B., Silverman, R., Nandakumar, R., Qian, X., & Hines, S. (2011). A comparison of difficulty levels of vocabulary in first grade basal readers for preschool dual language learners and monolingual English learners. *American Educational Research Journal, 48*, 421–461.

Linebarger, D., & Walker, D. (2005). Infants' and toddlers' television viewing and language outcomes. *American Behavioral Scientist, 48,* 624–645.

Loftus, S. M., & Coyne, M. D. (2013). Vocabulary instruction within a multi-tier approach. *Reading and Writing Quarterly, 29,* 4–19.

Loftus, S. M., Coyne, M. D., McCoach, D. B., Zipoli, R., & Pullen, P. C. (2010). Effects of a supplemental vocabulary intervention on the word knowledge of kindergarten students at risk for language and literacy difficulties. *Learning Disabilities Research and Practice, 25,* 124–136.

Lonigan, C. J., & Whitehurst, G. J. (1998). Relative efficacy of parent and teacher involvement in a shared-reading intervention for preschool children from low-income backgrounds. *Early Childhood Research Quarterly, 13,* 263–290.

MacGinitie, W. H., MacGinitie, R. K., Maria, K., & Dreyer, L. G. (2000). *Gates–MacGinitie reading test* (4th ed.). Rolling Hills, IL: Riverside.

Martin-Beltran, M., Daniel, S., Peercy, M., & Silverman, R. (2013, April). *"We're special buddies!": Examples of peer tutors providing cognitive, linguistic, and social support during interactions.* Paper presented at the annual meeting of the American Educational Research Association, San Francisco, CA.

Marulis, L. M., & Neuman, S. B. (2010). The effects of vocabulary intervention on young children's word learning: A meta-analysis. *Review of Educational Research, 80,* 300–335.

Marzano, R. J., & Marzano, J. (1988). *A cluster approach to elementary vocabulary instruction.* Newark, DE: International Reading Association.

Marzano, R. J., & Simms, J. A. (2013). *Vocabulary for the Common Core.* Bloomington, IN: Marzano Research Laboratory.

Mashburn, A. J., Pianta, R. C., Hamre, B. K., Downer, J. T., Barbarin, O., Bryant, D., et al. (2008). Measures of classroom quality in prekindergarten and children's development of academic language, and social skills. *Child Development, 79,* 732–749.

McKenna, M., & Zucker, T. (2009). Use of electronic storybooks in reading instruction. In A. Bus & S. B. Neuman (Eds.), *Multimedia and literacy development* (pp. 254–272). New York: Routledge.

Meier, J., & Sullivan, A. K. (2004). Spotlight schools: Success stories from high-risk kindergartens. *Reading and Writing Quarterly, 20,* 285–304.

Metsala, J. L., & Walley, A. C. (1998). Spoken vocabulary growth and segmental restructuring of lexical representations: Precursors to phonemic awareness and early reading ability. In J. L. Metsala & L. C. Ehri (Eds.), *Word recognition in beginning literacy* (pp. 89–120). Mahwah, NJ: Erlbaum.

Meyerson, M. J., & Kulesza, D. L. (2006). *Strategies for struggling readers and writers.* Needham Heights, MA: Allyn & Bacon.

Missall, K. N., & McConnell, S. R. (2004). *Technical report: Psychometric characteristics of individual growth and development indicators—picture naming, rhyming, and alliteration.* Minneapolis, MN: Center for Early Education and Development.

Moats, L. C. (2001). Overcoming the language gap. *American Educator, 25*(2), 5, 8–9.

Moll, L., Amanti, C., Neff, D., & González, N. (1992). Funds of knowledge for teaching: A qualitative approach to developing strategic connections between homes and classrooms. *Theory into Practice, 31,* 132–141.

Monopoli, W. J., & Kingston, S. (2012). The relationships among language ability, emotion regulation and social competence in second-grade students. *International Journal of Behavioral Development, 3,* 398–405.

Munro, N., Lee, K., & Baker, E. (2008). Building vocabulary knowledge and phonological awareness skills in children with specific language impairment through hybrid language intervention: A feasibility study. *International Journal of Language and Communication Disorders, 43*, 662–682.

Murphy, P. K., Wilkinson, I. A. G., Soter, A. O., Hennessey, M. N., & Alexander, J. F. (2009). Examining the effects of classroom discussion on students' comprehension of text: A meta-analysis. *Journal of Educational Psychology, 101*, 740–764.

Nagy, W. E. (2005). Why vocabulary instruction needs to be long-term and comprehensive. In E. H. Hiebert & M. L. Kamil (Eds.), *Teaching and learning vocabulary: Bringing research to practice* (pp. 27–44). Mahwah, NJ: Erlbaum.

Nagy, W. E., & Anderson, R. (1984). The number of words in printed school English. *Reading Research Quarterly, 19*, 304–330.

Nagy, W. E., Herman, P., & Anderson, R. (1985). Learning words from context. *Reading Research Quarterly, 20*, 223–253.

Nagy, W. E., & Scott, J. A. (2000). Vocabulary processes. In M. Kamil, P. Mosenthal, P. D. Pearson, & R. Barr (Eds.), *Handbook of reading research* (Vol. 3, pp. 269–284). Mahwah, NJ: Erlbaum.

Nagy, W. E., & Townsend, D. (2012). Words as tools: Learning academic vocabulary as language acquisition. *Reading Research Quarterly, 47*, 91–108.

Nash, H., & Snowling, M. (2006). Teaching new words to children with poor existing vocabulary knowledge: A controlled evaluation of the definition and context methods. *International Journal of Language and Communication Disorders, 41*, 335–354.

National Center for Education Statistics. (2012). *The nation's report card: Vocabulary results from the 2009 and 2011 NAEP reading assessments* (NCES 2013 452). Washington, DC: Institute of Education Sciences, U.S. Department of Education.

National Early Literacy Panel. (2008). *Developing early literacy: Report of the National Early Literacy Panel*. Washington, DC: National Center for Family Literacy.

National Governors Association Center for Best Practices and Council of Chief State School Officers. (2010). *Common Core State Standards for English language arts and literacy in history/social studies, science, and technical subjects*. Washington, DC: Author.

Ness, M. (2011). Explicit reading comprehension instruction in elementary classrooms: Teacher use of reading comprehension strategies. *Journal of Research in Childhood Education, 25*, 98–117.

Neuman, S. B. (1997). Television as a learning environment: A theory of synergy. In J. Flood, S. Brice Heath, & D. Lapp (Eds.), *Handbook of research on teaching literacy through the communicative and visual arts* (pp. 15–30). New York: Simon & Schuster.

Neuman, S. B., & Dwyer, J. (2009). Missing in action: Vocabulary instruction in pre-K. *Reading Teacher, 62*, 384–392.

Neuman, S. B., & Dwyer, J. (2011). Developing vocabulary and conceptual knowledge for low-income preschoolers: A design experiment. *Journal of Literacy Research, 43*, 103–129.

Neuman, S. B., Newman, E. H., & Dwyer, J. (2011). Educational effects of a vocabulary intervention on preschoolers' word knowledge and conceptual development: A cluster-randomized trial. *Reading Research Quarterly, 46*, 249–272.

Ortiz, A. A., & Artiles, A. J. (2010). Meeting the needs of ELLs with disabilities: A linguistically and culturally responsive model. In G. Li & P. A. Edwards (Eds.), *Best practices in ELL instruction* (pp. 247–272). New York: Guilford Press.

Paivio, A. (1986). *Mental representations*. New York: Oxford University Press.

Paley, V. G. (1981). *Wally's stories: Conversations in the kindergarten*. Cambridge, MA: Harvard University Press.

Parish-Morris, J., Mahajan, N., Hirsh-Pasek, K., Golinkoff, R. M., & Collins, M. F. (2013). Once upon a time: Parent–child dialogue and storybook reading in the electronic era. *Mind, Brain, and Education, 7*, 200–211.

Pearson, P. D., Hiebert, E. H., & Kamil, M. L. (2007). Vocabulary assessment: What we know and what we need to learn. *Reading Research Quarterly, 42,* 282–296.

Pearson Education, Inc. (2009). *Stanford achievement test series* (10th ed.). Upper Saddle River, NJ: Author.

Perfetti, C. (1985). *Reading ability.* New York: Oxford University Press.

Perfetti, C. (2010). Decoding, vocabulary, and comprehension: The golden triangle of reading skill. In M. C. McKeown & L. Kucan (Eds.), *Bringing reading research to life* (pp. 291–303). New York: Guilford Press.

Pianta, R., La Paro, K., & Hamre, B. K. (2008). *Classroom Assessment Scoring System.* Baltimore, MD: Brookes.

Proctor, C. P., Dalton, B., Uccelli, P., Biancarosa, G., Mo, E., Snow, C., et al. (2009). Improving comprehension online: Effects of deep vocabulary instruction with bilingual and monolingual fifth graders. *Reading and Writing, 24,* 517–544.

Purcell-Gates, V. (2007). *Cultural practices of literacy: Case studies of language, literacy, social practice, and power.* Mahwah, NJ: Erlbaum.

Restrepo, M. A., Morgan, G. P., & Thompson, M. S. (2013). The efficacy of a vocabulary intervention for dual-language learners with language impairment. *Journal of Speech, Language, and Hearing Research, 56,* 748–765.

Rice, M. L., & Woodsmall, L. (1988). Lessons from television: Children's word learning when viewing. *Child Development, 59,* 420–429.

Rose, D. H., & Meyer, A. (2002). *Teaching every student in the digital age: Universal design for learning.* Alexandria, VA: Association for Supervision and Curriculum Development.

Saint-Laurent, L., & Giasson, J. (2005). Effects of a family literacy program adapting parental intervention to first graders' evolution of reading and writing abilities. *Journal of Early Childhood Literacy, 5,* 253–278.

Salomon, G. (1981). *Communication and education.* Beverly Hills, CA: Sage.

San Francisco, A. R., Mo, E., Carlo, M., August, D., & Snow, C. (2006). The influences of language of literacy instruction and vocabulary on the spelling of Spanish-English bilinguals. *Reading and Writing, 19,* 627–642.

Segers, E. (2009). Learning from interactive vocabulary books in kindergarten: Looking back, looking forward. In A. G. Bus & S. B. Neuman (Eds.), *Multimedia and literacy development* (pp. 112–123). New York: Routledge.

Segers, E., & Verhoeven, L. (2003) Effects of vocabulary computer training in kindergarten. *Journal of Computer Assisted Learning, 19,* 559–568.

Semel, E., Wiig, E. H., & Secord, W. A. (2013). *Clinical evaluation of language fundamentals* (5th ed.). Minneapolis, MN: Pearson.

Shamir, A. (2009). Processes and outcomes of joint activity with e-books for promoting kindergarteners' emergent literacy. *Educational Media International, 46*(1), 81–96.

Shamir, A., & Korat, O. (2009). The educational electronic book as a tool for supporting children's emergent literacy. In A. G. Bus & S. B. Neuman (Eds.), *Multimedia and literacy development: Improving achievement for young learners* (pp. 110–124). London: Taylor & Francis.

Shamir, A., Korat, O., & Barbi, N. (2008). The effects of CD-ROM storybook reading on low SES kindergarteners' emergent literacy as a function of learning context. *Computers and Education, 51*(1), 354–367.

Shamir, A., Korat, O., & Fellah, R. (2012). Promoting vocabulary, phonological awareness and concept about print among children at risk for learning disability: Can e-books help? *Reading and Writing, 25*(1), 45–69.

Shamir, A., Korat, O., & Shlafer, I. (2011). The effect of activity with e-book on vocabulary and story comprehension: A comparison between kindergarteners at risk of learning disabilities and typically developing kindergarteners. *European Journal of Special Needs Education, 26*(3), 311–322.

Shanahan, T., Mulhern, M., & Rodriguez-Brown, F. (1995). Project FLAME: A literacy program for language minority families. In L. M. Morrow, S. B. Neuman, J. R. Paratore, & C. Harrison (Eds.), *Parents and literacy* (pp. 40–47). Newark, DE: International Reading Association.

Shedd, M. K., & Duke, N. K. (2008). The power of planning: Developing effective read-alouds. *Young Children, 63*(6), 22–27.

Silverman, R. (2007a). Vocabulary development of English-language and English-only learners in kindergarten. *Elementary School Journal, 107,* 365–383.

Silverman, R. (2007b). A comparison of three methods of vocabulary instruction during read-alouds in kindergarten. *Elementary School Journal, 108,* 97–113.

Silverman, R. (2009). *Martha Speaks website evaluation.* Unpublished report to WGBH. Washington, DC: Author.

Silverman, R. (2013). Investigating video as a means to promote vocabulary for at-risk children. *Contemporary Educational Psychology, 38,* 170–179.

Silverman, R., & Crandell, J. (2010). Vocabulary strategies in pre-kindergarten and kindergarten classrooms. *Reading Research Quarterly, 45,* 318–340.

Silverman, R., Crandell, J., & Carlis, L. (2013). Read alouds and beyond: The effects of read aloud extension activities on vocabulary in Head Start classrooms. *Early Education and Development, 24,* 98–122.

Silverman, R., & Hines, S. (2009). The effects of multimedia enhanced instruction on the vocabulary of English language learners and non-English language learners in pre-kindergarten through second grade. *Journal of Educational Psychology, 101,* 305–314.

Silverman, R., & Hines, S. (2012). Building literacy skills through multimedia. In A. Pinkham, T. Kaefer, & S. Neuman (Eds.), *Knowledge development in early childhood: Sources of learning and classroom implications* (pp. 242–258). New York: Guilford Press.

Silverman, R., Martin-Beltran, M., Peercy, M., & Meyer, A. G. (2014, April). *Using reading buddies to support vocabulary and comprehension development.* Paper presented at the annual meeting of the Council of Exceptional Children, Philadelphia, PA.

Sinclair, J. (Ed.). (2005). *Collins COBUILD student's dictionary* (3rd ed.). Glasgow, UK: HarperCollins.

Smith, M. W., Brady, J. P., & Anastasopoulos, L. (2008). *Early Language and Literacy Classroom Observation Tool, Pre-K.* Baltimore, MD: Brookes.

Smith, M. W., Brady, J. P., & Clark-Chiarelli, N. (2008). *User's guide to the Early Language and Literacy Classroom Observation Tool, K–3.* Baltimore, MD: Brookes.

Snow, C. E. (1991). The theoretical basis for relationships between language and literacy in development. *Journal of Research in Childhood Education, 6,* 5–10.

Snow, C. E., Barnes, W. S., Chandler, J., Goodman, I. F., & Hemphill, L. (1991). *Home and school influences on literacy.* Cambridge, MA: Harvard University Press.

Snow, C. E., Burns, S. M., & Griffin, P. (Eds.). (1998). *Preventing reading difficulties in young children.* Washington, DC: National Academy Press.

Stanovich, K. E., & Cunningham, A. E. (1993). Where does knowledge come from?: Specific associations between print exposure and information acquisition. *Journal of Educational Psychology, 85,* 211–229.

Strouse, G. A., O'Doherty, K., & Troseth, G. L. (2013). Effective coviewing: Preschoolers' learning from video after a dialogic questioning intervention. *Developmental Psychology, 49,* 2368–2382.

Swanson, E., Vaughn, S., Wanzek, J., Petscher, Y., Heckert, J., Cavanaugh, C., et al. (2011). A synthesis of read-aloud interventions on early reading outcomes among preschool through third graders at risk for reading difficulties. *Journal of Learning Disabilities, 44, 258–275.*

Sylvestre, A., Desmarais, C., Meyer, F., Bairati, I., Rouleau, N., & Mérette, C. (2012). Factors associated with expressive and receptive language in French-speaking toddlers clinically diagnosed with language delay. *Infants and Young Children, 25, 158–171.*

Thal, D. J., Bates, E., Goodman, J., & Jahn-Samilo, J. (1997). Continuity of language abilities: An exploratory study of late- and early-talking toddlers. *Developmental Neuropsychology, 13, 239–273.*

Townsend, D., Filippini, A., Collins, P., & Biancarosa, G. (2012). Evidence for the importance of academic word knowledge for the academic achievement of diverse middle school students. *Elementary School Journal, 112, 497–518.*

Tracy, K. N., & Headley, K. N. (2013). I never liked to read or write: A formative experiment on the use of a nonfiction-focused writing workshop in a fourth grade classroom. *Literacy Research and Instruction, 52, 173–191.*

van Steensel, R., McElvany, N., Kurvers, J., & Herppich, S. (2011). How effective are family literacy programs?: Results of a meta-analysis. *Review of Educational Research, 81, 69–96.*

Verhallen, M. J. A. J., & Bus, A. G. (2010). Low-income immigrant pupils learning vocabulary through digital picture storybooks. *Journal of Educational Psychology, 102, 54–61.*

Vygotsky, L. S. (1962). *Thought and language.* Cambridge, MA: MIT Press.

Walpole, S., & McKenna, M. C. (2007). *Differentiated reading instruction: Strategies for the primary grades.* New York: Guilford Press.

Wasik, B. A., Bond, M. A., & Hindman, A. (2006). The effects of a language and literacy intervention on Head Start children and teachers. *Journal of Educational Psychology, 98, 63–74.*

Wasik, B. A., & Hindman, A. H. (2011). Improving vocabulary and pre-literacy skills of at-risk preschoolers through teacher professional development. *Journal of Educational Psychology, 103, 455–469.*

Watts, S. M. (1995). Vocabulary instruction during reading lessons in six classrooms. *Journal of Reading Behavior, 27, 399–424.*

Wesche, M., & Paribakht, T. S. (1996). Assessing second language vocabulary knowledge: Depth versus breadth. *Canadian Modern Language Review, 53, 13–40.*

Whitehurst, G. J., Arnold, D. S., Epstein, J. N., Angell, A. L., Smith, M., & Fischel, J. E. (1994). A picture book reading intervention in day care and home for children from low-income families. *Developmental Psychology, 30, 679–689.*

Whitehurst, G. J., & National Center for Learning Disabilities. (2004). *Read together, talk together: Program guide.* New York: Pearson Early Learning.

Williams, K. T. (2002). *Group reading assessment and diagnostic evaluation.* San Antonio, TX: Pearson.

Williams, K. T. (2007). *Expressive vocabulary test* (2nd ed.). San Antonio, TX: Pearson.

Wood, J. (2001). Can software support children's vocabulary development? *Language Learning and Technology, 5, 166–201.*

Word Central. (n.d.) *www.wordcentral.com.*

Wordsmyth. (n.d.). *www.wordsmyth.net.*

World-Class Instructional Design and Assessment (WIDA). (2012). *2012 amplification of the English language development standards, kindergarten–grade 12.* Retrieved January 31, 2014, from *www.wida.us/downloadLibrary.aspx.*

Wright, T. S. (2012). What classroom observations reveal about oral vocabulary instruction in kindergarten. *Reading Research Quarterly, 47, 353–355.*

Wright, J. C., Huston, A. C., Murphy, K. C., St. Peters, M., Pinon, M., Scantlin, R., et al.

(2001). The relations of early television viewing to school readiness and vocabulary of children from low-income families: The early window project. *Child Development, 72,* 1347–1366.

Wright, T. S., & Neuman, S. B. (2013). Vocabulary instruction in commonly used kindergarten core reading curricula. *Elementary School Journal, 113,* 386–408.

Zeno, S. M., Ivens, S. H., Millard, R. T., & Duvvuri, R. (1995). *The educator's word frequency guide.* New York: Touchstone Applied Science Associates.

Zipoli, R., Coyne, M. D., & McCoach, D. B. (2011). Enhancing vocabulary intervention for kindergarten students: Strategic integration of semantically related and embedded word review. *Remedial and Special Education, 32,* 131–143.

Zevenbergen, A. A., & Whitehurst, G. J. (2003). Dialogic reading: A shared picture book intervention for preschoolers. In A. Kleeck, S. Stahl, & E. Bauer (Eds.), *On reading books to children: Parents and teachers* (pp. 302–320). Mahwah, NJ: Erlbaum.

Children's Literature

Aboff, M. (2008). *If you were a prefix*. Mankato, MN: Picture Window Books.

Aboff, M. (2008). *If you were a suffix*. Mankato, MN: Picture Window Books.

Aliki. (1989). *My five senses*. New York: Crowell.

Anderson, P. P. (2006). *Chuck's truck*. Boston: Houghton Mifflin.

Banks, K. (2006). *Max's words*. New York: Farrar, Straus and Giroux.

Barrett, J. (2001). *Things that are most in the world*. New York: Atheneum Books for Young Readers.

Barton, B. (1986). *Trains*. New York: Harper Festival.

Barton, B. (1998). *Boats*. New York: Harper Festival.

Barton, B. (1998). *Planes*. New York: Harper Festival.

Blackstone, S. (1998). *Bear on a bike*. New York: Barefoot Books.

Brett, J. (1989). *The mitten*. New York: G.P. Putnam's Sons.

Carle, E. (1997). *From head to toe*. New York: HarperCollins.

Choi, Y. (2003). *The name jar*. New York: Random House.

Cooney, B. (1982). *Miss Rumphius*. New York: Viking Press.

Cronin, D. (2000). *Click, clack, moo: Cows that type*. New York: Atheneum Books for Young Readers.

DeGross, M. (1998). *Donavan's word jar*. New York: HarperCollins.

DePaola, T. (1997). *Mice squeak, we speak*. New York: Penguin.

Dorros, A. (1997) . *Abuela*. New York: Penguin.

Floca, B. (2003). *The racecar alphabet*. New York: Atheneum Books for Young Readers.

Floca, B. (2007). *Lightship*. New York: Atheneum Books for Young Readers.

Floca, B. (2009). *Moonshot: The flight of Apollo 11*. New York: Atheneum Books for Young Readers.

Freeman, D. (1968.) *Corduroy*. New York: Penguin.

Freeman, D. (1978). *A pocket for Corduroy*. New York: Penguin Books.

Gibbons, G. (1981). *Trucks*. New York: Holiday House.

Gibbons, G. (1983). *The boat book*. New York: Holiday House.

Gibbons, G. (1988). *Trains*. New York: Holiday House.

Gibbons, G. (1991). *From seed to plant*. New York: Holiday House.

Gibbons, G. (1995). *The bicycle book*. New York: Holiday House.

Graves, K. (2010). *Chicken Big*. San Francisco: Chronicle Books.

Holland, S., & Lofthouse, A. (2003). *Rivers and lakes*. New York: DK Publishing.

Jordan, H. (1992). *How a seed grows*. New York: Harper Trophy.

Kalman, B. (1997). *How a plant grows*. New York: Crabtree Publishing.

Kates, B. (1996). *We're different, we're the same*. New York: Random House.

Keats, E. J. (1962). *The snowy day*. New York: Viking Press.

Krauss, R. (2004). *The carrot seed*. New York: HarperCollins.

Lewis, K. (1999). *Chugga-chugga choo-choo*. New York: Hyperion Books for Children.

Lewis, K., & Kirk, D. (2002). *My truck is stuck*. New York: Hyperion Books for Children.

Lionni, L. (1986). *It's mine*. New York: Knopf.

Lobel, A. (1979). *Frog and Toad together*. New York: HarperCollins.

Loomis, C. (1996). *Rush hour*. Boston: Houghton Mifflin.

Malyan, S. (2005). *Sea creatures*. New York: DK Publishing.

Martin, B. (1992). *Brown bear, brown bear, what do you see?* New York: Henry Holt.

Martin, B., & Archambault, J. (1988). *Listen to the rain*. New York: Henry Holt.

Marsh, L. F. (2010). *Great migrations*. Washington, DC: National Geographic.

Marsh, L. F. (2012). *Weird sea creatures*. Washington, DC: National Geographic.

Mayo, M. (2002). *Dig dig digging*. New York: Henry Holt.

Mayo, M. (2004). *Choo choo clickety-clack!* Minneapolis, MN: Carolrhoda Books.

Mayo, M. (2012). *Zoom, rocket, zoom!* New York: Walker.

Meddaugh, S. (1995). *Martha speaks*. Boston: Houghton Mifflin Harcourt.

Medearis, A. S. (1999). *Seeds grow!* New York: Scholastic Press.

Morris, A. (1990). *On the go*. New York: Lothrop, Lee & Shepard Books.

National Geographic. (2010). *Amazing planet: Creatures of the deep* [videorecording]. Washington, DC: Author.

Numeroff, L. (2010). *If you give a mouse a cookie*. New York: HarperCollins.

Polette, N. (2003). *Mae Jemison*. New York: Children's Press.

Prince, A. J. (2006). *What do wheels do all day?* Boston: Houghton Mifflin.

Pulver, R. (2011). *Happy endings: A story about suffixes*. New York: Holiday House.

Rathmann, P. (1995). *Officer Buckle and Gloria*. New York: Putnam.

Rosen, M. (1997). *We're going on a bear hunt*. New York: Little Simon.

Schertle, A. (2009). *Little blue truck leads the way*. Boston: Harcourt Children's Books.

Schotter, R. (2006). *The boy who loved words*. New York: Schwartz & Wade Books.

Schreiber, A. (2008). *Sharks!* Washington, DC: National Geographic.

Seeger, P. (1986). *Abiyoyo*. New York: Aladdin.

Seuss, D. (1968). *The foot book*. New York: Random House.

Smith, P. (2012). *Animal hide and seek*. New York: DK Publishing.

Stewart, M. (2010). *Dolphins*. Washington, DC: National Geographic.

Tarpley, N. A. (2001). *I love my hair!* New York: Little, Brown Books for Young Readers.

Van Dusen, C. (2005). *If I built a car*. New York: Puffin Books.

Viorst, J. (1972). *Alexander and the terrible, horrible, no good, very bad day*. New York: Atheneum Books for Young Readers.

Weatherby, M. A. (2004). *The trucker*. New York: Scholastic Press.

White, E. B. (1952). *Charlotte's web*. New York: Harper & Row.

Youngdahl, K., & Grupper, J. (2004). *Deep sea dive* [videorecording]. Washington, DC: National Geographic.

Zion, G. (2006). *Harry the dirty dog*. New York: HarperCollins.

Index

Page numbers followed by *f* indicate figures.